A Reading of Anxiety

A Reading of Anxiety follows the sessions of Lacan's Seminar X, examining its presentation of the structure of anxiety, step by step.

Christian Fierens considers why and how the structure of anxiety always depends on speech even if it remains on the threshold between the symbolic and the real and explains that there is a genuine connection between anxiety and the Lacanian object *a* which puts in doubt the obviousness of any object. The book then explores the importance of anxiety for the practice of the analyst, determines that the object *a* is fundamentally void and discusses encountering nothingness. Finally, Fierens establishes that this nothingness inside the object and inside anxiety leads to the truth of anxiety.

A Reading of Anxiety will be an essential book for students as well as clinicians to find a practical way to cope with anxiety as a clinical approach to the real in psychoanalysis. It will be relevant to all readers interested in the work of Lacan.

Christian Fierens is a psychoanalyst and psychiatrist based in Belgium. He holds a PhD on psychosis in Freud's work and has published several books on Freudian and Lacanian psychoanalysis, including *The Soul of Narcissism* and *The Jouissance Principle*, both published by Routledge.

"This fluent, clear, readable translation by Patricia McCarthy of Christian Fierens' *Lecture de l'Angoisse* provides an essential resource for any serious clinical investigation of anxiety. Fierens' *Lecture* provides an effective tool for working psychoanalytically with anxiety in an epoch when the dominant reaction is to remove it, to delete the cause. It is not proposed as a definitive reading but as Fierens' own taking on the questions Jacques Lacan articulates in his *Seminar* and making them his own. In turn, this translation allows readers in English to take on these questions and make them their own. In a way that can only be fruitful, it demands a serious engagement by the reader, an engagement singular to each which will contribute crucially to the reader's formation and the articulation of their relation to psychoanalysis."

Barry O'Donnell, Ph.D., practises psychoanalysis and is a member of the *Irish School for Lacanian Psychoanalysis (ISLP)*. He is Director of Psychotherapy Programmes in the School of Medicine, University College Dublin and Director of the School of Psychotherapy at St. Vincent's University Hospital, Dublin.

"A helpful and challenging book is this *Reading Anxiety* by Christian Fierens. Its importance goes far beyond Lacan's Xth seminar whose sessions it follows in order to comment explicitly on them. Very well documented, with references to Freud and to Lacan's own sources of inspiration, it is an indispensable work not only for those who want to get to know Lacan, but also for those who want to explore the clinical and theoretical wiring of anxiety from a Lacanian point of view, including questions of the object (a), desire and Jouissance, the Real, the Symbolic, the Imaginary."

Gertrudis Van de Vijver, Professor in philosophy, Ghent University, practicing psychoanalyst.

"*Reading Anxiety* is an intricate appraisal of Jacques Lacan's *Seminar X,* in which Lacan produces the central notion of the 'object cause of desire'. The beauty of Christian Fierens' approach is that it is not an explication, but rather a creative reading that invents a new methodology in its theoretical elaboration. Fierens stresses, moreover, the necessity for each reader of Lacan's work to produce his or her own original reading."

Michael Gerard Plastow, Psychoanalyst (The Freudian School of Melbourne, Association Lacanienne Internationale) and child psychiatrist (Alfred Child and Youth Mental Health Service).

"This book presents a comprehensive and engaging reading of one of Lacan's key seminars by one of the finest practicing analysts and teacher of psychoanalysis in the Lacanian community today. Rigorous and admirably accessible, it gives an excellent account of an intricate development of Lacan's notion of anxiety by situating it in the gap between *jouissance* and desire. There are a few books devoted to Lacan's seminar on anxiety. In a clear and careful reading, Christian Fierens offers insightful treatment of the role of anxiety in Lacan's theory of the subject of the unconscious by illuminating the theoretical elaborations introduced by Lacan in his seminar on anxiety and exploring their clinical implications with remarkable perspicacity."

Jelica Šumič Riha, Institute of Philosophy, Research Centre
of the Slovenian Academy of Sciences and Arts.

A Reading of Anxiety

Lacan's Seminar X

Christian Fierens

Translated by Patricia McCarthy

Routledge
Taylor & Francis Group

LONDON AND NEW YORK

Designed cover image: Getty | Jackyenjoyphotography

First published in English 2025
by Routledge
4 Park Square, Milton Park, Abingdon, Oxon OX14 4RN

and by Routledge
605 Third Avenue, New York, NY 10158

Routledge is an imprint of the Taylor & Francis Group, an informa business

Christian Fierens, Lecture de L'angoisse – Le séminaire X de Lacan, Louvain-la-Neuve, Éditions EME, 2023

British Library Cataloguing-in-Publication Data
A catalogue record for this book is available from the British Library

ISBN: 9781032762777 (hbk)
ISBN: 9781032762760 (pbk)
ISBN: 9781003477822 (ebk)

DOI: 10.4324/9781003477822

Typeset in Times New Roman
by codeMantra

This reading of Lacan's Seminar on Anxiety is a reprise of a seminar given by videoconference from January to June 2022. I would like to thank the seminar's participants for their commitment and support throughout this work.

Contents

The vocal object   155

 9   The central role of the vocal object   157

10   The vocal object *a* in the structure and in the clinic   173

PART SIX
The truth of anxiety   195

11   Obsessional neurosis in the structure   197

12   From anxiety to the Names-of-the-Father   218

       References   *233*
       Index   *235*

Introduction

With the major contribution to psychoanalysis of Lacan's Seminar X, anxiety can no longer be treated simply as a symptom, a negative phenomenon or a pathological manifestation. On the road to the constitution of the subject by the signifier in the locus of the Other, anxiety sustains the gap between mythical *jouissance* (the very principle of the functioning of the unconscious) and the avatars of *desire* where the barred subject appears. It is at the heart of this anxiety, as the gap between *jouissance* and desire, that Lacan's *object a* and the barred Other (the non-response of the Other) emerge. From *jouissance*, anxiety produces the object *a* which causes desire. From then onwards, the psychoanalytic act will consist in supporting anxiety and overcoming it (*aufheben*) in and through transference love. "Only love allows *jouissance* to condescend to desire".

My reading of the seminar is divided into six parts, each comprising two chapters:

1 *Anxiety and the real.* On the path to the constitution of the subject by the signifier at the heart of the Other, anxiety depends on the *real*. Anxiety and its relation to the real come about starting from the signifier (Chapter 1, Lessons 1 and 2). The real of anxiety implies a not-knowing (Chapter 2, Lessons 3–5).

2 *Anxiety and its action involve the object a.* The structure of anxiety and its action is differentiated from *desire* and involves the object *a* (Chapter 3, Lessons 6 and 7). The object *a* is at the heart of transference (Chapter 4, Lessons 8 and 9).

3 *The desire of the analyst.* The *analyst's desire* can only be introduced as a function of lack (Chapter 5, Lessons 10–12, Seuil Chapters 10 and 11). Desire can only be articulated by taking account of anxiety, situated in the *gap between jouissance and desire* (Chapter 6, Lessons 13 and 14, Seuil Chapters 12 and 13).

4 *Minus phi and the object a.* *Women analysts* are immediately drawn to the questioning of desire, which implies a new approach to the body (Chapter 7, Lessons 15 and 16, Seuil Chapters 14 and 15). *Minus phi* insinuates itself into all the forms of object *a*, including the scopic form or the look (Chapter 8, Lessons 17 and 18, Seuil Chapters 16 and 17).

5 *The voice or the vocal object.* The introduction of *the vocal object* through the *shofar* is central to Lacan's entire teaching. The centrality of the vocal object *a* (Chapter 9, Lessons 19 and 20, Seuil Chapters 18 and 19) engages the whole

structure and a new clinic (Chapter 10, Lessons 21 and 22, Seuil Chapters 20 and 21).

6 ***The truth of anxiety***. Despite the repression proper to desire, as in the obsessional problematic, we must support the place of anxiety which re-situates desire in its dependence on *jouissance* (Chapter 11, Lessons 23 and 24, Seuil Chapters 22 and 23). The truth of anxiety lies in the overall structure of *jouissance-anxiety-desire;* it is expressed in the 'Name-of-the-Father' (Chapter 12, Lesson 25, Seuil Chapter 24, introduced in the single lesson of the following year's seminar *Les Noms-du-Père*).

Approaching the seminar on Anxiety requires a reading, that's to say, a reading by a true reader.

The reader of this book should not simply learn or store up Lacan's questions but make them his own. He or she must embark on the adventure of a genuine discussion with Lacan. Without this critical, inventive and unwavering questioning, the journey through Lacan's writing serves nothing. One must redo the work oneself so that such a reading might be fruitful. The integral transmission of the Lacanian contribution implies the 'matheme', but the matheme should never be understood as the borrowing of a mathematical formula to be pasted onto a psychoanalytic problem. The matheme is the process *whereby one does it by oneself,* by tracing, even questioning the path which invents the answers (this is what happens in mathematical practice) and these answers re-launch the questions.

This is the sense of my reading of this seminar: *Anxiety* invites the reader to read and reread the text *for himself,* to trace his own path, to rediscover how things intersect and don't intersect, and *by these means*, to move forward in the richness of an inventive reading.

Part One

Anxiety and the real

Chapter 1

Anxiety as "real", starting from the signifier

LESSON 1[1]: FROM THE SIGNIFIER TO THE REFERENCE
TABLE (INHIBITION/SYMPTOM/ANXIETY)

1 How to understand the signifier?

The seminar on *Anxiety* is situated in the direct line of its predecessor, the seminar on *Identification*. A phrase hovers above the latter: "the subject is that which is represented by a signifier for another signifier". If this is so, if the subject needs an identification in order to exist, it is because, in the first place, it, the subject, is non-existent. *It must be made*, because it is in no way some substance supposedly already there that the signifier would come to comment on secondarily. The subject is *only* represented by the signifier for another signifier. If the subject is completely dependent on the signifier, how are we to understand this signifier?

To understand "the signifier" and the expression "a signifier for another signifier", two completely different ways are proposed and opposed.

1 First of all, this expression can be understood as implying a *signifying chain*, a sequence of signifiers or words, a sentence or a discourse. Each word in the sentence only takes on its sense in relation to the other words in the sentence. Each part of speech takes on its sense only in relation to the other components of speech. Each signifier (word, part of speech) has meaning only in relation to at least one other signifier, which itself has another meaning. With this understanding, we should rather talk about the *signifying chain* and the signifiers that go to make a sentence or a discourse to convey a message, a hidden message, a message that we could interpret with the big Other, the big Other being the whole of the code, of the knowledge of language. Everything functions here, starting from the first level of Lacan's graph of desire[2]: the intention to signify has employed the big Other (A)[3], the code of language, to produce the message s(A) enunciated in the signifying chain, and this message can be interpreted, decoded or deciphered through the intermediary of the big Other. This decoding takes place on what is called in the graph the "signifier" line, starting from the signifying chain present in the message (Figure 1.1).

DOI: 10.4324/9781003477822-2

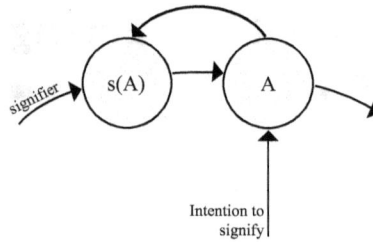

Figure 1.1 Coding and decoding of the signifier.

This understanding of the 'signifier' corresponds to what happens in a psychoanalysis, an interpretation that deciphers the hidden, repressed message. The 'subject' carrier of this hidden message situates himself in relation to the big Other and expects him to decipher his own repressed message. The topology of the intertwined toruses provides an illustration where the subject's hidden desire as revealed by the demand of the Other is illustrated by the turn of the axis of the torus of the subject corresponding to the turn of the winding of the torus of the Other (Figure 1.2).

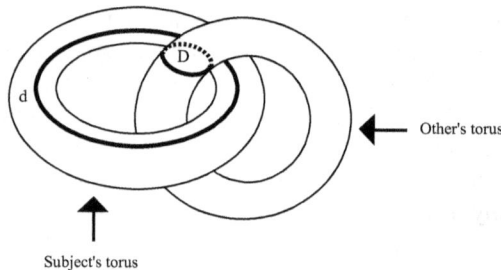

Figure 1.2 Intertwining of subject's torus with Other's torus.

Whether the Other is taken to be the analyst or something else, the intertwining of the two toruses supports the interpretation or the decoding of the message with the big Other enabling us to *know*: the signifier remains a function of its own signified, of its signification or meaning, and its hermeneutic interpretation leads to a knowledge that could ideally become absolute.

2 The second conception of the signifier is introduced in a radical fashion in the Seminar on *Identification*. The signifier is for another signifier, which itself is nothing other than the first signifier *repeated* and, in this repetition, emptied of all that is imaginary. We regularly experience this loss of the imaginary at the very heart of the signifier: 'Good morning' wishes us a good day.

To repeat 'Good morning' is to insist on the real that the first 'Good morning' was not heard, and that the Other did not respond. By the second round of the refrain, the signifier has lost its signified and all of its imaginary. Any signifier can thus be valid for another signifier, which is no more than a trait of this first signifier, repeated and devoid of any imaginary: a 'unary trait'. If we question the big Other about the meaning of this unary trait or of this other signifier, the Other does not answer. The "other signifier', the unary trait or S_2, stripped of all its imaginary flesh, refers only to a zero, to a void of meaning or of knowledge.

In this second conception, our starting point is no longer a message to be interpreted, but the experience of S(Ⱥ), the hole in the imaginary. In Lacan's graph of desire, we are at the level of the top line "of *jouissance*". With S(Ⱥ) comes the need to *do* something without the help of knowledge or the response of the big Other. This necessity to invent is at the heart of the drive (still on the line of *jouissance*): \$ ◊ D. D is the demand coming from the big Other insofar as it does not respond to what it demands. In the demand or absolute command supposedly decreed by the big Other "you shall not desire she who has been the object of my desire", the Other gives us no answer to the question of what we must do. We will have to construct something new with this non-answer. This is what is already at stake in the writing of the drive \$ ◊ D, where it is not a question of situating the subject in laws already given. It is a question of letting it emerge in its own law (autonomy = self-legislation) from the demand of the Other that remains without an answer, from the absolute nothing, according to the principle of *jouissance*.[4] (Figure 1.3).

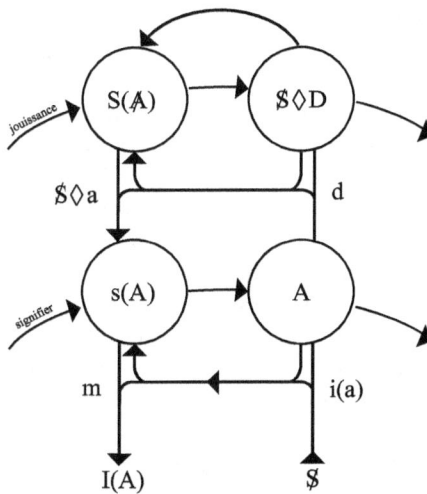

Figure 1.3 Lacan's graph of desire.

Starting from *jouissance*, the invention at the heart of the drive always implies the real of non-response (R), which is said in the midst of the symbolic (S) along with the imaginary effect (I) of invention, in other words the triad of the Borromean knot (RSI). Starting from the signifier, the first signifier (charged with the imaginary) will only really be for another signifier (symbolic) as this other signifier refers back to the void (the real) provoking invention (ISR).

The second conception of the signifier gives rise to the topology of the cross-cap, as we saw in the seminar on *Identification*. To summarise: the large loop of the first signifier charged with the imaginary and the small loop of the other signifier emptied of the imaginary (and repeating the first) together form an interior eight. By connecting the two loops of the interior eight with ties, we form a Moebius strip; and by closing the single edge of this Moebius strip in on itself, we form the cross-cap or the projective plane. In *Identification*, this served as the figure for the fundamental *phantasy* (starting from the imaginary of the signifier ISR). But starting from the real of non-response (RSI), it is the invention inherent in the *drive* that is written in the topology of the Borromean knot and in that of the cross-cap.

The difference or the floating between the *drive* and the *phantasy* will enable us to situate anxiety more precisely.

2   How do we approach anxiety?

In *Identification*, anxiety is introduced from the perspective of the intertwined toruses of the subject and the Other and is defined as the feeling of the desire of the Other. The big Other is first assumed to be perfectly consistent. Lacan, for example, represents it in the figure of the praying mantis, ready to devour its mate, or again, in 'The Subversion of the Subject and the Dialectic of Desire', in the apparition of Beelzebub in the form of the camel in Cazotte's *Le diable amoureux*, who, in his cavernous voice, roars out *Che vuoi*, What do you want? Anxiety would arise from a monstrous form – a praying mantis, Beelzebub's camel – in the locus of the big Other, who is supposed to speak and think.

The question of the big Other rises above the lower line of the signifier, implicating desire and aiming to become fixed in the phantasy. This is why anxiety must be situated at the level of phantasy, where, like the phantasy, it is played out in the in-between of the lower line of the signifier and the upper line of *jouissance*, or, in the in-between of the first and second conceptions of the signifier. We can already suspect that the method essentially, for treating neurotic anxiety, revolving around desire and phantasy and the line of the signifier, will consist in bringing the upper line of *jouissance* into play.

Let us start, however, from the lower line, from the big Other supposed to know.

2.1   Anxiety based on knowledge

The "subject supposed to know" is explained in Hegel's *Phenomenology of Spirit*. The first part (A) deals with *consciousness* in general (with the triad of sensation, perception and understanding). The second part (B) deals with *self-consciousness*, notably with the dialectic of the master and the slave. The third part (C) brings together consciousness and self-consciousness in *reason* (all the reality of consciousness is rational in self-consciousness, and all the rationality of self-consciousness is the reality of consciousness). Reason is then the starting point

(AA) of a new dialectic that leads to absolute knowledge. The fourth part (BB) takes up the whole dialectic of reason at the level of society and the state: this is the *spirit* itself. The fifth part (CC) relates, links and internalises the whole process in *religion*. Finally, the sixth part (DD) takes up the whole of all the parts articulated together in *absolute knowledge*. According to Lacan, self-consciousness (*Selbstbewusstsein*) is exactly the same as the subject supposed to know. Supposed knowledge is thus polarised towards and in absolute knowledge. In principle, there is no anxiety in all of this great chariot of knowledge. Everything seems well articulated in such a consistent big Other.

However, this whole cartage, this whole harnessing of knowledge composed by Hegel is called into question and disarmed by the highlighting of a fundamental unknown at the very root of this knowledge. With Kierkegaard and the existentialists (including Sartre), absolute knowledge goes awry: this is disarray; disorder insinuates itself into knowledge and this is anxiety. Lacan associates this disarray of knowledge with the misadventures of Little Hans' phobic object: the horse falls and is dislodged from its cart; the disarray of the horse makes Hans anxious.

Three attempts to deal with anxiety in and through knowledge or "the reason for failure".

1   Sartre's *seriousness*. Starting from disarray, a first way of dealing with anxiety would be to put the horse back in its shafts, to put anxiety back in the shafts of knowledge, to take anxiety seriously – that is, in the series of the development of knowledge and history – as Sartre wants to do in the *Critique of Dialectical Reason*.
2   Heidegger's *concern*. In *Being and Time* (first section), concern is the existential that takes up the condition of being-in-the-world that is *Dasein* and it is at the interior of this concern that anxiety appears, thus allowing us situate anxiety as an essential element in the perspective of the knowledge inherent in being-in-the-world.
3   Freud's *expectation*. After considering anxiety as the product of the automatic transformation of unused libido, Freud considers anxiety as a signal of danger, as the expectation of danger with a view to being able to avoid it or to, at least, prepare for it. We remain still within the perspective of the knowledge of danger.

These three ways of dealing with anxiety consist each time in identifying it and finally reducing it to the seriousness of an object of concern and the expectation proper to the mechanism of phobic defence. With these three approaches, it seems that we might have cornered this famous anxiety. We haven't immobilised anything at all; the bird has flown, we haven't even approached it; we've simply re-established a knowledge. Now, we have to work without these nets of knowledge. We can't approach anxiety by holding on to the net of the bottom line of the signifier in the graph (the first conception of the signifier as a signifying chain).

2.2   Anxiety starting from the second conception of the signifier

The three discourses given in Rome by Lacan in 1953, 1967 and 1975 mark the advances involved in the introduction of the second conception of the signifier, the signifying process. The first discourse (1953) introduced the report "The Function and Field of Speech and Language in Psychoanalysis"[5] and, with it, the realisation of the *subject by means of the signifier*. The second discourse (1967) takes account of a *failure* in the field of psychoanalysis and finds the reason for this in the fact of wanting to understand psychoanalysis *in terms of knowledge*. The third discourse (1974) introduces the *jouissance* at the very heart of the Borromean structure of R, S, I.

With reference to the Second Rome Discourse, we have just seen how anxiety cannot be treated as a function of knowledge (seriousness, concern or expectation). We need to situate anxiety *not in relation to knowledge* itself, but in relation to the *difficulty of knowing* (including the unconscious).

With reference to the Third Rome Discourse, we are going to see how anxiety must be situated in *relation to jouissance*, which is fundamental and foundational for the question of *movement*.

Anxiety in the movement of the Borromean Knot (The Third Rome Conference, La Troisième)

With *La Troisième*, anxiety is situated very precisely in the perspective of *jouissance*. The flattening of the Borromean knot captures a series of *jouissances*, and not just the classic three: phallic *jouissance* (at the intersection of S and R), *jouissance* of the Other (at the intersection of R and I) and *joui-sens* (at the intersection of I and S). This triad has become classic because they alone are explicitly inscribed in the drawing of the Borromean knot in *La Troisième*. But the text of the same lecture also explicitly mentions the *jouissance* of the body (the imaginary I, to the exclusion of R and S) and the *jouissance* of life (the real R, to the exclusion of I and S) and it would be easy to inscribe the *jouissance* of death (the symbolic S, to the exclusion of R and I).

Far from being explained in an inert schema, with inert boxes, anxiety implies movement in the structure of the Borromean knot. At first, we might think that anxiety should be inscribed in the *jouissance* of the body insofar as it could be circumscribed in the seriousness of a knowledge, in the concern of being-in-the-world and in the prudent expectation of anything that might threaten the body (1). However, from the *jouissance* of the body, the bird of anxiety has flown, bypassing the question of the absolute nothing, the object *a* at the centre of the drawing of the Borromean knot (2). Anxiety would then run counter to the *jouissance* of the body, into phallic *jouissance* (in the intersection of S and R, to the exclusion of I) alongside what Freud already called "castration anxiety" (3). This movement continues in the questioning of phallic *jouissance*, *in the dimension of the real* (4). In its movement, anxiety then appears in the tangential wake of the *real* loop (4), inscribing itself in the *jouissance* of the body (1) via object *a* (2) and via phallic *jouissance* (3) (Figure 1.4).

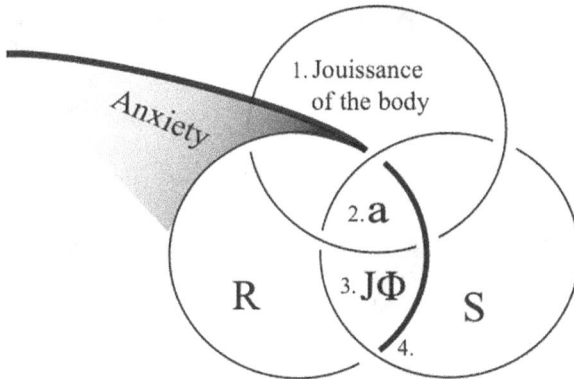

Figure 1.4 Movement of the anxiety from the *jouissance* of the body (1), through the object *a* (2) and the phallic *jouissance* (3) until the tangential wake of the *real* loop (4).

3 The reference table inhibition, symptom and anxiety

If anxiety is situated in the wake of the real, how can we specify this real?

On the one hand, anxiety completely escapes knowledge; it will have to be grasped in non-knowledge and the difficulty of knowing taken to its extreme (the unconscious). On the other hand, anxiety implies movement, the radical movement of structure (the drive), explained in particular in the Borromean knot. With these two ways of specifying the real (in the difficulty of knowing and in the question of movement), we have identified the two axes by which Lacan will specify anxiety in the trio ISA (inhibition, symptom, anxiety). We are going to see that on both axes, the trio ISA corresponds strictly to the trio ISR of the three dimensions of the imaginary, symbolic and real.

The two conceptions of the signifier determine two approaches to anxiety. The first (that of the lower line of the signifier in the graph) presupposes a possible knowledge, but anxiety escapes knowledge: the first axis of approach to anxiety is determined by the difficulty of knowing. The second conception of the signifier (that of the upper line of *jouissance*) presupposes movement, which will determine the second axis of approach to anxiety. These two axes concern not only the analysand, but first and foremost the analyst himself and with them, we can construct the reference table inhibition, symptom, anxiety. This table should not be understood as a classification of the pathological phenomena from which the patient or analysand suffers, but as a marker in the approach to the *listening* of the analysand and of the analyst. Anxiety can certainly be taken as an inhibition, but it is also a symptom and it must be supported as anxiety. The analyst would have to pose himself the question of his possible inhibition and of what constitutes a symptom in the direction of the treatment; above all, he would have to support the real of anxiety, his own and that of the analysand. Such is the sense of the seminar *Anxiety* and its reference table: (Figure 1.5).

	Difficulty of knowledge 1	Difficulty of knowledge 2	Difficulty of knowledge 3
Movement 1	**Inhibition**		
Movement 2		**Symptom**	
Movement 3			**Anxiety**

Figure 1.5 Inhibition, symptom and anxiety in the frame of movement and knowledge.

On both axes, we have three positions. These three positions are not on a continuum of difficulty of knowledge or of movement. They correspond each time to the trio of the imaginary, the symbolic and the real (Figure 1.6).

	Knowledge **I**	Knowledge **S**	Knowledge **R**
Movement **I**	**Inhibition**		
Movement **S**		**Symptom**	
Movement **R**			**Anxiety**

Figure 1.6 Inhibition, symptom and anxiety in the frame of imaginary, symbolic and real.

We could also show how the first position – for the two axes – implies the pleasure principle, the second, the reality principle and the third, the *jouissance* principle: (Figure 1.7).

	Pleasure Principle	Reality Principle	Jouissance Principle
Pleasure Principle	**Inhibition**	...	...
Reality Principle	...	**Symptom**	...
Jouissance Principle	...	...	**Anxiety**

Figure 1.7 Inhibition, symptom and anxiety and their own principle for the movement as well as for the knowledge.

By erasing the column and row entries, we obtain a reference table with nine cells: (Figure 1.8).

Inhibition	Impediment	Embarrassment
Emotion	Symptom	*Passage à l'acte*
Émoi	Acting out	Anxiety

Figure 1.8 Complete reference table of "inhibition, symptom, anxiety".

We now need to determine the value of each of these cells which serve as an entry point on the axis of the difficulty of knowing and on the axis of movement.

Three levels in the axis of the difficulty of knowledge

1 *Inhibition* is the point of origin of the two axes. Nothing moves and there is nothing to know. There is no difficulty at all on the side of knowledge: knowledge is only the image of reality (imaginary), it is a non-knowledge.

2 But *to say* that one is inhibited, to *talk* about inhibition, is already to pass to a certain form of knowing and to the symbolic. It is *an impediment*: you're trapped. The Latin verb *impedicare* means entrapment; more precisely, *impedicare* means to get caught in the *pedica,* in a snare, a foot trap. In impediment, the subject gets caught up in his own symbolic system. He is entangled. The subject is caught in the symbolic and in the principle of reality; at the same time, he is immobilised (in the axis of movement), trapped in his own immobile image. To think about impediment, the symbolic has to be there at the same time (at the median level of the difficulty of knowledge) and immobilised in the imaginary (at the level of movement).

3 In *embarrassment*, the difficulty of knowing is at its greatest. The subject can no longer find his way; the subject is blocked by a *real* that effaces him. The *embarazada*, the pregnant woman, is embarrassed by her foetus, by the child she is carrying inside her. Her being as a (symbolic) subject is barred by the real of a birth that has not yet taken place (movement is arrested), not only of the birth of her child, but also of her own birth *as a mother*, which questions her very status as a woman. Embarrassed, I can no longer know, and the big Other doesn't respond S(Ⱥ). I am confronted with the real and the principle of *jouissance* (a radical bar on the subject and the big Other), from this radical non-knowledge and this real, I am invited to create, but I don't know how to respond (movement is completely arrested).

Three tiers in the axis of movement

It is not a question of measuring movement – is it fast or slow? – but of understanding the different kinds of movement and their nature. For Aristotle, movement can be understood in four different ways: according to quantity (getting bigger or smaller), according to quality, an alteration (for example, the caterpillar that becomes a butterfly), according to place (it is now a transport or a translation), and finally, according to substance (movement here implies the birth and death of substance: *genesis* and *phtora*). This fourth kind engages the reality of creation, invention and the principle of *jouissance*; it corresponds to the third degree on the axis of movement. The other three movements, according to Aristotle, correspond to the second degree. And the absence of all movement corresponds to the first degree.

1 *Inhibition* is defined as the stoppage of movement.

2 *Emotion* involves movement, *motion*, but something disturbs normally regulated movement: e-motion. Here, movement is triggered by an external factor which involves an alteration, a change of place and a change of magnitude. For example, the crisis of hysteria attempts to change things, to alter, displace, increase or decrease the desire of the Other and one's own desire.

3 *Émoi*. According to Bloch and Von Wartburg's *Dictionnaire étymologique de la langue française*, "émoi" comes from the old verb *esmayer*, to trouble, to frighten, to dismay and is related to *mögen* in German and, in English, to *want*, to the modal verb *may*. *Émoi* implies the most profound movement; it implies the emergence of birth and the corruption of death, but in the form of pure unrealised potential. Presented in the facile dimension of the imaginary, it is not questioned and remains in the field of naive non-knowledge.

Lacan challenges the first French translation of Freud's *Triebregung* as 'motion pulsionnelle' (*Triebregung* is translated as "instinctual impulse" in both Strachey's *The Complete Psychological Works of Sigmund Freud* and Laplanche and Pontalis's *Vocabulary of Psychoanalysis*). "Motion pulsionnelle" in French could be justified if we consider that the drive in its dynamic sense, life drive and death drive, responds in the graph to S(O), at the real level of the line of *jouissance*. With *émoi*, it is the creative potential of the drive that appears in its raw state, without knowing it. And, if "esmayer" is linked to *mögen*, to desire, we can also understand, with Heidegger, that *émoi* is at the source of what we can achieve, of what we are really capable of, *vermögen* (having means), at the creative and inventive level; we are only capable, *vermögen*, of what we desire, *mögen*, coming from the creative force inherent in *mögen* and *émoi*.

For Freud, anxiety is an *affect*, accounting for one of the two representatives (*Repräsentant*) of the drive. The drive cannot be perceived directly as such; it can *only* be *represented* (*repräsentiert*) by its two representatives (*Repräsentant*), the representation (*Vorstellung*) and the affect. Representation is the signifier, as first conceived in the signifying chain dominated by the subject supposed to know, where the little pegs fit into the little boxes. But when the little pegs no longer fit into the boxes provided by knowledge, when the principle of reality breaks down and the real of non-knowledge imposes itself, it is the affect of anger or anxiety that appears, obliging us to revise our way of conceiving the signifier and to introduce the second conception of the signifier, the question of the real and of *jouissance*.

By addressing anxiety *as a real affect* (and not as an emotion or an impediment), Lacan elevates it to the third level both in the order of difficulty of knowledge (embarrassment) and of movement (*émoi*), that is, to the level of embarrassment where there is no response from the Other S(Ⱥ) and to the level of *émoi*, where the root of movement is summoned (according to the principle of *jouissance*). At these outer extremes of the two levels of the reference table, a new erotology is required for psychoanalysis; this consists in supporting anxiety as a conjunction of *émoi* with movement at its root and of embarrassment corresponding to the maximum difficulty in knowing.

LESSON 2[6]: ANXIETY AS THE TRUTH OF DESIRE

1 How to approach anxiety – three methods

Starting from the dimension of the unspeakable *real* highlighted in the first lesson, the question arises: is the teaching of psychoanalysis still possible? Has it a sense?

Teaching presupposes the transmission of a knowledge, placing us in the median level of the difficulty of knowing. More fundamentally, as opposed to a knowledge that is given and acquired, teaching as a process always first presupposes non-knowledge, not only the non-knowledge of the one who is learning, but also the non-knowledge of the one who is teaching.[7]

Should the analysand be made to know something? That is what the neurotic expects from analysis: that his case will be explained to him and that he will in any case be let off the hook. Because he wants to know, in the sense of the median level of the difficulty of knowing, and at the same time, he doesn't want to know in the sense of repression: he doesn't want the fundamental question that is repressed, to be touched. The not-knowing of the neurotic is situated in the column of inhibition.

The analyst's non-knowledge, however, is radically out of step with regard to the position of a subject supposed to know; it takes account of the radical non-response of every big Other as an instance of supposed knowledge: the signifier of the Other barred $S(\cancel{A})$ on the top line of the graph, the line of *jouissance*.

By approaching non-knowledge in this way, to teach is to aim at taking hold by allowing oneself to be caught up in the movement of the real and of what this implies. To take hold in the form of 'letting oneself be taken hold of' is already an "understanding", but not at all an understanding at the level of knowledge: above all, it is necessary *to not understand* at the level of knowledge, above all, to not remain tangled up in the first conception of the signifier, to not remain at the line of the signifier in the graph where the message could be interpreted by the common sense of the big Other. If Lacan regularly insists on "not understanding", it is to avoid remaining on the line of the message (the first conception of the signifier) and to open up access to the line of *jouissance* (the second conception of the signifier). In this way, we will be able to orient ourselves in the right method for approaching anxiety, for "understanding" anxiety.

1 *The catalogue method* consists in classifying or categorising anxiety by a series of concepts and sub-concepts, of genera and of species – subspecies. We could represent this method as a series of concentric circles that would end up pinpointing exactly what anxiety is. In this way, anxiety is a psychoanalytic concept, a concept representing the drive, a concept representing the drive by means of an unpleasant affect, for example. In this sense, anxiety would finally be the little peg that fits perfectly into the right hole defined in the series of concentric circles (concepts, sub-concepts, sub-sub-concepts, etc.). But anxiety arises precisely when the little pegs *don't fit* into the little holes!

2 *The analogy method* consists in approaching anxiety from different points of view (biological, sociological, philosophical, etc.) and then establishing a series of analogies between these different approaches. This method was already in play in the approach to anxiety as seriousness (with Sartre), as concern (with Heidegger), as expectation (with Freud and Lacan) and the resonance between these different perspectives. This method is built around knowledge and is not the right approach for addressing anxiety: "the bird has flown".

3 *The method of the key* will be the only right approach. The key here is the method of how the signifier functions as understood in the second conception. The key is presented as an interior eight, whose large loop is S_1, charged with an entire imaginary, and whose small loop S_2 is a repetition of S_1 freed of all imaginary. In S_2, all that remains is a trait, a unary trait, empty of all imaginary and all meaning. The key is the production of S_2, of the unary trait, not S_1. Take any signifier and it can serve as S_1. The question is to draw the S_2 from it, in other words to empty S_1 of its imaginary. The process may seem absolutely abstract. Listening

to our analysands, we can hear that they themselves provoke the emptying of the imaginary of the signifier. When an analysand contradicts himself (and free association inevitably leads to this), the signifier involved loses its imaginary consistency. Thus, in the conjunction of "it's my mother" and "it's not my mother", "my mother" becomes an S_2 signifier, a unary trait with no imaginary to speak of.

"In the beginning is the unary trait" is not to say that with unary traits we would have the elementary parts from which we could assemble a drawing or a more complex structure. "In the beginning is the unary trait" means that with the unary trait (the production of S_2 from any S_1 emptied of its imaginary), we have the key that will accompany us from the beginning to the end. From then onwards, instead of trying to find the imaginary coherence that could be constructed from what the analysand says, the analyst will seek instead to support the incoherence – the contradiction that unmoors the signifier from the imaginary, without knowledge – and which is the place for invention.

2   Anxiety as the truth of desire

"In the beginning is the unary trait" in the beginning is the big Other, in the equivocation of the subject supposed to know (the lower line of the signifier in the graph) and of a radical non-knowledge that gives no answer (the upper line of *jouissance* in the graph). This equivocation produces the "dialectic of desire" depending on the phantasy, at the intermediate line between the phantasy and of desire in the graph, where the "subject" is the subject engendered by the signifier ("subversion of the subject"). Desire and the subject appear in the dialectic that implies the Other and the desire of the Other.

The desire of man is the desire of the Other.[8]

Taken out of context, the phrase is perfectly Hegelian, and Lacan might seem fundamentally Hegelian. For Hegel, and for many a certain way of practising psychoanalysis, the Other is *consciousness* or what can become conscious; it is the subject supposed to know that dominates all history up to absolute knowledge (consciousness, self-consciousness, reason, spirit and religion, and absolute knowledge). The Other is here – for Hegel – the Other of the line of the message, who will be able to interpret the message.

Put back into its explicit context, the same sentence is preceded by explicit mention of the *unconscious*: "the unconscious is the discourse of the Other", where the "of" must be understood as an objective determination: it is not the Other who speaks, but the unconscious speaks of the Other, who does not respond $S(\cancel{A})$; the result is that the business of the Other agitates us and pushes us towards invention and creation. For Lacan, the Other is the Other barred by the line of *jouissance*. The Other implies the unconscious, that is, non-knowledge, absolute non-knowledge. It is a hole at the level of knowledge, at the level of the explanation of what I am, a hole at the level of interpretation. It is illusory to think that psychoanalysis is going to lead to an explanation of what I am, in an analysis or even in the pass; it is completely contrary to the process of psychoanalysis.

Far from being a question of the history of philosophy, the difference between Hegel and Lacan, between the Hegelian and Lacanian interpretation of desire in relation to the Other, is fundamental to the practice of the signifier: are we to understand it according to its first conception centred on absolute knowledge (the lower line of the signifier in the graph, Hegel) or according to the second conception centred on absolute non-knowledge (the upper line of *jouissance* in Lacan's graph)? By following the conception of the signifier as a signifying chain, we rely on the hypothesis of a possible interpretation based on the big Other, who is the subject supposed to know. The big Other exists, personified or not, thanks to which the subject can identify and find the interpretation that suits him or her before leaving analysis and acting on it. For Lacan, for true psychoanalysis, what is really at stake is S_1–S_2, the interior eight and the movement of creation stating from $S(\cancel{A})$.

But between Hegel's desire and Lacan's desire, where is the truth? How can it be right to hold as true, desire according to Hegel or according to Lacan? It is not just a question of formulating the structure of desire according to one or the other, but rather the truth of this desire on both sides, and it is anxiety that offers the truth each time: (Figure 1.9 and 1.10).

1. The structure of desire in Hegel	3. The truth of Hegelian desire: anxiety
2. The structure of desire in Lacan	4. The truth of desire according to Lacan: anxiety

Figure 1.9 Structure and truth of desire by Hegel and Lacan.

1. $d(a) : d(A) < a$	3. $d(x) : d(\cancel{A}) < x$
2. $d(a) < i(a) : d(\cancel{A})$	4. $d(0) < 0 : d(\cancel{A})$

Figure 1.10 Formulae of the structure of desire and of its truth for Hegel and for Lacan.

The passage from the structure of desire to the truth of desire consists each time in a loss of imaginary substance, corresponding to the signifying process S_1–S_2. In the Hegelian formulae (1 and 3), the "a" is replaced by an "x" and the "A" by an " $\cancel{A}$ "[9]. In the Lacanian formulae (2 and 4), "a" is replaced by zero 0, and similarly "i(a)".

Besides the literal expressions, $d(a)$, $d(A)$, a, $d(x)$, $d(\cancel{A})$, x, $i(a)$, $d(0)$ and 0, each of the four formulae contains two operators, ":" and "<". The operator ":" is read as "in other words", "equivalent to", or even "confronted with", not without making the difference between the two expressions linked by the operator resonate. The second operator "<" is read as "institutes", "leads to" or even "produces".

2.1 The Structure of desire in Hegel

Let's read these formulae. Hegel's first formula reads then as: the desire of the little other confronted with the desire of the big Other produces the consistency of the little other. Replacing the "little other" with man then becomes "the desire of man is the desire of the Other", meaning that the desire of man confronted with the desire of the Other produces the consistency of man. In the master-slave dialectic, the confrontation of the desire of the slave and the desire of the master produces the slave's consistency. And the whole dialectic is played out in self-consciousness, self-awareness, in the perspective of knowledge.

2.2 The structure of desire in Lacan

The desire of the little other necessarily culminates in the confrontation between, on the one hand, the ideal ego, dependent in the graph on the lower line of the signifier and, on the other hand, the desire of the barred big Other, dependent in the graph on the upper line of *jouissance*. Desire (d) – inscribed in the graph on the intermediate line linking it to the phantasy ($ ◊ a) – leads to the double conception of the signifier, understood at times in the signifying chain, as one signifier among others and sometimes in the S_1–S_2 movement, the movement of the interior eight, creator of the Moebius strip, then of the cross-cap. Desire produces the confrontation between, on the one hand, the imaginary ideal Ego and, on the other, d(A), which determines the structure of the fundamental phantasy ($ ◊ a), hence of S_1–S_2, of the interior eight, thus of the second conception of the signifier.

The ideal ego, presented in the form of the specular image, is not simply the image in the mirror, it is the imaginary of all explanations that are held, of all interpretations that provide a landscape, a vision of what the subject could be on the basis of the signifying chain (Figure 1.11).

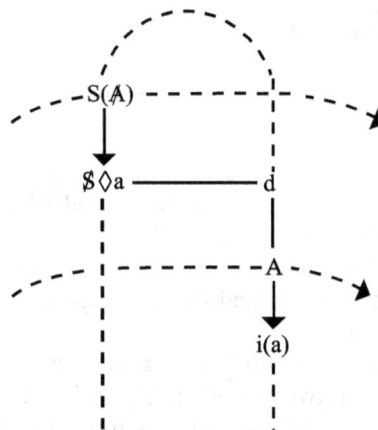

Figure 1.11 The desire between the second conception of the signifier (depending on the signifier of the big Other) and the first one (depending on the big Other and the ideal Ego), presented in the Lacan's graph.

And the fundamental phantasy, insofar as it depends on S(Ⱥ), reprises the fundamental structure of the unconscious starting from the upper line of *jouissance*. Desire is thus produced and constructed in the in-between of the unconscious that can be interpreted (the first conception of the signifier) and the dynamic unconscious (the second conception). All that follows of the seminar on Anxiety will not cease from insisting on the necessity to understand desire by taking *jouissance* and the gap between desire and *jouissance* into account.

While, in Hegel, desire, as equivalent to the desire of the Other, produced the consistency of man, of the little other in consciousness and in, supposedly, absolute knowledge (at the level of the line of the signifier), in Lacan, desire writes the dialectic that articulates man's imaginary consistency, the dialectic of the little other with the unconscious and the radical non-knowledge inherent in *jouissance* (line of jouissance).

What is the truth of these two positions?

2.3   The truth of desire in Hegel

On the one hand, he who was presented as the little other or man is only an unknown x. On the other hand, the big Other as absolute knowledge is only an imaginary construction; it is in fact barred: Ⱥ. The great haulage of the *Phenomenology of Spirit* is unravelling; this is the disarray introduced into the history of philosophy with Kierkegaard in the *concept of anxiety*. While Hegel masters the difficulty of knowledge in the median position of the reference table (by explaining the series of *impediments* that provoke the course of the different figures of History), with Hegel's truth, unveiled by Kierkegaard, we have passed into maximum *embarrassment*: the consequence of the entire structure of desire in Hegel no longer leading to knowing what the little other, man, is, but to an unknown, to x.

At the same time, the passage from knowing to not-knowing, from impediment to embarrassment, from the big Other supposed to know to the barred big Other (Ⱥ), and the reduction of man (a) to a pure unknown (x), already introduces Lacan's structure of desire, which, from the outset, implied Ⱥ.

Which is the truth?

2.4   The truth of desire in Lacan

The desire of the *little other* is the desire for zero d(0). The starting point of desire is found in this zero, which already resonates with the object *a*, in its radical form: there is nothing and there will be nothing because the enterprise of knowing necessarily engenders contradictions that annihilate all imaginary consistency. This zero is the object *a* in its vocal form, underlying S(Ⱥ) (there will be no response from the big Other). Very concretely, this zero can be constructed in mathematics; for Frege, zero is defined as identical to that which is not identical to itself: there is nothing that falls under this concept, it is zero, it is a contradiction as when one might say a "wooden stone", a "square circle". Such formulae can be very useful in analysis to clarify the value of the multiple contradictions that inevitably arise. And they place us in the truth of the treatment. It is object a, it is zero, it is the starting point, which engenders the two-sided, janus-like face of the moral law and desire (moral law = repressed desire), commanding every movement of creation and invention.

The ideal ego, i(a), is replaced by zero. This is not just the "specular image", but also the whole imaginary of coherent explanations of what it is to be an individual and of all the interpretations that hold up well. It is all worth zero: the passage from the structure of desire to the truth of desire, i(a) is, for Lacan, replaced by zero.

This zero, as the value of i(a), is confronted and brought into resonance with the desire of a big Other that does not exist.

2.5   The reversal of the formula of the truth of desire

With this reversal, the formula of the truth of desire must now be read from right to left: the desire of the barred Other gives way to the desire of a (d(a)), but this d(a) is no longer the desire of man, but desire starting from nothing, desire that starts from the object a in its vocal form. In other words, the desire of the analyst has become the desire of what holds the place of the semblance of object a in psychoanalytic discourse. In Part Three, we will return to this question of the desire of the analyst starting from nothing. The place of the semblance as d(a) that comes in the place of d($Å$) is confronted with the zero of the "specular image", including the interpretations that claim to give the image of the analysand's psychological structure. And this resonance between d(a) and 0 on the analysand's side is merely the product of the desire from zero that is inherent in the analysand's work: it is produced in and with desire arising from 0, from the vocal object on the analysand's side.

With this 0 and this d(0), desire is selectively (punctually) indicated; it is not of the order of the infinite, but locally engendered in the signifying process, in the movement of the interior eight, in the movement of the signifier for a single signifier. The classical dimension of the so-called infinitude of desire is a theological dimension, which trusts in God, who is founded on a big Other. Situated on the lower line of the graph, it is a false infinitude based on the indefinite signifying chain, on signifiers that, in their metonymy, can never stop.

In contrast to the infinitude of desire, the unary trait – always singular – must be understood as starting from zero and not from one. Because if we understand the unary trait as a unit, it becomes possible to add signifiers indefinitely, allowing us to remain with the first conception of the signifier, that of the signifying chain.

Therefore, let us start again with the Other and the barred Other insofar as it indeed allows the subject, as represented by a signifier for another signifier, to emerge.

3   The division of the Other by the question of the subject

How do we conceive of the Other? As a given consistency, as the big Other that is not barred, as the locus of the code? It then corresponds to the first conception of the signifier. Or, in the division of the Other, which annihilates it and makes it a barred big Other? Then, it corresponds to the second conception of the signifier.

How do we situate the subject in the field of the Big Other?

With this question, we are already engaged in the first conception of the signifier (we will see later how Lacan proposes another schema of the division of the Other, corresponding to the second conception of the signifier in the line of *jouissance*). We can imagine *this* division of the field of the Other as a mathematical division, the division of 19 by 3, for example, gives us 6 and 1 remaining. We have only divided 18 and 1 remains (Figure 1.12).

19	3
18	6
1	

Figure 1.12 19 divided by 3 gives quotient 6 and leaves a remainder 1.

Similarly, the division of A by S the subject (who does not yet exist and who only appears in the signifying process approached here by the schema of division) gives us a divided A, or a barred A (this is one way of seeing A: a divided A that remains within the framework of the first conception of the signifier and of an essentially unbarred big Other). In *this* division, we have only divided the barred subject (barred by the signifier) and what remains is "a": (Figure 1.13).

A	S
$	Ⱥ
a	

Figure 1.13 The division of the big Other A by the subject S. A divided by S gives quotient barred A and leaves a remainder *a*.

The two lower terms in the left-hand column provide us with the two terms of the phantasy, $ and a. But here, the phantasy is still grasped in terms of the signifying chain (the first conception of the signifier) and not as the "fundamental phantasy" set out in the topology of the cross-cap (the second conception of the signifier).

Recall that the Hegelian formula of desire was centred on the desire of the Other where the desire of the Other (the master) was only a form of *love*, and if the man (the slave) did not want it, that changed nothing about the love of the Other: "*I love you even if you don't want it*". The love of the Other, of the master (d(A)), imposes itself in all consciousness in the face of the slave's (d(a)) unwillingness, and this is what determines what man is. Here, love is more important than desire, and not-wanting more important than not-knowing; for *love* and *will* appear in the Hegelian dialectic centred on the absolute knowledge of the Other. In other words, Hegelian desire is not a true desire.

The Lacanian structure of *desire* begins with unconscious desire: "*I desire you even if I don't know it*". Desire (d(a)) has the consequence that all imaginary explanations (i(a)) are no more than veils that hide radical not-knowing and resonate with it (d(A̶)). *We are already at the level of the line of jouissance* and desire depends on it. Engaging desire beyond awareness, beyond interpretation, beyond explanation is played out with the force of the unconscious inherent in the non-knowledge of the Other himself ("even if I don't know it"). *Desire* depends on the non-knowledge of the Other, fundamentally barred (Lacan's reversed formula for the truth of desire).

Later on, we shall see how the real question of love will be introduced starting from *jouissance*, that is, from S(A̶). "Only love allows jouissance to condescend to desire". Desire is understood in its dependence on jouissance *by means of love*. And love depends on a process that does not begin with persons and self-consciousness, but with the signifying process $(S_1–S_2)$ the second conception of the signifier) where *jouissance* is primary. None of this comes about without a revision of the schema of the division of the Other, which implies another way of understanding desire and love, beyond the will that always lags behind knowledge.

Identification is no longer played out in knowledge and in the imposition of the love of the Other that is stronger than the will of the subject to be identified (Hegel). It is the identification to the unknown object of my desire, to this zero, to the object that you lack and that I also lack. From this void, from this zero, the invention of the one who loves and the one who is loved is played out in a reciprocal action that precedes the constitution of personalised desire (in the subject or in the Other, as supposed in the topology of the intertwined toruses).

Notes

1 Lesson of 14 November 1962.
2 Jacques Lacan, "Subversion of the Subject and the Dialectic of Desire" in *Écrits*, Paris, Seuil, 1966, p. 808.
3 Other or Autre? All uses of the Other are equivalent to l'Autre in Lacan's sense, hence, the use of the symbols A or a instead of O or o in diagrams, schemata and formulae throughout the text.
4 Christian Fierens, *Le principe de jouissance, Louvain-la-Neuve*, EME, 2020. *The Jouissance Principle,* London, Routledge, 2022.
5 Jacques Lacan, "Subversion of the Subject and the Dialectic of Desire" in *Écrits*, Paris, Seuil, 1966.
6 Lesson of 21 November 1962.
7 Cf. Jacques Rancière, *Le maître ignorant*, Paris, Fayart, 1987.
8 Jacques Lacan, "Subversion of the Subject and the Dialectic of Desire" in *Écrits*, Paris, Seuil, 1966, p. 814.
9 Here, we follow the Staferla version: http://staferla.free.fr/S10/S10%20L'ANGOISSE.pdf

Chapter 2

The real and non-knowledge

We have seen in the previous lessons that the key to approaching anxiety was the signifier, more precisely the second conception of the signifier, "a signifier for another signifier", in which the first signifier, S_1, charged with the imaginary is repeated in S_2, emptied of all imaginary. In the seminar on *Identification*, Lacan uses the example of his grandfather, who was an obnoxious *petit bourgeois*: "a grandfather (S_1) is a grandfather (S_2)", to be understood as "my grandfather who was an obnoxious petit bourgeois" (S_1 loaded with the imaginary) is a "grandfather" (S_2, which no longer has any meaning and who's signified is a question mark). In this process, the imaginary I is already articulated in S_1, the symbolic S in the passage from S_1 to S_2 and the real R with the void of meaning in S_2. The triad of R, S and I allows us to radically differentiate the first conception of the signifier (in which the real is absent) from the second (in which the real is present), and to differentiate the Hegelian conception of desire, revolving around consciousness and absolute knowledge (I and S), from the Lacanian conception of desire, involving non-knowledge S(Ⱥ) and the real (I, S and R).

This differentiation between the Hegelian and Lacanian conceptions of desire is illustrated by our ISA reference table (inhibition, symptom, anxiety), now *doubly* organised around the difficulty of knowing and of movement, by ISR (the imaginary, the symbolic and the real). A Hegelian conception and a conception of psychoanalysis revolving around a signifying chain to be interpreted (thereby excluding consideration of the real) do not take embarrassment, *émoi* and anxiety into account. The reference table is then reduced to the four boxes of inhibition, of impediment, of emotion and of the symptom, where everything pretends to function according to the pleasure principle (I) and the reality principle (S) without taking the *jouissance* principle (R) into account (Figure 2.1).

Inhibition	Impediment
Emotion	Symptom

Figure 2.1 The reference table reduced to four boxes.

DOI: 10.4324/9781003477822-3

Such a table (corresponding to the first conception of the signifier according to Hegel) makes it impossible to understand anything about psychoanalysis. Lacan insists from the outset that he is not Hegelian, that he has never been Hegelian and that his 1946 article *Presentation on Psychical Causality* already implied the real and the articulation R, S, I. The real falls outside the Hegelian framework and Hegel's four-square diagram fits into the Lacanian nine-square framework as a reduction of the latter.

In this session of the seminar, Lacan is going to accentuate a double articulation of the real, on the one hand starting from the symbolic and, we might say, from reason, and on the other, starting from the imaginary and the mirror where, in each case, the key to the signifier is at stake.

1   The symbolic and the real

Claude Lévi-Strauss's *La pensée sauvage* (1962) had just been published, the last chapter of which was a critique of Sartre's *The Critique of Dialectical Reason* (1960). As we have seen, from Sartre's point of view, to deal with anxiety, we would have to put history back in its shafts along with seriousness and consider the individual in terms of society, of the history that shapes him. A Hegelian perspective, this dialectises the individual side of the ego, the side of the pure for-oneself *pour soi* (cf. Hegel's consciousness and self-consciousness) with the collective, societal side (cf. Hegel's spirit and religion) by way of reason and from the perspective of knowledge (cf. Hegel's absolute knowledge). From the point of view of the symbolic (and of knowledge), Sartre may well contrast the primitive and the civilised. But this distinction is fallacious according to Claude Lévi-Strauss, because from the outset, a fundamental opposition imposes itself between, on the one hand, the real of exchanges that are spontaneously given in praxis and, on the other, the symbolism of pre-conscious, pre-meditated structures and rules. The real is very present in Levi-Strauss's thinking, even if *The Elementary Structures of Kinship* (1945) lends itself too easily to reducing the question of the real of exchanges to a (symbolic-imaginary) *reality*, rather than highlighting their articulation with the symbolic of pre-conscious, pre-meditated rules.

For Sartre, the opposition between *analytic reason*, which analyses the facts of *reality* (including exchanges), and *dialectical reason* (the rules that are symbolically structured in history) remains in the Hegelian perspective of knowledge and the symbolic. Let us add here that *analytic reason* and *dialectical reason* resonate with Kant's division of *transcendental logic* (in *The Critique of Pure Reason*) into two major parts: *transcendental analytic* and *transcendental dialectic*. The *transcendental analytic* analyses and deals with the categories and principles that condition all knowledge. The *transcendental dialectic* dialectises the inevitable tendency of reason to imagine itself knowing what is impossible to know; reason thus produces three fundamental imaginary illusions, reason's three pure ideas: the imaginary of the soul, the imaginary of the world and the imaginary of God, which, respectively, plug the inevitable hole, the real of what would be the ultimate substance, the ultimate cause and the ultimate reciprocal action.

Let us now start from the inevitable imaginary of the *world* and successively bring into play the symbolic of the stage and the real of the scene on the stage.

1.1   The world, the stage and the scene on the stage

The world presents itself as a reality already structured by the certain conditions of experience, but it is an *imaginary* requirement, on the basis of which the symbolic can make its entrance. Any S_1 is a constituent part of the world, but serves as the entrance on stage of the signifying process; it is for the stage.

The stage. What distinguishes the world from the stage is that on the stage, things come to be *said*. This saying cannot be reduced to the saying of science or to any other form of communication. Saying, as *symbolic*, is the word that gives birth to the "actor", the *parlêtre*, including all the history that needs to be put back into its shafts.

The scene on the stage is redoubled here in a way similar to the second conception of the "signifier for another signifier". For Freud, quoting Fechner, the scene of the dream is another scene, *ein anderer Schauplatz*, a scene other than the scene of vigilant representation.[2] Out of synch with the symbolism of the day before, the other scene already indicates the *real* of the unconscious. Thus, the young Descartes advances onto a hidden stage: "*larvatus prodeo*"[3] "onto the (symbolic) stage of the (imaginary) world *I advance masked* (real?)".

But is it enough to quote Freud's other scene or Descartes' *I advance masked* to touch on the real? Or again is it enough to note with Freud that an event appearing as a "dream within a dream" "is the most decisive confirmation of the reality of this event" and can be taken for the real itself of this event? It is nothing of the sort. As we will see with Shakespeare, the simple duplication of the scene and the simple repetition of the signifier do not immediately open the dimension of the real.

1.2   The scene on the stage in Hamlet

Claudius has killed Hamlet's father and married Gertrude, his father's wife. In the first act, the ghost of Hamlet's father appears to his son, revealing to him that he has been murdered by Claudius and asking him to avenge him and spare his mother Gertrude. To comply with his father's request, Hamlet is going to pass himself off a madman.

In Act II, Claudius and Gertrude worry about Hamlet's madness, try to bring him to his senses sending him to England with his childhood friends, Rosencrantz and Guildenstern. In the same act, a gentleman, Polonius, explains that if Hamlet has gone mad, it is because Ophelia, Polonius' daughter, has refused his advances.

In Act III (where the question *to be or not to be* is raised), Hamlet hires professional actors to perform a scene all together similar to the actual murder of Hamlet's father by Claudius: Hamlet's aim is to capture Claudius' unease and feelings of guilt at seeing this scene, thereby reminding him of his crime. Claudius is indeed troubled by this theatrical performance and withdraws with the Queen. He then implores heaven to pardon him for his crime. Hamlet surprises Claudius in prayer, but refuses to kill him at the very moment that Claudius is repenting, reasoning that to kill him at that moment would be to send him straight to heaven. Later, while strongly reproaching his mother for her part in the crime, he hears a noise behind a curtain. Believing it to be Claudius spying on the discussion, he drives his sword into the curtain and kills the man who is not Claudius, but Polonius.

The fourth act recounts, among other things, the suicide of Ophelia following the death of her father, Polonius.

In the fifth act, the duel between Laertes, son of Polonius, and Hamlet ends in the death of both (because the blades have been poisoned). Having fatally wounded Laertes and before dying himself, Hamlet stabs King Claudius, who immediately dies.

In the scene on the stage, the play in a play, Lucianus, actor, who is to kill the king does not appear as Claudius the brother of the King, but as his nephew (Hamlet's son). In this scene on the stage, Hamlet thus aims to give body to his own specular image (i(a)) in the person of Lucianus. It is not his attire, as Lacan presents it, that allows Lucianus to be identified as Hamlet's specular image, but Hamlet's own words; in his introduction to the play, which serves as the scene within the scene (scene 2 of act 3), Hamlet introduces Lucianus as the "the nephew of the king"! when it is in fact, Hamlet the son, who has to kill his uncle Claudius at the end of the tragedy, whereby, on this introduction of Lucianus by Hamlet, Ophelia comments: "You are a good as a chorus, my lord".

However, Hamlet's identification by means of the specular image represented by Lucianus in the scene on the stage is by no means sufficient to allow Hamlet take action to avenge his father, even as, in Scene III, in the act of praying and repenting, his neck already presented to his sword, Hamlet holds back and refuses to slay Claudius.

What does Hamlet lack in order to have the courage to avenge his father? An imaginary identification with Lucianus is not enough. So that he can kill Claudius, Hamlet must identify with Ophelia, the victim to suicide, who has herself identified with the *object* of her grief, that is, with her father Polonius. In this last identification, Ophelia allows the destructive shadow of the lost object to fall on her. It is a mourning that could be called melancholic. But the only outcome of identification with the lost object is not melancholy or the suicide that would follow (as for Ophelia). Another outcome of identification with the lost object is to give the lost object the positive value of the dead person as having been alive and as having already achieved glory. This heralds the whole importance of the object *a*.

That identification with the specular image does not suffice, and that it must pass by way of identification with the lost object (all is lost) is made clear in the last act, where Hamlet has to kill his specular image Laërtes before he can stab Claudius.

Here, according to Lacan, we find the formulae of the structure of desire and of its truth. Desire leads to or produces a contrasting equivalence between the specular image and the desire of the barred big Other. Recall that for Lacan, the formula of desire is written "d(a) < i(a): d(A̶)". Imaginary identification with Lucianus and even with Laërtes is not enough for Hamlet to engage in the act of avenging his father. Identification with the object of desire, object *a* is also required. But it is only insofar as this object of desire has just disappeared (Ophelia's suicide) that it takes on its full value as the object cause of desire, rather than the object that is aimed at by desire. The object *a* thus resides in the suspended dimension of the *im-parfait*, the not-perfect. Analysis of the *im-parfait* reveals the non-knowledge inherent in object *a* as when, the sentence "the moment after the bomb was to explode", taken out of context, opens up a knowledge in suspense, where *we don't know* whether the bomb exploded or whether the explosion was narrowly avoided. This "we don't know" can be heard in Freud's interpretation of a son's dream about his father who was still alive, being dead, but who "didn't know he was dead". We recall that this suspension in not-knowing uniquely concerns the position of desire: "he did not know that he was dead according to the dreamer's wish".

The position of not-knowing implies that the big Other, the subject supposed to know, does not know, S(A̶), and will never answer the question. The object of desire is introduced by the scene on the stage i(a), by the specular image, including the whole world of imaginary explanations and interpretations (in the signifying chain), but it must be placed in resonance with the subject supposed to know (A), *who does not know*, S(A̶), in other words with the desire of the barred big Other, d(A̶). It is from here that we can situate anxiety.

Let's start again from the imaginary at play in i(a).

2 The imaginary and the real

The second part of Lesson 3 is built around the schema of the two mirrors or the optical schema.[4] Lacan had already introduced this schema in Seminar I, *Freud's Technical Writings*,[5] a large part of which was explicitly devoted to Freud's article *Introduction to Narcissism* (1914).

For Freud, the ego is nothing other than the *development of the Ego*. The ego starts from a question: what am I? What am I worth? It finds support in the past, in an ideal ego i(a) in what it would ideally have been; having lost this past and imaginary ideal ego, it can do only one thing which is to project it into the future i'(a) in the form of the ego ideal I(a) in an attempt to find it again in a renewed way. This ego ideal is not the imaginary double of the ideal ego; it is an ideal ego emptied of all imaginary. The development of the ego thus corresponds to the S_1–S_2 symbolic process. "The signifier (S_1) is what represents the subject for another signifier (S_2)" reads here: "the ideal ego (S_1) represents the subject for the ego Ideal (S_2)". The ideal ego is indeed imaginary (S_1), and the ego ideal is the repetition of an ideal ego, which, in this repetition, is emptied of all imaginary and organises a large hole in its middle.

The schema for the development of narcissism can be illustrated as follows: (Figure 2.2).

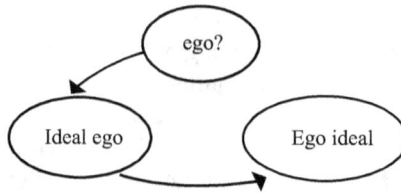

Figure 2.2 The development of narcissism.

It can also be presented in the simplified form of the optical schema with mirror S, forming i(a), the ideal ego, and mirror A, transforming i(a) into i'(a), which transforms the ideal ego into the ego ideal (Figure 2.3).

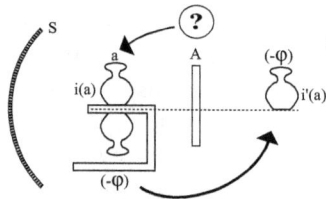

Figure 2.3 The schema of the two mirrors (S and A), forming the ideal ego (i(a)) and transforming it into the ego ideal (i'(a)).

On the left-hand side of the schema, i(a) should not be understood simply as a specular image in the restricted sense of the term, but also as a whole way of understanding and explaining it in the field of the look and of absolute knowledge.

By virtue of the spherical mirror, the different flowers marked "a" in the complete schema are brought together in *the real image* of the vase situated in the underlying box (let us note that what is called a "real image" in optical physics has nothing to do with Lacan's real; it is an imaginary image that can be fixed, for example, as in a film). The specular image i'(a), in the broadest sense of the term, is an optical phenomenon that we can see and know. Specularisation, or rather specularity in general, consists in being able to insert these flowers or these different objects into knowledge, into a "real image" (properly imaginary!) produced by means of the spherical mirror (absolute knowledge). This specularisation is also at play in the two toruses of the neurotic structure and in the explanations where everything can be shown, demonstrated and made visible: the demand of the subject is explained by the desire of the Other and the demand of the Other by the desire of the subject, each time reciprocally.

But the spherical mirror in the mirror stage is only the first part of the exposition of the mirror stage. There, we have indeed a specularisation of the body, of the structure of the body, of the bodily image for the child who sees himself in the mirror. But this is only the first aspect of this bodily unity. Because i(a) is referred onto i'(a) by the plane mirror, which thus makes it possible to sketch I(A), the ego ideal. In the "development of the ego", the image formed in the past of the ideal ego is transformed in the future, always depending on the present question: What am I? What do I desire? What does the Other desire? The plane mirror allows us to see i'(a), which is a *purely virtual* image, because where it is shown on the schema, there is no image; it can only be seen by an eye sufficiently well placed to see i(a) reflected in the plane mirror. In the meantime, it represents the question: what does the Other desire? What does the Other desire as far as I'm concerned? Now, with the signifier (the second conception of the signifier), the Other is fundamentally barred, and there is a hole, impossible to fill, at the heart of i'(a): here, we find the lack of the phallus that was supposed to be used for everything, to explain everything. The phallus is lacking: minus phi.

Let us now return to the tragedy of Hamlet, which is supposed to illuminate "the scene on the stage", in other words the real on the basis of the symbolic. Hamlet's specular identification with Lucianus i(a) is completely insufficient to engage Hamlet's act of avenging his father. So that the act might take place, it must be initiated starting from the question of the subject's being (*to be or not to be*), in other words from the development of the ego, already understood as a signifying process (S_1–S_2 or the passage from the ideal ego to the ego ideal). For this to happen, the entire imaginary of S_1 must be summoned, certainly, but above all it must be unleashed, as is the case with the death of Polonius, and the mourning and suicide of Ophelia. Only then does the possibility of invention, of creation in the act itself, appear.

The positive side, where everything can be explained in an absolute knowledge, can be written as i(a); the negative side of the lost object (minus phi), where meaning fails and non-knowledge imposes itself, can be written as *a*, or object *a*. These two sides – i(a) and *a* – are the two supports of the function of desire. They are both represented as an imaginarisation, on the one hand, i(a) dependent on the lower line of the unbarred big Other (the first conception of the signifier) and on the other hand, *a* dependent on the upper line of the barred big Other (the second conception of the signifier), that is, on S($\bar{A}$).

These two sides are represented, on the one hand, in the topology of the intertwined toruses (i(a) and the first conception of the signifier) and, on the other, in that of the cross-cap (*a* and the second conception of the signifier). In the topology of the cross-cap or fundamental phantasy, the signifying process (S_1–S_2 represented by the stamp of the phantasy) articulates S and the object *a*. The first term of the phantasy is the Moebius strip, the subject who replaces all explanation by turning in on himself (like the said strip), who can still be presented as an exercise in knowing; the second term is the object *a*, outside knowledge, minus phi, which precisely implies commitment to the act (for example, Hamlet's act of avenging his father).

Anxiety always recalls and rekindles the dependence of the phantasy on the signifying process (the second conception of the signifier) and the line of *jouissance* in the graph. It arises at the intersection of the maximum difficulty of knowledge (radical non-knowledge) and of maximum movement (the very motor that allows Hamlet to act). Anxiety occurs in the complex structure of desire shared between i(a) and *a*, when something comes to occupy the place of the hole, the place of *minus phi*; this is the experience of the *Unheimlich*, where the lack comes to be lacking, where an ordinary object comes to fill the hole. If we understand narcissism as a perfectly imaginary structure, we short-circuit the question of narcissism itself. Because we fill up the ego ideal or i'(a), – yes, we fill it up – this filling up of *minus phi*, the plugging of the hole, is precisely the source of anxiety.

LESSON 4[6]: UNHEIMLICHKEIT

1   The home of the speaking being

We need to familiarise ourselves with the development of the ego, which entails the passage from i(a) to i'(a), that is, from the ideal ego to the ego ideal. And this passage essentially presupposes the signifier in its second conception, the imaginary S_1 signifier, which in its repetition empties itself of all that is imaginary to become pure S_2. S_2 repeats S_1 and S_1–S_2 forms an interior eight, the S_2 loop becoming much smaller since it has lost all its imaginary. This interior eight loop delimits a Moebius strip, created by the crossings or resonances between the small loop S_2 and the large loop S_1. A surface with a single edge and a single face (S) asks only to be closed by a bilateral surface with a single edge (the object *a*). Here is the structure of the fundamental phantasy at the same time as the engendering of the cross-cap by the signifier.

We need to familiarise ourselves with this structure *in movement*, because it is here that the ego as well as the subject have their home (*Heim*) and their secret (*Geheimnis*). And it is from this familiarity or homeliness (*heimlich*) that the unfamiliar, the "uncanny", the strange (*unheimlich*) can appear. In his 1919 article, *The "Uncanny"* (*das Unheimliche*, also translated into French as "the disquieting strangeness"), Freud draws on philological considerations to show that the word *heimlich* has two distinctly foreign spheres of meaning, "that of the homely, the comfortable, and that of the concealed, the hidden. *Unheimlich* would come to be used as the opposite of the first of these meanings, not of the second".[7]

A feeling of unhomeliness, of disquieting strangeness is provoked (among other examples) by an automaton about which we wonder whether it is a living being with a psyche or whether it is a lifeless object without a psyche. Freud relies on Hoffmann's *The Sandman* to show that, even if the story contains an automaton (Olympia), the disturbing strangeness or anxiety is provoked by *castration anxiety* (in *The Sandman*, the anxiety for Nathaniel of losing his eyes, being a substitute for castration anxiety).

For his part, Lacan, in the seminar on *Identification*, develops the structure of the fundamental phantasy and of the cross-cap, which applies to the normal structure for all the psychopathologies. It is here – in the normal structure (\$◊a) – that the dwelling place of the speaking subject, whoever he may be, is to be found: it is his *Heim*, his home, where the *Unheimliche*, the uncanny and anxiety have their place. Each of the three terms of the fundamental phantasy can be accentuated, in turn, and thus given an imaginary consistency. The pervert is characterised by the fact that he prioritises what lies at the heart of the object *a* and gives it imaginary consistency in the phallus. The neurotic is characterised by the fact that he gives all importance to the lozenge (*le poinçon*), to the signifying process, that is, to the big Other and to the imaginary consistency of the big Other. The psychotic gives all importance to the $ and gives it its imaginary consistency in the body.

With the familiar dwelling of the speaking being in the fundamental phantasy, the final impasse of the neurotic is not castration anxiety. It consists rather in giving an entirely imaginary consistency to the big Other; it is from this imaginary that the neurotic structure presents itself as the structure of two intertwined toruses, the torus of the subject and the torus of the Other. With and in the consistency of the Other, the subject supposed to know (the first conception of the signifier), the neurotic wants to know, he wants to know with all of the imaginary linked to this knowledge, imagined as full of sense. If, in the second conception of the signifier, S_2 is emptied of all its imaginary and is a non-knowledge, the neurotic does not want to take this into account, *he wants to know*, he wants to fill in the knowledge. The hole in the Other S(A) is filled by the phantasy of the neurotic, which is a consequence of the fundamental phantasy when we give imaginary consistency to the signifier and the Other. The neurotic does not recoil before his own castration, his shortcomings, his limitations. He accepts all this willingly, as long as the Other is not castrated. He refuses to make of his own castration "what the Other lacks", he refuses to use his own castration in support of the castration of the Other S(A). The neurotic avoids the line of *jouissance* that starts from S(A). In place of the *jouissance* of the barred Other, he invents another *jouissance* of an Other that is not barred.

In the optical schema or the development of the ego, it is essential to keep the place of a hole at the level of i(a) as much as at the level of i'(a), and at the level of the ideal ego as much as at that of the ego ideal. This is the importance of the object *a* and of *minus phi*. In his imaginarisation of the signifier and the big Other, the neurotic plugs up these holes. And this is anxiety, not the anxiety of losing his positivised eyes or the phallus, but the anxiety of having already positivised them (and of being able to lose them secondarily). The neurotic thus creates his own anxiety by giving imaginary consistency to the Other and plugging the holes in object *a* and *minus phi* with a positivised object *a* and an imaginary *plus phi*. We can now return to *The Sandman* and examine how anxiety as *Unheimlich* arises in the structure of the *Heimlich*, the optical schema, the development of the ego and the first conception of the signifier.

2   The Sandman

The story begins with three letters which take up roughly two fifths of Hoffman's text.

The first letter is from Nathaniel, the unhappy hero of *The Sandman*, to Lothaire, the brother of Clara, Nathanial's sweetheart. Nathaniel is writing to explain the reason for his absence and why he is keeping his distance. It is because he has been in a state of anxiety (*unheimlich*) ever since a merchant named Coppola (later incarnated as Coppelius) turned up at his house to sell him a barometer. At the time, Nathaniel dismissed the merchant, but an anxiety persists, and he offers Lothaire the following interpretation. When he was a child, his mother was wont to say, at nightfall, that the sandman (surely a person in his imagination?) would come by to put him to sleep by throwing sand in his eyes, until Nathaniel discovered that the sandman had indeed become a real person who one evening came to do business with Nathaniel's father. Determined to know who he was and what he was doing with his father, Nathaniel hid behind the curtains to see what was going on. It was the old lawyer Coppelius, whom he knew well and who practised alchemy, during which he cried out "Give me some eyes". Frightened, little Nathaniel cried out in anxiety from his hiding place, prompting Coppelius to try to tear out the child's eyes. The father then begged his master to spare little Nathaniel. During a final alchemy session, his mother having persuaded his father to stop these experiments, Nathaniel heard a terrible explosion, which killed his father.

This first letter serves as a letter of interpretation, of explanation (the first conception of the signifier), highlighting the imaginarisation of the big Other in the figure of Coppelius, which precedes and conditions the threat to gouge out the eyes ("a substitute for castration" according to Freud). Intended for Lothaire, who acts as a double, as Nathaniel's specular image, Nathaniel, in error, addresses the letter to Clara, sister of Lothaire but also his beloved.

The second letter is Clara's reply to Nathaniel's letter, sent to her inadvertently although intended for her brother. Written in a reasonable tone of explanation, Clara replies to Nathaniel in an effort to ease his anxiety: "Your father is dead through his own fault, forget this Coppelius, forget the merchant of barometers, forget it all and think of yourself". Common sense advice, you might say, not exactly what you'd expect from a beloved.

The third letter, like the first, is written by Nathaniel to Lothaire, his mirror image, to now explain that he has moved on and is taking classes run by someone named Spalanzani (the name of an Italian biologist who pioneered the experimental field of artificial fertilisation for animals). Remaining with the communication of facts, Nathaniel recounts how, through a narrow slit, he was able to catch a glimpse of a beautiful girl who seemed to be sleeping with her eyes open, learning a little later that she was Spalanzani's daughter. Once again, this is a letter of explanation to his double or mirror image, Lothaire.

2.1   The rest of the story

In the second part of the story, the narrator first explains why he couldn't begin otherwise than with these three letters. Unable to compose an account that reflected the brilliant colours of the internal image of his tale, the letters would serve to sketch out an image to which he will now add more and more colours.

---

1   The letters date from a time when Nathaniel had left to study elsewhere, during which he met Professor Spalanzani.

2 On his return, Clara throws herself into his arms and Nathaniel tries to forget the lawyer Coppelius and Clara's reasonable letter. But Nathaniel continues to be haunted by the figure of Coppelius qua Coppola, composing around them a whole system of mystical exaltation (*Schwärmerei*) and a poem, which the rational Clara tries to oppose. To no avail. Nathaniel and Clara drift apart.

3 Nathaniel leaves for another year of study, during which time, from his bedroom window he observes Spalanzini's daughter, the magnificent Olympia. He ends up buying a telescope from the famous Coppola to gaze with fascination at this woman, who appears to him to be absolutely frozen. Invited to a ball organised by Spalanzani in his "daughter's" honour, Nathaniel falls in love with her. The beautiful Olympia reads Nathaniel's gloomy writings responding to them with stereotypical phrases. In a delirious scene, Spalanzani battles with Coppola, who gouges out Olympia's eyes, revealing Olympia to be nothing more than an automaton built by Spalanzani, whence Coppola screams endlessly: "Wooden doll, turn, turn, wheel of fire, turn, turn".

4 Nathaniel awakes from his terrifying dream. All traces of madness have disappeared. The two sweethearts, Nathaniel and Clara, are reunited.

5 They climb the local town's belfry where Clara draws Nathaniel's attention to a moving mass below. Nathaniel taking out his spyglass and sees that it is Coppelius. He roars "Wooden doll turn, turn, wheel of fire turn, turn" and tries to hurl Clara down, Clara who he now supposes to be a wooden doll, and who is narrowly saved by her brother. Nathaniel jumps into the void.

3 Anxiety and phantasy in neurosis (anxiety does not initially arise as castration anxiety)

From this story, we can discern that the big Other is personified several times as supposed knowledge: in the field of alchemical magic, the big Other is Coppelius; in the field of the spyglass or telescope and of meteorological knowledge, it is Coppola; in the field of knowledge to create a living being, it is Spalanzani. From this point of view, the imaginative emphasis is indeed *neurotic*. The letters and the rest of the account accentuate an interpretive function and the specular image, these conforming to i(a) whose hole is potentially filled every time.

Following this imaginarisation, it is the *eye*, a particular organ of the body that is accentuated, chosen here to represent the subject insofar as it is confronted with knowledge. The accentuation here is *psychotic* (resonating with the language of the organ, *Augenverdreher*, the eye-twister, as in the case identified by Tausk[8]). This leads to a fascination with the invention of a new subject, the automaton Olympia. But such an accentuation of the subject and of the body, which is psychotic, depends on the imaginative accentuation of the signifier and the big Other.

As for the accentuation of object *a* with the imaginarisation of the phallus, this is absent. The eye is not the phallus, but it is in the continuity of knowledge (neurosis) and while Olympia is not a phallic character, the question of the subject's body and soul is nonetheless emphasised psychotically. The object *a* is not accentuated in the person of Clara, Nathaniel's beloved at the very moment when it could have been.

On each of her appearances in the story, she is reduced to a rational, somewhat distant person.

Contrary to the Freudian thesis of "anxiety as castration anxiety", anxiety emerges in *The Sandman* as neurotic anxiety, which goes hand in hand with the imaginarisation of the signifier and the big Other or, secondarily, as psychotic anxiety, which goes hand in hand with the imaginarisation of the subject and the question of the body.

In the general structure of the dwelling place (*Heim*) of the speaking subject, we can accentuate and imaginarise the two parts of the signifying process, on the one hand "the signifier represents the subject" and we can write S in place of i(a) or the ideal ego, and on the other hand, "the signifier represents the subject for another signifier", but this "other signifier" is imagined by the neurotic in the form of the phantasy (the barred subject and a certain form of the object *a*, oral, anal, scopic) and we can write "a S" in place of i'(a) or the ego ideal: the phantasy is all on the side of i'(a) or the ego Ideal. In other words, the neurotic chases after the phantasmatic realisation of what he imagined himself to have been in his past. Nathaniel's story is primarily neurotic in structure (Figure 2.4).

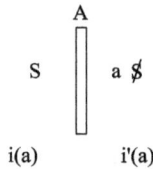

A

S   a $\bar{\$}$

i(a)   i'(a)

Figure 2.4 The neurotic phantasy or the phantasy on the side of the ego ideal (i'(a)).

In the same general structure of the dwelling place (*Heim*) of the speaking subject, we can accentuate object *a* under the form of the imaginary phallus where object *a* is inscribed in the place of i(a) and the S is inscribed in the place of i'(a). It is perversion that reveals the true structure of the phantasy, as we can read in *Kant with Sade*[9] in Schema Z, which is equivalent to Schema L: (1) object *a* in the place of the big Other, (2) passes to the Ego or the will, (3) then to the subject-object victim of sadism, to produce (4) the purified subject.[10] The pervert gives full importance to the phallus, which is the forbidden centre of object *a*. So, by starting from the centre of object *a*, the pervert is at the heart of the functioning, not of the subject, not of the signifier, but of what makes up the consistency of the cross-cap (Figure 2.5).

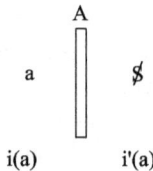

A

a $\bar{\$}$

i(a)   i'(a)

Figure 2.5 The true structure of the phantasy revealed by perversion.

If it weren't for the neurotics, we would never have known anything of this, because it is they who provide the articulation of the fundamental phantasy through the signifier S_1–S_2. In contrast to the engendering of the structure of the phantasy in the Sadean experience, phantasy in the neurotic fills the hole in the Other as best it can, that is, with a fiction. The knowledge of the phantasy is a knowledge cobbled together by the neurotic, a knowledge that fits him "like gaiters on a rabbit": the neurotic doesn't do much with his phantasy, because it serves to counteract, to plug anxiety and at the same time to provoke it.

The neurotic's phantasy is integrally oriented towards the big Other; he addresses the Other and tries to spark the Other's demand, using the object of desire of his phantasy to entice the Other into asking for something, only to refuse it from him afterwards. Always to support the consistency of the big Other. In her dream, the butcher's beautiful wife elicits the demand of the Other (her friend, but also her husband, the butcher, and Freud himself, to whom the dream was addressed) to give consistency to the desire of the Other. She has not been unsuccessful, insofar as her dream becomes the cornerstone that allows Freud to develop the entire structure of his *Interpretation of Dreams*, a structure which gives imaginary consistency to the signifier.

The neurotic affair does not go without the articulation of the two toruses: the desire of the torus of the neurotic subject is intertwined with the second torus, with the demands of the Other. The neurotic subject doesn't want to pay the price himself, he doesn't want to give anything away, not even his anxiety, not even the question of the real that is at stake. Therefore, he begins by bringing his symptom to the analysis (at the symbolic level). It is here where the impact of the part taken by the analyst in the treatment appears, along with the question of the desire of the analyst who accepts the symptom. But the neurotic wants more, he wants that the analyst demand and, says Lacan, since the analyst doesn't demand anything of him, he begins by modulating his own demands, which come from the *Heim-Unheimlichkeit*, that is, from the central hole, even if plugged in his case. It must be understood that all demands are always articulated with *minus phi*, with the central void. Whatever they may be, demands do not regress towards the oral object (as is traditionally thought); they regress fundamentally towards the absolute nothing, towards the demand for zero.

Starting from this zero, we can question the five origins of anxiety that Lacan identified in the Freud's text *Inhibitions, Symptoms and Anxiety*: (1) the loss of the uterine milieu at birth (oral object), (2) the loss of the mother as an object (anal object), (3) the loss of the penis (phallic object), (4) the loss of an object of love (scopic object) and (5) the loss of the love of the superego (vocal object). Is the danger of losing one or other of these objects what generates a corresponding anxiety? No, as we have seen in the story of Nathaniel it is when there is no possibility of lack that anxiety arises, when all the holes are plugged by imaginarisation sometimes at the level of the signifier and the big Other (neurosis) or at the level of the subject and his body (psychosis). With the omnivorous eye continually present in the story, lack can come to be lacking, and there, anxiety arises.

LESSON 5[11]: NOT-KNOWING AND THE VOID

1 Not-knowing in philosophy

Is there specifically a genuine desire to know? Is there an epistemophilic drive? Psychoanalysis – which, as we have seen, must be centred on not knowing – should radically call into question these two notions. And if all philosophy is focused on knowledge and founded on the tendency to know (desire or drive), then psychoanalysis departs radically from any philosophical approach.

From *The Critique of Pure Reason* onwards, the philosophy of Kant seems to be centred on the question of knowledge. Kant says it himself: this first critique deals with the question: *what can I know?* And the answer is: *nothing*, if it does not correspond to the spatio-temporal conditions of sensibility (*Transcendental Aesthetics*) and *nothing*, if it does not correspond to the logical framework of understanding, itself structured by the categories from which the principles derive (*Analysis of Concepts* and *Analysis of Principles* in the *Transcendental Logic*). With these two versions of "nothing, if it's not...", the response to the question *what can I know?* Appears to be a "brainwashing", as evoked by Lacan at the beginning of the next lesson (Lesson 6), to rid psychoanalysis of all the cumbersome knowledge that would situate it in metaphysics (including Hegel).

Kant concludes his analysis with his table of nothings,[12] in which the third and fourth forms repeat the two "nothing if it's not..." of the answer to the question "What can I know?" The third form of nothing is the spatio-temporal framework, which is itself empty, an *ens imaginarium* without object (empty intuition). The fourth form of nothing is the logical framework of understanding, empty because it defies the conditions of knowledge, which must always be rooted in sensibility; it is a *nihil negativum*. These two "nothings" correspond strictly to the scopic and vocal forms of Lacan's object *a*.[13] (Figure 2.6).

Transcendental aesthetics		*Ens imaginarium*
Transcendental logic	Transcendental Analytic (concepts and principles) Transcendental Dialectic	*Nihil negativum*

Figure 2.6 The third and the fourth forms of nothing in relation with the structure of pure reason (Kant).

The rest of Kant's questioning, starting with the fourth form of nothing, opens onto two divergent paths.

1 The first path remains in the question of knowledge (*The Critique of Pure Reason*). In the second part of the *transcendental logic*, the *transcendental dialectic*, *reason* (altogether very unreasonable) undertakes to construct ideas without any roots in sensibility, based on the pure concepts of understanding alone, of the

categories alone. These are the three pure ideas of reason: the soul (or the subject), the world and God. These three ideas are the subject of the three branches of metaphysics: rational psychology, rational cosmology and rational theology. Metaphysics or ontology thus presents itself as a vast body of knowledge (an absolute knowledge), but it is in fact no more than a pseudo-knowledge encompassing the whole universe of the subject, the world and even of God. It is, in reality, nothing but a radical non-knowledge.

2 The second path opens onto another question, starting from non-knowledge (*The Critique of Practical Reason*). Based on the question "What must I do?", Kant distinguishes a doing that is conditioned by knowledge rooted in sensible experience, a technical or pragmatic doing (corresponding to the principles of pleasure and reality) from a moral doing, which is imperatively imposed without concessions to extenuating circumstances and which takes note of radical non-knowledge. Ethics imposes itself imperatively (we understand this to mean the imperative duty to give its rightful place to the ethical unconscious according to the principle of *jouissance*[14]). *The Critique of Practical Reason* thus opens up a philosophical field outside of the question of knowledge, starting from a radical non-knowledge (we would say from the unknowable unconscious, *Unbewusst*).

The question of truth is no longer to know what I can know, in correspondence with transcendental aesthetics and transcendental analytics. The truth, to be found in the "nothing…", is not what leads reason to invent a metaphysical pseudo-knowledge. It is the opening up of an ethics starting from nothing. For this opening truth, *minus phi* especially should not be forgotten, the radical hole (which does not come from the subtraction of a supposedly primordial *plus phi*).

With non-knowledge, the Other as supposed knowledge is radically barred: S($\bar{A}$). The non-knowledge included in the ethics of the unconscious is radically opposed to Hegel's philosophy, which is centred around self-consciousness *Selbstbewusstsein* (refer to the second part of *The Phenomenology of Spirit*). This self-consciousness is precisely the subject supposed to know within which any knowledge of the object could be inscribed. It is a short step from thinking we could know any object (absolute knowledge) to the jubilation of being able to know everything. This is the jubilation of the mirror stage, where the subject imagines being` transparent to himself: knowing everything about himself, knowing everything about the world reflected in him. Except that the subject has a back, the reverse side of the shiny medal of knowledge.

In the neurotic and toric perspective of the big Other that is not barred (the Hegelian perspective), anxiety could be defined, in *Identification*, as "the feeling of the desire of the Other".

2 The nightmare and anxiety

Continuing with this lesson, anxiety is presented, by means of the nightmare, in the sense that it evokes the *jouissance* of the Other. In other words, the question of *jouissance*, which implies the barred Other S($\bar{A}$), is substituted for the simple desire in the formula "the feeling of the *desire* of the Other", which seemed to imply the *unbarred* Other. If the barred Other is incarnated, it will always be in the more or less frightening figure of a monster. The etymology of *Nightmare* attests to this. In English, a mare is a female horse of course, but it is also a sexual demon, male or female, incubus or succubus, who violates the sleeper during the *night*, the night of the not-knowing of the unconscious. The etymology of nightmare (cauche-mar) in French borrows from mare in English, while *night* in English gives way to "cauche", from the verb "caucher", which means to tread on, to press, not neglecting the question of pleasure embodied in the sexual demon. Füsseli's painting *The Nightmare* depicts the scene of a woman with an incubus crouching on her chest while she is asleep.

The question of *jouissance* is always at stake in the nightmare. The nightmare embodies the barred big Other (*jouissance*) in the *form* of an unbarred big Other (desire). The Sphinx at Thebes, the figure of the nightmare, embodies a big Other who enjoys (non-knowledge: *jouissance*) in the form of a figure who poses an enigma to which she knows the answer to be desire. Another figure of the nightmare is taken by Lacan from Cazotte's *Diable Amoureux*: at the call of the main character of the story, the demon Beelzebub in the form of the head of a camel summons desire, but also *jouissance*, with his question: *Che vuoi?* what do you want? In these examples, the subjacent *jouissance* takes the form each time of a question. "What animal walks on all fours in the morning, on two legs at noon and on three legs in the evening?" asks the Sphinx. This question summons man and comes back to posing the question of desire and *jouissance Che vuoi?* This remains the initial question in the development of narcissism – who am I? – and it already implies *jouissance*. This question is the primordial experience hidden in any true demand whatsoever, a question without an answer, a question inexhaustible in knowledge, in other words the true question. However, the big Other, *represented as unbarred,* is supposed to know the answer. On the side of the Sphinx, the answer is man; on the side of the camel Beelzebub, it is phantasy.

With the nightmare and the primordial question, we can situate anxiety and neurosis at the same time and in the same place, notably *by the response*: the phantasy, which would give the true nature of man.

3   Neurosis and its treatment of the void

The great hysterics of Freud's time, with their paralyses, their anaesthesias, their scotomata, were unaware of their lack; hence, they had no anxiety. The hysterical process consists in transplanting the question of anxiety onto the Other, in making the Other anxious.

The obsessional turns around the signifier and calls it into question because the signifier is a fiction, it is a trick, it is a trickery. The obsessional has good reason to put the signifier in question. But how? For want of a reliable realistic signifier, the obsessional wants to return to the sign (and this is a return to the first conception of the signifier). The sign itself, for the obsessional, comes to plug the hole in the signifier (S_2 as empty of signified). And it is from filling this hole that anxiety arises.

Let us recall the second conception of the signifier, where the signifier must again be called into question. It begins with a trace, a sign that already has the value of S_1: by erasing the trace, by erasing the signified of the sign, we move on to S_2 as the emptying of the imaginary consistency of the signifier. We thus arrive at a certain "knowledge", but it is a knowledge without any imaginary consistency, the zero degree of knowledge where all meaning is erased. It is a "*pas de sens*", a "no sense": this suppression of sense allows for the invention and passage to a new sense. The "*pas de sens* or absence of sense" becomes the "*pas de sens*", the step of sense, or the passage to sense. Having erased the true traces, the way is free to invent false ones. From the point of view of truth as the adequation of the said to the thing, this is a lie. But the *invention* of these false traces is the emergence of a new sense of the truth starting from non-knowledge, of opening to the creative side of the ethical unconscious. This is what is at stake in the concept of "*cause*": within the framework of knowledge (*The Critique of Pure Reason*), the cause is fundamental to knowing the object; it determines its object as well as its effect. From the moment when the whole imaginary support of knowledge breaks down, the cause reveals its gap (*béance*) and appears as the cause of freedom (*The Critique of Practical Reason*). Not the freedom of a subject, however transcendental, but the freedom of the unconscious, as non-knowledge, not known, unaware, *Unbewusst*. It is the opening up of a new field, outside consciousness, outside the subject supposed to know.

The fundamentally false part of the neurotic's demand is not due to the fact that it is a fiction and a lie, but to the fact that the neurotic is on the side of knowledge, on the side of consciousness, of self-consciousness, on the side of Hegel, on the side of the specular image, of explanation, etc. He wants to know. And anxiety is directly linked to this side which is a lure. Instead of being something that would calm anxiety by covering over the hole, the plugging of non-knowledge by knowledge is what fundamentally provokes it.

From this hole, from this $S(\bar{A})$, the question of the drive – $S \lozenge D$ – is opened. This is where the big D is indeed the primordial demand, the demand of the Sphinx, the *Che vuoi* demand, a demand without response, that is, the absolute zero. It is to the extent that our demands addressed to the big, unbarred Other (A) cannot count on any response $S(\bar{A})$, that the demand *to* (A) is inverted into a demand *for*, a demand that arises from the void, from $S(\bar{A})$, the primordial demand at the heart of all demand. It will be clear that, for Hegel, this inversion is never produced, for the simple reason that we remain in absolute knowledge always hoping for an answer to the question.

The primordial demand is already in play with the oral object, the teat, the substitute for the mother's nipple, *dummy* in English. The infant is not yet there as someone with a demand: there is no demand of somebody. But the question already arises of the demand *for*, the demand for what might be at play in the *dummy*: what is the supposed demand coming from the *dummy*? what does it want of me? *Dummy* means both the fake object that replaces the nipple, but also any fake object, a mannequin, a puppet, Olympia in *The Sandman*. The *dummy* in its broadest definition corresponds strictly to the definition of the object *a* in its oral form, a dummy object, a well-constructed concept that remains a dummy, *fake*, in other words unable to be the object of perfect satisfaction. *Fake news* presents itself as the oral form of object *a*: empty concepts without an object, well-constructed concepts, but remaining empty because we can't find an object that corresponds to them in reality. This is the definition of the oral object *a*: the object that assures satisfaction, perfect pleasure, but, no object, in reality, can correspond to it At the next stage, the anal stage, a reversal explicitly brings the actors into play, who, through toilet training, acquire their ownership of the subject: the mother's demand is reversed into a demand *of* the mother.

With this reversal, in the *dummy* as well as in the anal object, the non-response is what can be highlighted each time, the primordial demand at the heart of all demand, the demand that starts from S(Ⱥ) and remains unanswered at the level of knowledge. This is the *empty* space that will be accentuated later in the phallic (*minus phi*) form of object *a* and in its vocal form.

It is this empty space that is important to desire. Blaise Pascal, who was interested fundamentally in desire, could not but be interested in the question of the void. By contrast, the scholars of Pascal's time were probably not interested in desire, and the presupposition that "nature abhors a vacuum" can have meant nothing more than "the scholars abhor desire".

Notes

1 Lesson of 28 November 1962.
2 Sigmund Freud, The Interpretation of Dreams" in *The Standard Edition of the Complete Psychological Works*, Volume 4 and 5, translated and edited by James Strachey, London, Hogarth Press, 1953, p. 536.
3 "I advance masked".
4 Jacques Lacan, *Le séminaire livre X, L'angoisse*, Paris, Seuil, 2004, p. 50.
5 Jacques Lacan, *Le séminaire livre I, Les écrits techniques de Freud*, Paris, Seuil, 1975, pp. 125–163.
6 Lesson of 5 December 1962.
7 Sigmund Freud, "The Uncanny" in *The Standard Edition of the Complete Psychological Works*, Volume 17, translated and edited by James Strachey, London, Hogarth Press, 1955, pp. 224–225.
8 Sigmund Freud, "The Unconscious" *The Standard Edition of the Complete Psychological Works*, Volume 14, translated and edited by James Strachey, London, Hogarth Press, 1957, pp. 197–198.
9 Jacques Lacan, "Kant avec Sade" in *Écrits*, Paris, Seuil, 2004, p. 774.
10 Christian Fierens, *Le principe de jouissance*, Louvain-la-Neuve, EME, 2020, pp. 173–183. *The Jouissance Principle,* London, Routledge, 2022, pp. 133–141.
11 Lesson of 12 December 1962.
12 Immanuel Kant, *Critique of Pure Reason*, in *Œuvres philosophiques I*, Paris, NRF La Pléiade, 1980, pp. 1010–1011.
13 Cf. Christian Fierens, *Lecture de L'identification de Lacan. De l'utopie d'identité au moteur de l'invention*, Louvain-la-Neuve, EME, 2020.
14 Christian Fierens, *Le principe de jouissance*, Louvain-la-Neuve, EME, 2020. *The Jouissance Principle,* London, Routledge, 2022.

Part Two

Anxiety and act involve object *a*

Chapter 3

Anxiety, act and object *a*

LESSON 6¹: ANXIETY, ACTING OUT AND *PASSAGE À L'ACTE*

1 The structure of anxiety

The structure of anxiety presupposes (1) an empty space, (2) a framing and (3) what appears in the frame.

1 *The empty space* has already been introduced by *the* signifier (singular), "the signifier for another signifier", S_1 for S_2: S_2 being the space emptied of the imaginary inherent in S_1. The place is left vacant by the non-response of the Other: $S(\cancel{A})$. It is from this place that the line of *jouissance* starts in the graph. Here, the empty space and *jouissance* are approached through the lens of female genital sexuality, with reference to Ferenczi's book *Research into a Theory of Genitality*. According to Lacan, Ferenczi's entire construction defined and pinpointed the development of male sexuality within the framework of a mediation, a thesis-antithesis-synthesis articulation that is clearly situated in the Hegelian perspective of the subject supposed to know (the big Other is not barred). However, Ferenczi indicates that, for women, this entire construction – which applies both to the development of male sexuality and to the learned construction of the psychoanalyst – undergoes an interruption *without any possible mediation*. While male sexuality can be approached through a mediation involving knowledge and the big Other that is not barred, for women this does not work and non-knowledge and *jouissance* have to be taken into consideration. *Jouissance* is a feminine affair, and Tiresias, the transgender of mythology, confirms this: feminine enjoyment is clearly superior to the aforementioned masculine enjoyment.

The empty space inherent in feminine *jouissance* can be addressed by the bodily organ and the hysterical structure in concert. The vagina comes into play in the genital relationship through a properly hysterical mechanism. Lacan insists that the vagina is a completely insensitive organ (as is the case for the remote part of the perineum). Despite this organic insensitivity, the vagina is the locus of so-called vaginal *jouissance*. Under "normal" conditions of experience,

DOI: 10.4324/9781003477822-5

enjoyment would have to pass through something that is properly sensitive. The vagina as a place empty of all sensibility, by being the locus of *jouissance*, contradicts the conditions of experience. It is not that we need to reconsider these conditions of experience in sensibility, the touchstone of all knowledge; it is that *jouissance* is situated outside knowledge and outside sensibility, even if we insist endlessly on reducing it to sensibility. Now, what contradicts the conditions of sensible experience is the radical nothingness, the *nihil negativum*, absolute nothingness, which is equivalent to the vocal object, to the voice. All this is not to say that, from a sexological perspective, vaginal *jouissance* should absolutely be promoted in preference to clitoral *jouissance*. What matters is the highlighting of *jouissance* in general with the void and the fourth form of object *a*.

Hysteria precisely summons the *jouissant* body, the body that *essentially* enjoys; that is, *on the model of the vagina*. In *On Narcissism an Introduction*, Freud spoke of the generalised erogeneity of the body based on the model of the *male sex* (plus phi). With Lacan, erogeneity is displaced and elevated to *jouissance*, with the primordial accentuation in the body of the empty place, the hollow, the absence of sensitivity, etc. Hysteria – derived etymologically from the uterus – thus presents itself as the neurosis closest to genital completion in the question of *jouissance* and the object *a* in its vocal form. But hysteria is also the neurosis closest to the most primary thing, insofar as the privileged form of the object *a* in the hysteric is also another form of emptiness, the oral form of the object *a* (cf. Dora). In hysteria, the first and last forms of the object *a* resonate.

In the diachronic perspective of "normal" human development, where the stages follow one another (oral, anal, … ending with the genital), hysteria is both at the beginning and at the end. This is because it is essentially animated by a synchronic structure already at play in the *parlêtre*, the speaking being, inherent in the signifying process. This is why hysteria gives rise to a specific *discourse*, the hysterical discourse. It is the only pathology that gives its name to one of the four discourses. We could therefore say quite simply: hysteria is the only pathology. It serves as the basis for the whole of psychopathology, in the explanation of obsessional neurosis, in its proximity to psychosis and schizophrenia, in the discursive approach to any suffering of the speaker (Figure 3.1).

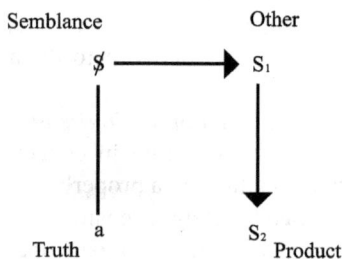

Figure 3.1 Structure of the hysterical discourse.

The synchronic structure of the hysterical discourse has the characteristic of producing S_2. The product of hysterical discourse is S_2, is knowledge. But what knowledge? The hysteric produces no positive knowledge, no treatise on psychology or psychoanalysis. Socrates, the perfect hysteric, did not produce any positive knowledge. What the hysteric produces is the emptying of knowledge, an emptied knowledge, a purified S_2. This we hear very clearly when we open the *Traumdeutung*, where Freud had his own idea, his own positive knowledge, "every dream is the fulfilment of a wish" with all the parade of imaginations and interpretations that can be attached to it. This knowledge of Freud's can be inscribed as S_1 in the hysterical discourse of the butcher's beautiful wife who, through her dream,[2] completely empties the Freudian thesis of its content: her dream is a non-fulfilment of desire. Freud's knowledge (S_1) is a hollow knowledge, a non-knowledge. What the hysteric produces is an S_2, a knowledge, but a knowledge reduced to zero, the zero degree of knowledge.

2 *The framing* is both spatial and temporal. Here, we leave behind the strict question of empty space, non-knowledge and enjoyment, space-time being the primordial condition of all knowledge.

From a spatial point of view, the frame is represented by the mirror in the mirror stage and the two mirrors in the optical schema: the mirror has an edge that is a frame. Now, the mirror and the optical schema illustrate any attempt at explanation: any explanation, any interpretation is always played out within a frame. At the same time, this window frames the whole of reality, insofar as reality is always seen as what can be explained in intuition and understanding (cf. Kant's transcendental aesthetic and transcendental analytic). The phantasm itself appears like a framed painting and counts as the window that opens onto all reality. Anxiety appears in the frame specific to phantasy, the frame that determines the place of reality. A number of René Magritte's paintings evoke the framed structure of phantasy: a painting comes to be placed in the frame of a window, the image of an apparent reality is prolonged in a painting or in clouds, and so on. Magritte called a certain number of these paintings *The Human Condition*. The frame of the mirror, the frame of phantasy, determines the human condition.

The Wolfman's famous dream illustrates this framing: the wolves perched on the walnut tree appear through a window, which serves both as the frame of the phantasy and as the frame of the anxiety of the nightmare, the anxiety of being devoured by the wolves, the anxiety of the *jouissance* of the Other presentified by the wolves.

Spatial framing is played out in seeing: mirror, window, painting, image, phantasy. I am how I am seen or how I see myself. Seeing is the frame of *The Sandman*: Nathaniel's spyglass, the window through which he sees Olympia, and so on. But where does this framework of phantasy for all reality and anxiety come from?

The framework of the phantasy is produced in the S_1–S_2 signifier process. The interior eight, Moebius strip and finally cross-cap, the signifier *produces* the fundamental phantasy on which the seminar on *Identification* ended: $S \lozenge a$.

What frames both S and a is their edge. For both, their only edge is the interior eight that separates them. Written as the lozenge ◊ of the formula of the phantasy $ ◊ a, the lozenge, now as the equivalent of the signifying process (S_1 becomes S_2) is a temporal process: framing is founded *in temporality*.

Framing from a temporal point of view is not a matter of timing between two well-defined moments (between 2 and 3 hours, between 4 and 5 years, etc.). Temporal framing is the emergence of the possibility of invention, one could say of metaphor. The opening of the frame is the moment when all explanation fails. In the dream of the Wolfman, the temporal framing is the *sudden* of *suddenly the window opens*; it is the opening of the stage onto the world. The stage is upon us, an opening for a *saying* (*un dire*) that doesn't remain at the level of the world; it is the breaking in of a temporality, which is not the temporality of the world, but a new temporality in which the freedom of the invention of the unconscious is situated.

In *Inhibitions, Symptoms and Anxiety*, the temporal framing of anxiety was conceived as *Erwartung*, the expectation of the loss of the object that matters, whatever it may be, the breast, the mother, the phallus, etc. The loss of such an object would leave the child *hilflos*, defenceless, without recourse; hence, anxiety arises. But not all waiting is anxiety-provoking and not all anxiety is fundamentally about waiting. The temporal framework of anxiety cannot be defined by waiting. It is given by the signifying process S_1–S_2 at play, in the passage from the ideal Ego (S_1) to the Ego Ideal (S_2). This passage is an interruption of the knowledge underlying S_1 to open an empty space S_2, another stage for the invention of a new saying. This interruption of the ordinary course of things (the world) for a new saying is at play in the three strikes announcing the play: the first strike could be by chance, the second strike signals that it is not by chance (it is an S_1) and the third strike, as pure repetition, opens up the empty place (S_2) where the play can be performed.

3   *What appears in the frame* is the *Heim*, the home, but at the same time the home with its disquieting side, *Unheimlich*, the unease in the home, the disquieting that gives you the shivers. The host (on the side of the *Heim*) has the same root as the hostile (on the side of the *Unheimlich*): the host is fundamentally the hostile, but the hostile, softened and appeased. These two faces in the *Heim*, the host and the hostile, support each other as in an original repression. It is the face of the hostile that must be kept secret. The secret, *Geheimnis* (always the same root), is that in the home, the hostile has been coaxed into becoming a guest. What has never passed through the networks of recognition is the uninhabited, the uninhabitable, the hostile that is always there at the heart of the home. Anxiety is not without an object, and that object is the *Heimlich-Unheimlich-Geheimnis*.

We have seen how the signifier erases the trace, and the void of signification specific to S_2 makes room for the invention specific to the unconscious. It invents any imaginary; it is the locus of fiction, but also of lies. The signifier is infinitely deceptive. The structure of anxiety does not directly imply invention; in pure anxiety, the signifier charged with the imaginary does not appear in any framing. All we have is the radicality of the S_1–S_2 signifier with this fundamental void which always there and not malleable by any thought, therefore always unthinkable, the place of presentiment, of something that precedes (imaginary) feeling: there is nothing imaginary about anxiety.

Anxiety is what does not deceive. What does not deceive is always outside of doubt. Would it be enough to add doubt to reduce anxiety? Doubt about the cause of anxiety cannot diminish it. Rather, the opposite is true: it is from anxiety that we must understand doubt and doubt in general. Anxiety is the cause of doubt, not the deterministic cause, but a cause that invents in the very place of emptiness, outside the sensible series and outside the experience of knowledge. We could undoubtedly reread Cartesian doubt from the perspective of anxiety. To ensure certainty, not on the basis of doubt, however hyperbolic, but on the basis of the anxiety that precedes it, beyond the question of doubt, anxiety lends its certainty to action. If action suggests certainty, this it draws from anxiety, but not without at the same time summoning the deceit of the signifier.[3]

2   Action and stumbling against a background of anxiety: acting out and *Passage à l'acte*

The certainty of anxiety is the structure of the real, developed in the three points of the structure of anxiety: (1) the empty space on the side of the real, (2) its framing by the signifying process on the side of the symbolic, (3) in this framing, an imaginary deceit coming to fill the hole, notably through the phantasy of the neurotic. This structure of anxiety links up perfectly with the nine-square grid and its two axes, these being the axis of the difficulty of knowing (horizontal) and the axis of movement (vertical).

The greatest difficulty in knowing is on the side of the real, and that is *embarrassment*. We imagine something *en-trop* or too much, something that exceeds every possibility of knowing. The greatest mobilisation implies the radical principle of movement, where death and generation are at stake. But action does not develop, it is only *émoi*. We imagine that there is something *less*, something *en-moins*. These two positions in the nine-square grid determine the real axis of the greatest mobilisation (*émoi* = *en-moins*) and the real axis of the greatest difficulty in knowing (embarrassment = *en-plus*); anxiety lies at the intersection of these two axes of *émoi* and embarrassment. Starting with anxiety and moving towards either *émoi* or embarrassment, we can see how the initial certainty inherent in anxiety (which does not deceive) is transmuted into certainty of action in two completely different ways (acting out on the side of *émoi* or *passage á l'acte* taking action on the side of embarrassment), but not without once again summoning the signifier (which deceives). From then on, the certainty of action will always be tinged with deception and lies.

The first transference of certainty (based on anxiety), a symbolic transference involving the signifier, remains in the major difficulty and embarrassment of a something in excess *(en-plus)*, somewhat forced. But it avoids the question of the real of movement as genesis and decay ... to replace it with a movement of the signifier, a movement of change corresponding to external entreaties. We will compare this signifier *en-plus* to the first conception of the signifier. It is *passage à l'acte*: instead of supporting the movement of life and death in its radicality, we pass to action where the action is merely a modification in the movement, a reaction.

The second transference of certainty (based on anxiety), also a symbolic transference involving the signifier, remains, on the contrary, on the question of life and death, of *mè phunai*, of *émoi*, of the radical questioning of life, but it sidesteps the radical dimension of not-knowing (the third degree of the difficulty of knowing) by emphasising the signifier in suspense of its radical passage from S_1 to S_2: the real is symbolised, but S_1 has not yet really passed to S_2. This signifier *en-moins* can be compared to the second conception of the signifier. It is *acting out*.

Most of Hamlet's tragedy is played out at the level of *acting out* and the signifier *en-moins*. The major example of this is Hamlet's mortal wounding of Polonius, who symbolises the one who is killed (S_1), but the stakes of death (S_2) remain in suspense. It is only a shadow of the act by which Hamlet should avenge his father. The act can only take place – at the end of the play – when Hamlet will have exhausted all the tricks of knowledge to no avail, to finally give the driving impetus to his major embarrassment beyond possible knowledge.

These two transferences of anxiety – *passage à l'acte* as a signifier *en-trop* or acting out as a signifier *en-moins* – are not categories that would allow us classify acts as either one or the other. On the contrary, the point is to understand how these two dimensions can come into play, and how we can bring them into play in every example of an act we come across. If we point to the dimension of continual acting out in the tragedy of Hamlet, it is in function of the central question of *passage à l'acte*. We could in general characterise the obsessional side of the neurotic by the signifier *en-trop* and acting out, but this is only because it avoids the fundamental question for him and in him, which revolves precisely around the signifier *en-moins* of death. We could characterise hysteria as a discourse commanding the approach to all psychopathologies through the signifier *en-moins* and acting out, but nothing is ever taken for granted and everything is always in counterpoint to the other position, the signifier *en-trop* constantly spotted by the hysteric in her partner.

In *passage à l'acte*, we keep the real side of anxiety in total difficulty while reducing movement to a simple change, an alteration in the movement. It is a radical deception to reduce the radical nature of movement to a simple change, an alteration. This deception, which would capture anxiety by means of a reaction, is present in all scientific approaches to anxiety. In the "scientific" approach, anxiety is reduced to a change in movement, to a reaction, where the question of life and death disappears.

Whatever the action, *passage à l'acte* or acting out, it can be said that the certainty of action is always borrowed from anxiety. Stronger than the certainty provided by knowledge alone, the certainty of action is always weaker than the certainty of anxiety. It is the latter that is at the centre of psychoanalysis.

The certainty of anxiety displaced onto the signifier *en-trop* (*passage à l'acte*) and onto the signifier *en-moins* (acting out) is played out in the very logic of the psychoanalytic discourse. Let us follow the logic of little Hans. *First,* the encounter with the real (anxiety) as impossible is the encounter with the real of sex as impossible: it is impossible to encounter a single living being without a penis. This leads him to formulate a universal affirmative proposition: "all living beings have a penis", which can be written "for all x phi of x". In this proposition, the phallus is introduced as a signifier en-plus, *en-trop*, an embarrassing signifier. He then encounters another form of the impossible with the mother without a penis, and this is an *en-moins* signifier. The real now appears as the answer "for all x phi of x", but not without provoking *émoi*. This real poses the true question at the level of movement: that there should be a living being without a penis calls into question the very principle of the living (as having a penis). It is the radical question of movement that is imposed in the contradiction of "for all x phi of x": if having a penis is no longer the criterion for life, the whole of life collapses; it is life and death. This reasoning takes the form of an acting out, based on the median position on the axis of the difficulty of knowing and on the third position in the axis of movement.

In his reasoning, little Hans stumbles from one formula to another turning around this question of anxiety with the phallus, too much and too little, and it is anxiety that makes this encounter with the impossible, with the real as impossible, work from stumble to stumble. "*I understumble you perfectly*" harmonises well with "*I understand you perfectly*", shifting understanding towards stumbling: "I stumble over you in my understanding". Understanding can no longer be reduced to the insertion of things, ideas and all that there is, to grasp and contain into sets that include elements, into Euler circles that include points or into concepts that include objects. Understanding is nothing but a series of stumblings whose centre is the void, and it is in the stumblings that the very principle of movement is played out.

Stumbling rediscovers the double circle, the interior eight: the large circle stumbles into the small circle, and only there can the encounter with the real, which torments logic and man, be played out. Lacan could have followed this stumbling in Heidegger's development of *Dasein* as concern, and *concern* (the last chapter of the first section of Being and Time) would have stumbled into *being-for-death* (the first chapter of the second section). Lacan prefers to make philosophy and its knowledge stumble. The *Qoheleth* introduces the question of *jouissance* and the real.

3   Jouissance, desire and the law

The *Qoheleth* is a small book in the Bible commonly named "Ecclesiastes" after the preacher who wrote it in the 3rd century BC. He presents himself as the son of David and king of Jerusalem. The adages "all is vanity", "nothing new under the sun" and "dust thou art and unto dust shalt thou return" are taken from this little book, which may seem moralising. But Chouraqui points out that the book is far more *metaphysical*, rather "all is vanity" should be translated as "all is smoke", revealing the true nature of things: "smoke of smoke, all is smoke".[4]

Lacan essentially extracts one phrase from this little book: *Jouis*, the command-ment to enjoy pronounced by God. Two points need to be made here. *Firstly*, it is not God who tells me to enjoy myself, it is *Qoheleth* who speaks throughout the book (verse 1,1). *Secondly*, "Enjoy" seems to be a simplified translation of verse 9:9: "Live life with the woman you love all the days of the smoke of life given to you under the sun". This can be understood as: "*Enjoy the* woman you love every day of your life that vanishes into smoke under the sun". On the one hand, Lacan introduces a consistent big Other in the form of God, who is absent from the text. On the other hand, he suppresses the mention of woman, retaining only "jouis".

All of the *Qoheleth* is played out against a backdrop of smoke, of the evanes-cence of all imaginary values and consistencies. And it is in this emptiness that joy can and must emerge an enjoyment *for everything* under the sun. *For every-thing*, is then a principle of *jouissance* independent of people and circumstances. How can I respond to God's command, "enjoy"? Here, it is not the big Other who doesn't respond to the demand, it is "I" who can but respond without any imaginary meaning added "I hear - message received loud and clear 5/5", without adding any imaginary meaning: *j'ouïs*. This redundant response to the demand nevertheless introduces the symbolic (and with it a double shift): the pure real of "jouis" is on the one hand preserved, and on the other taken up at the symbolic level of "*j'ouïs*". The pure "jouis" must be seen at the source, at the origin of all anxiety. But the anxiety of *enjoy (jouis)* (in the maximal difficulty of knowing and of radical movement) does not remain there, it is taken up again in a *I hear (j'ouïs)*, where *jouissance* is sometimes displaced and reduced to some kind of movement, (the *passage à l'acte* side of "j'ouïs") is sometimes transferred into the field of ordinary knowledge (the "acting out" side) (Figure 3.2).

(Inhibition)		
	(Symptom)	J'ouïs (I hear) – *passage à l'acte*
	J'ouïs (I hear) - acting out	Jouis (Enjoy) – (anxiety)

Figure 3.2 "passage à l'acte" and "acting out" in the reference table (inhibition, symptom, anxiety).

In "J'ouïs – *passage à l'acte*", *jouissance* is understood as radical non-knowledge, and its movement of life and death is reduced to one movement among others. In the "J'ouïs – acting out", *jouissance* is understood as the very principle of the living (life and death) and is assumed to be solvable through knowledge.

If the "woman" mentioned in the *Qoheleth* can be erased, it is because *jouissance* – introduced as feminine – concerns all *jouissance*. Lacan adds that the God who commands "jouis (enjoy)" also commands *circumcision*, but he immediately speci-fies that this circumcision has nothing to do with castration, the cutting off of an essentially masculine attribute: "nothing [is] less castrating than circumcision", the point here being to define object *a on the* basis of the primordial function of the cut, and not on the basis of the positivisation of the phallic object, which could be cut secondarily. This is the key importance of *minus phi* that we will return to later in the Seminar.

Despite his keen interest in the sacred text, Lacan defends himself against being a cabalist in the calculation of signifiers, signifiers that would arrive at a meaning or a cabalistic interpretation, corresponding to the first conception of the signifier. Contrary to any search for meaning, he understands the signifying process as the producer of the void, of S$_2$ (as in the hysterical discourse), and it is this void that can enlighten us. Reversing the usual meaning of the expression "*taking bladders for lanterns*" (which consists in denouncing so-called enlightenment based on hollows, on emptiness, on nothing), he takes charge of the emptiness that illuminates the whole dialectic of desire as a function of *jouissance*. The lantern of knowledge has to fail, my lantern of knowledge has to fail, to allow recognition of the empty place, that is really the central place, the heart of the question of *what does he want? Che vuoi?* God does not answer, S(Å).

Desire in its relation to the law depends on the question of *jouissance*, addressed by Lacan in the *Qoheleth*. But it is also articulated in a moment of the philosophical tradition (contrary to what Lacan says, p. 97); it is articulated in that great turning point in the history of ethics that is the *Critique of Practical Reason*, which questions action: what should I do? Kant distinguishes between the lower faculty of desire, subject to the vagaries of sensibility and knowledge, and the higher faculty of desire. It is the latter that interests us here where desire is intimately linked to the moral law, not as something that the moral law should combat and curb, but as desire inherent in the creation of the law in complete autonomy, dependent on the empty place, the *nihil negativum*. The moral law raised up in this way is neither a search for pleasure nor an adaptation to reality. It is the emergence of a new law and a new desire, an emergence in the ethical and dynamic unconscious, operating according to the principle of *jouissance*.[5]

In *Totem and Taboo*, Freud addresses the question of desire and the law on the one hand, and that of *jouissance* on the other. This he does is through his myth. The myth of the father of the primal horde who enjoyed all the women of the horde. The murder of the father by the rebellious sons opens the way to both their desire and at the same time their guilt, which is simply the other side of the law and the establishment of social order. Before the murder of the father, it is the reign of the *jouissance* of one, that of the personified Other, but it is an imaginary *jouissance*, degraded in the sense that it presents itself as the maximum of *pleasure*, total and boundless. With the murder of the father, it is the big Other that is barred; and it is only here that the real question of *jouissance* begins: given that the big Other does not respond S(Å), it is the question *What should I do?* that opens onto desire and the law starting from the principle of *jouissance* opened up by the murder of the father.

Desire and law are like two sides of the same coin. Desire and law bar access to the Thing. Desire must conform to the supreme commandment: *Thou shalt not desire thy mother*; the Thing (the mother) is forbidden, and it is as such that she remains outside the law and outside desire. But more fundamentally, the interplay of desire and law prevents us from seeing *what is at stake*, from seeing how desire and law depend on the Thing and *jouissance*. Desire and law are played out at the level of the structure of repression: the law is nothing but repressed desire, and desire is nothing but the law unleashed. But the question of the void, of the nothing, of the *Qoheleth*, is, in principle, set aside. It is not a thing that is repressed; it is the very principle of the functioning of the unconscious (the principle of *jouissance*) that is set aside in the interplay of repression, desire and the law.

In the meantime, the two sides of desire and the law illuminate two classic ways of looking at the object in psychoanalysis, namely the fetishistic object and the phobic object. The law channels desire in that the forbidden object and the phobic object appear as the object to be avoided, the wolf, for example. Pure desire attaches itself to the object that would be adequate to it, the object that fills the hole and hides the dependence of desire relative to the hole of *jouissance*; this object is the fetish as a positive condition for the choice of the object of love (where the castration of the Other is in brackets): the little shoe. Are we caught between the phobia of the wolf and the fetishism of the little shoe? Between the wolf and the shepherdess?

Lacan ends the session making a rendezvous with the killing of the wolf. We will hunt the wolf. With the death of the wolf, we will cease thinking of anxiety in terms of phobia and the phobic object. Because phobia, which pertains to desire and the law, in fact conceals the question of anxiety and *jouissance*.

LESSON 7[6]: AROUND OBJECT *a*

1   Presentation of object *a*

Two of Freud's major texts could serve to introduce Lacan's object *a*: *An Introduction to Narcissism* (1914) and *Inhibitions, Symptoms and Anxiety* (1926).

On the side of narcissism and the development of the ego, the ideal ego and the ego ideal, in other words i(a) and i'(a), sum up the whole of the libido: the ideal ego would be the libido of the body itself and the ego ideal would open up the libido on the side of the object. But on both sides, we must not forget *the hole*. Recalling the optical schema, on the side of the ideal ego i(a), object *a* can be inscribed, it seems positively, in the neck of the vase (of the ideal ego), but this is a construction that implies *minus phi* as such, the hole in the vase (the hole whose specular image cannot be synthesised). On the side of the ego ideal i'(a), it is the void (*minus phi*) that is inscribed as the place for a making, in place of what would appear as a positive object *a* in the ideal ego (Figure 3.3).

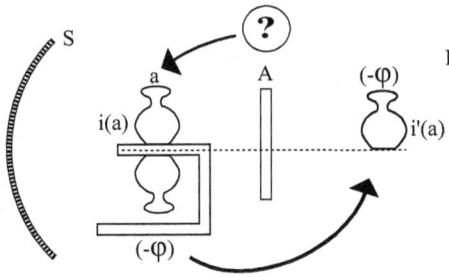

Figure 3.3 The schema of the two mirrors (S and A), forming the ideal ego (i(a)) and transforming it into the ego ideal (i'(a)).

With this difference between the ideal ego and the ego ideal, object *a* appears, at times, as something full in the ideal ego, which we can imagine in the past, and at times, as empty, *minus phi*, which inspires any veritable act in function of this hole in the ego ideal. Narcissism is simply the development of the ego which, having lost the ideal ego, tries to find it again in the ego ideal.[7] And object *a* is inscribed in this development of the ego as something on the side of the ideal ego, as an absolute (and productive) nothing on the side of the ego ideal.

In *Inhibitions, Symptoms and Anxiety*, Freud presents anxiety as the signal of the possible loss of a primordial positive object, cf. the five fundamental losses: oral, anal, phallic, scopic and vocal. But, according to Lacan, anxiety occurs only when object *a* as *emptied*, is replaced by a positivised object: lack is lacking, the hole is plugged, anxiety is provoked.

In function of the question of narcissism (what am I?) and the unsettling nature of anxiety, object *a* appears only at the same time as a radical questioning of the subject in one form or another. Object *a* appears only with S barred. This object, says Lacan, we designate by a letter: *a*, a single letter indicating the identity of the object in all its various effects and forms (oral, anal, etc.). Lacan introduced this letter *a* in the seminar *L'identification*: *a*, alpha, the first letter of the alphabet, abstracts all the differences between all the little letters, all the letters of the *alpha-bet*. Thus, object *a* ignores all the qualities of an object, whether oral, anal, scopic, phallic or vocal, in order to designate, in a single movement, that which takes up all these divergences, all these different faces. Applicable to all objects in general, every object is subject to this *objet petit a*.

According to Kant, the object in general, only appears in transcendental aesthetics, in other words in space and time. All this is called into question by object *a*. On the one hand, time is not the time of past, present and future instances; as we have seen, it is the time of the sudden appearance in the temporal framing that characterises anxiety: the wolves in the window frame appear "suddenly", for example. On the other hand, the object cannot be identified in the three classical dimensions of space, thereby calling space into question. The importance of the unconscious is that the subject cannot be in consciousness and object *a* is not reducible to the possible field of space-time and transcendental analytics, or to the structure through which we perceive all phenomena. The absolute nothing, the object *a*, is what is *outside* transcendental analytics, outside all phenomena we can perceive.

The absolute nothing is aimed at and encountered with *the* signifier and not in the signifying chain, with the inventive process of the ethical unconscious and not in the unconscious as a reservoir-depository. "The signifier must be embodied in the body", but the "body" is not Descartes' *res extensa* as outlined in geometry. The body: "it comes". In other words, the purchase of the body, incarnation, is the purchase in *jouissance* that is played out in the development of the ego, in the schema of the two mirrors, where object *a* finds its place. Object *a* finds its place only in the movement, in the beat, in the oscillation, in the flashing between, on the one hand, the ideal ego or the left side of the optical schema (what is given as i(a), as what can be completely explained, circumscribed, etc.) and, on the other hand, the ego ideal with this emptiness, with *minus phi*, with this hole that, of course, cannot be explained. Object *a* is embodied only in the oscillation between something on the side of the ideal ego (always supposed to be identifiable, explicable, etc.) and this hole that is inexplicable on the side of the ego ideal. Between something and nothing.

"Anxiety is not without an object". Such a phrase suggests that anxiety has an object. More radically, it says that it first concerns the hole, the lack. And we must first understand the object *a* as *minus phi*. Everything revolves first around *minus phi* and nothingness: the phallus is *minus phi* before we can see the slightest positiveness of a *plus phi* appear. It is something that doesn't exist except through the movement of relaunching produced by lack. Minus phi, in the seminar on *Anxiety*, has the place and function of highlighting the primordially empty, negative side of object *a* (without this primacy, it is meaningless). The primacy of *minus phi* also makes it possible to revise the castration complex.

2   The castration complex and the primordial cut

In the story of little Hans, the phallus appears as something that is present, then hidden and absent. It is the mother who does not have the phallus: this raises a question. But the castration complex itself takes the form of a threat. "It's going to be cut off": it is going to be cut it off from the body, from the body where it is enjoyed. Once cut off, the phallus becomes an ordinary object, exchangeable like all other objects, and we quite frequently encounter the phantasy of the phallus cut off from the body, which is in the hand or in the pocket, which can be exchanged, which is, says Lacan, *zuhanden*, something close to hand, to use Heidegger's term, which can be put in a toolbox, in one's pocket, etc. This is what is at stake with the phallus. This is what is at play for little Hans in the plumber phantasy.

The cut at stake in the castration phantasy distinguishes between two types of object: ordinary objects, on the one hand, objects that we can have and know, that we can share, that we can exchange and manipulate (in Lévi-Strauss's kinship systems, women are valued as such, as objects of exchange, assumed to be equivalent to a certain form of phallus) and on the other hand, objects, insofar as they derive from object *a* that are grasped in their emergence, prior to the consistency of any commonplace object. Object *a* is not, then, an additional object that is added to the set of objects in the world. It is prior to them, it is there before any ordinary object.

Freud imagined the cut and castration as the separation or loss of a positive object. Thus, in *Inhibitions, Symptoms and Anxiety*, the child risks losing five main types of object in the course of its development: (1) the breast and the fully satisfying foetal environment, (2) the person who demands cleanliness, (3) the penis, (4) the esteem of the person who sees me and (5) the person who represents the super-ego. In each case, the positive object, reduced to an unquestioned reality, precedes the cut (and castration), which is merely one of several possible manipulations of the object. By contrast, to understand the five forms of object *a* (oral, anal, phallic, scopic and vocal), each must be radically questioned in terms of the nothing, in terms of the primordial void.

To bring the primordial cut into play, the one that *makes* the difference between object *a* and the common object through the intermediary of the nothing, the castration of the mother is the most effective, because the phallus object of the mother has no reality, no positivity, other than what is imaginarily attributed to it... with the precise aim of missing out on the radical *minus phi*. The castration of the big Other seems to start out from the positivity of a big Other supposed to know (absolute knowledge), but this supposition of knowledge is nothing other than the avoidance of *non-knowledge* (radical and primordial *minus phi*).

In *On the Universal Tendency to Debasement in the Sphere of Love* (1912), Freud deals firstly with the "most general of the debasements of love", male impotence, which he interprets as follows. An impotent man's love for his wife depends on his incestuous attachment to his mother and exists only as a substitute for an incestuous attachment which has not been overcome. Since the cut that differentiates between object *a* and the common object has not taken place (which is what constitutes the "incestuous relation"), it is the symptom of impotence that is operating: the man can love his wife (who has replaced his mother), in a tender current, as an ordinary object, but he cannot love her in the sexual current with all the force summoned from object *a*. The sexual current is repressed, forbidden; the man is completely impotent with his wife, who can be loved as a mother is loved, and he seeks his sexual satisfaction with prostitutes. In Freud's interpretation, the man in question is still caught up in the underlying belief of the uncastrated mother and the fear of castration of his own primordially positive object (*plus phi*) and, secondarily, he must act out the cut by distinguishing the ordinary object of love and the sexual object *a* represented in prostitutes. But Freud follows the same schema as the impotent man he analyses: promoting the positive phallus where the mother is not castrated, then the cut between the tender current and the sexual current, (these two currents corresponding to the drive for self-preservation and the sexual drives of Freud's first theory of the drives).

Lacan takes up the question of *sexual impotence* in another way. In the literature, attempts are made to explain it as an impediment to orgasmic discharge within the framework of the pleasure principle. Lacan draws attention to the preliminary pleasure, which does not lead to orgasmic release, but rather to increased stimulation and excitation. Yet, the function of the Other must be introduced not on the basis of discharge, but on the basis of this preliminary "pleasure". The latter must be relocated in the optical schema (the schema of narcissism), where the tilting of the plane mirror makes it possible for i'(a) to appear-disappear and invoke the hole in i'(a), i.e. the hole in the ego ideal: *minus phi*.

The question of male impotence revolves around the mother insofar as she is the primordial object of a man's love life. But this object is primordial in that it already contains *within itself* the cut and the entire structure of the two-mirror schema, in other words, of narcissism. On the one hand, the mother appears as part of the positive landscape of the ego ideal, a figure who is supposed to know what the child should and should not do. On the other hand, she is perforated, "castrated", without knowledge and without response, yet not absent, and it is then that the commandment of purified *jouissance Jouis*, of the emptiness of jouissance, which opens up the inventiveness of her child's unconscious, can be understood as coming from her.

Two mechanisms come into play to avoid the question of the mother's not-knowing and castration. On the one hand, the relationship with the prostitute (who replaces the mother and provides a proxy sexual satisfaction) is part of a *phobic* mechanism, which consists of avoiding the mother as sexual. On the other hand, degrading and demeaning behaviours in relation to the sexual object make it possible to veil the emptiness, the *minus phi*, to avoid it, while presenting these as the very conditions of the choice of the object of love; this is the *fetishistic* and perverse mechanism. These two mechanisms, of the phobic object and the perverse object, are involved in all sexual manifestations. These two processes of avoidance come into play in any "explanation" about sexuality: "from top to bottom", that is, at the level of thought as well as at the level of the sexual act, in Freud's thought as well as in the conduct of the one who is impotent. They intervene in the transference for the analysand and for the analyst. But they are not enough to define what is at stake in transference.

3 Object *a* and the transference

Transference cannot be defined by the repetition of feelings of love, hate, avoidance and ignorance, or by the repetition of facts in a given diachronic history. Transference must be situated in relation to the S_1–S_2 signifying process, constantly at play in the synchronic relationship between analysand and analyst, which involves love. Transference love is not the repetition of feelings or facts, it is a metaphor: a loving hand (the analysand's or the analyst's?) reaches out towards a log (the analyst or the analysand?), the log ignites with love, another hand emerges from the burning log and reaches out towards the first hand. The loved log becomes loving.

It is not love (the flame) that springs from the beloved (the hand), it is the hand that springs from the flame: the beloved appears only because there is love. Therefore the analysand and the analyst only appear because there is *first of all transference love*. Love is always reciprocal; it is the movement that permits the analysand to come into being at the same time as the analyst in the reciprocal action of love, in the reciprocal action of the transference.

The metaphor of love and love as reciprocal action make it possible to overcome the "rock of castration" on which Freud's analyses stumbled, not unrelated to Freud's limited conception of the transference. In *Analysis Terminable and Interminable*, Freud describes how analysis regularly comes up against the "rock of castration", the "original rock[8]", *gewachsenen Fels*. The French translation proposes translating *gewachsenen* as "of origin", whereas *wachsen* actually means "to grow". The "rock of castration" is thus a rock "that has grown" in the sense that we would say a plant has grown. Its growth depends on the formation of a conception of castration. Thus, the woman conceived as always in the grip of penis envy (*Penisneid*) waits endlessly and indefinitely for the penis to be given to her by the analyst, in the form of a gift, in the form of interpretations, in the form of answers that would suit all her worries. The woman doesn't give up, she stumbles on this rock of castration, still waiting for this gift from her analyst. The man, however, doesn't want to receive it because he doesn't want to be dependent on another man, he wants to do everything himself and he dismisses his analyst and the phallic interpretation, ending his analysis prematurely.

In this presentation, not only has the phallus been positivised *plus phi* at the outset, but also the supposition of knowledge has been assured. In his approach to transference, Freud remained at the level of knowledge: he had the phallus of knowledge, and the patient – woman or man – would have done better to take advantage of this. Freud's phallus-knowledge, the big Other, thus plugs the hole in the subject's desire. The big Other and the subject, Freud and his analysand, are articulated like two intertwined toruses where the knowledge of one fills the provisional non-knowledge of the other. And if analysis lends itself to the analysand's transferential phantasies, these phantasies remain on the side of possible knowledge. Love as a reciprocal action in which the analysand and the analyst are created, is left to one side. Freud's interpretation then largely equates to the veneer of the phantasy covering over the true function of the void, thereby closing off the true function of the analyst, which is that of the semblance of object *a*, namely, of this urgency, of having to hasten (s'embler): *to hasten into the opening of minus phi*. The *semblant* – or semblance – (or *s'emblant*, "to hasten upon" in a movement of haste) the semblance of object *a* in analytic discourse, has as its truth S_2, non-knowledge, the zero degree of knowledge.

The idea is to promote from the outset, something other than a change of object in order to avoid anxiety. Phobic and counterphobic practice avoids the wolf. Lacan announced that he was going to sound the death knell for the wolf: one must kill off this phobic practice of avoiding anxiety and the object of anxiety, and engage *in haste* (d'emblée) in the semblance of the object *a*, in transference love, including in the reciprocal causality of the analysand and the analyst.

4   Topology: object *a* and the cross-cap

The last part of Lesson 7 is based on the topology of the cross-cap. An interior figure-of-eight cut separates two different surfaces on the cross-cap: a Moebius strip (= S) and the residual part ("I give it to you like a host" = object *a*). In the seminar on *Identification* (lesson of 6 June 1962), Lacan had presented a Moebius strip as a *specularisable* surface. "Specularisable" is defined by "the irreducibility to its own specular image"; the specular image of a right glove presents itself as a left glove; similarly, the specular image of a right Mœbius strip would present itself as a left Mœbius strip. But this is not true, and in *Anxiety,* Lacan rightly states, without mentioning its reversal, that the Moebius strip *is not* specularisable. What is the point of this? In *Identification,* the connection between the Moebius strip and the specular image through its supposedly specularisable character allowed the question of the subject (Moebius strip) to *directly* connect with the ideal Ego and its imaginary. However, this direct connection is merely an illusion that short-circuits the complex movement of transformation of the Moebius strip into the *neurotic torus.*[9] The false thesis of the specularity of the Moebius strip led us to believe that we could deal with the subject, its reversals and contradictions within the framework of a coherent seeing and knowing. Yes, we can attempt to do that, but, at the same time it means foundering in a maze of explanations, interpretations and pseudo-justifications that are properly neurotic and that continuously reveal the *fundamental* not-knowing at the very heart of an enterprise of absolute knowledge.

   To measure the revolutionary impact of the introduction of the object *a* in the approach to every object and every *parlêtre*, let's start with the ideal ego, the specular image, the supposed knowledge through which we could encircle the question of the subject, enclose it as in the vase of the optical schema. This vase is topologically equivalent to a sphere with a hole in it. Let's close the hole in the vase with a cross-cap, which contains the object *a* within itself. We obtain the projective plane: the starting surface has acquired the very properties of the cross-cap and the projective plane (Figure 3.4).

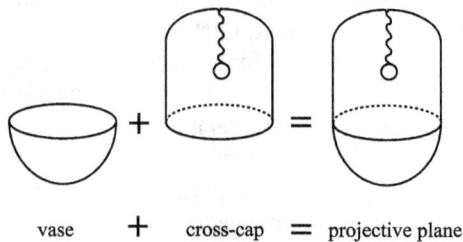

vase   **+**   cross-cap   **=**   projective plane

Figure 3.4 Structure of the projective plane in relation with the cross-cap.

   On the projective plane thus obtained, let us now effect a double cut (interior eight); we thereby separate the Moebian surface S (unilateral and non-specularisable) and the residual surface, the "host" or sliver of object *a* (bilateral and non-specularisable). If we reject object *a*, all the rest of the surface is reduced to a Moebius strip (Figure 3.5).

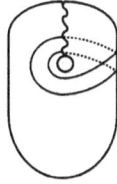

Figure 3.5 A Moebius strip on a projective plane.

The projective plane is a real revolution: we are no longer dealing with a spherical bilateral surface, we are definitively in another universe, the one engendered by the S_1–S_2 signifier (interior eight, Moebius strip, then cross-cap), even if we can always close our eyes and not be satisfied with removing a small piece of surface, and this piece can be presented as spherical and treated in a corresponding logic.

However, in the attempt to take a small piece of spherical, specularisable surface from the order of the specular image i(a), "the strange and invasive image of the double" may appear, like Maupassant's doubling at the end of his life, but also like the doubling of the phallus, from the moment it is apprehended as *plus phi* (its ordinary mode of appearance). It is enough to make a spherical cut that twice traverses the line of penetration of the cross-cap for the single hole of the spherical cut to appear as *two* holes. On the side of the vase and i(a), the spherical cut always appears as *one* hole. On the side of the projective plane or cross-cap and i'(a), the hole of the spherical cut may duplicate itself. To see this, all you need do is make the cut as a cross-section through the neck of the vase and through the "neck" of the cross-cap (and this neck implies the double crossing of the penetration line by the cut): (Figure 3.6).

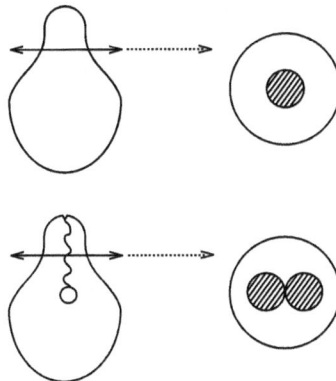

Figure 3.6 Duplication of a spherical hole on the top of a projective plane.

Maupassant's doubling, personality splits, the narcissistic splits in the two mirrors involve the cross-cap. In other words, they always come within the framework of the structure engendered by the signifier (second conception of the signifier: interior eight, Moebius strip, cross-cap and object *a*), conditioning every object and every question of the subject.

Transference is the enactment of the structure of the cross-cap. It takes place both in the analysand and in the analyst. By right, it precedes everything, including those phenomena of splitting that we can too easily place on the side of the imaginary, which are merely the consequence of a spherical cut, admittedly a little particular, on a structure that depends fundamentally on the signifying process (S_1–S_2). From the outset, we always have this structure of the signifier S_1–S_2.

Notes

1 Lesson of 19 December 1962.
2 Sigmund Freud, *The Interpretation of Dreams*, London, Hogarth Press, 1953, p. 146ff. Jacques Lacan, *The Direction of the Treatment and the Principles of its Power*, in *Écrits, The First Complet Edition in English,* translated by B. Fink in collaboration with H. Fink and R. Grigg. New York, W.W. Norton & Company, 2006, p. 620ff.
3 The signifier seems destined to produce the signified that would respond to it exactly by the truth that would match it. In vain. That is its inevitable lie.
4 "Qohèlèt, Ecclésiaste" in *La Bible,* translated and presented by André Chouraqui, Paris, Desclée de Brouwer, 2003, p. 1350.
5 Christian Fierens, *The Jouissance Principle*, London, Routlege, 2022.
6 Lesson of 9 January, 1963.
7 Sigmund Freud, "On Narcissism: An Introduction" in *The Standard Edition of the Complete Pychological Works*, Volume 14, translated by J. Strachey et al., London, Hogarth Press, 1957.
8 Sigmund Freud, "Analysis Terminable and Interminable", in *The Standard Edition of the Complete Psychological Works,* Volume 23, translated by J. Strachey et al., London, Hogarth Press, 1964.
9 Jacques Lacan, "L'Étourdit", in Seuil (Ed.) *Autres Écrits*, Paris, Seuil, 2001, p. 469.

Chapter 4

Object *a* and the transference

LESSON 8¹: INTRODUCTION OF OBJECT *a*

LESSON 8¹: INTRODUCTION OF OBJECT *a*

1 Object *a* as the cause of desire

We are tempted in psychoanalysis to accord primacy to *the subject*, which corresponds to the Moebius strip that, at the end of the seminar on *Identification* Lacan called specularisable, this, a specularisable subject of explanation and knowledge, in a toric and neurotic topology. But the subject – represented "by a signifier for another signifier" (second conception of the signifier, S_1–S_2) – is in fact non-specularisable as he said in Lesson 7. Lacan's hesitation in saying that the Moebius strip is specularisable (Seminar IX) or non-specularisable (Seminar X) indicates that the question of the subject falls between a practice of explanation and knowledge (along the lines of the specular image i(a)), and psychoanalytic practice itself where the radically non-specularisable object *a* is central: outside explanation and outside knowledge. Psychoanalysis as a practice of the signifier (S_1–S_2) revolves around the object *a*. And "anxiety is not without an object" (on the side of the object *a*) while presenting itself as something eminently subjective (on the side of $) : "anxiety is the only subjective translation of *objet petit a*". As we have seen, anxiety articulates object *a* and the subject, at the very locus of the phantasy between the top two lines of the graph.

In everyday experience, we generally place ourselves in a perspective that focuses on the structure of the subject, the subject made explicit through *intentionality*. Intentionality concerns the subject: if a being is conscious, he must be nothing other than a web of intentions. We encounter intentionality in Husserl and Merleau-Ponty. It is already present in Descartes with the question of doubt and the *Cogito*. It is central to Kant, with his three questions that define man: what can I know, what must I do, what can I hope for? It is fundamental in Hegel's *Phenomenology of Spirit* and also in *The Science of Logic*. The originality of Husserl however lies in his elaboration of an intentionality *outside representations*, something like a more profound intentionality. From the point of view of the intentions of intentionality, the object of desire is the object that is there before the intention. It presents itself as the goal of desire, of the intention of desire; it is there before

DOI: 10.4324/9781003477822-6

desire as the goal to be achieved. Assuming the primordial subject in relation to the object of desire implies that the object is the goal of the intention of desire.

Now, the object of desire, Lacan's object *a*, does not fit into the general schema of intentionality. It is precisely not the object targeted by desire as its goal or intention, but rather *the cause of desire*.

Let's introduce causality through *Aristotle's four causes*. Four causes explain the emergence of a statue. *First,* the material cause of the statue is the marble from which it is made. *Second,* the formal cause, the form of the statue, the statue of a god, for example. *Third,* the efficient cause is the sculptor who modelled it. *Fourth,* the final cause is the purpose of the statue, which is to place it in a temple, for example. The object of desire is not the final goal, it is not the final cause of intentional desire, and the other three Aristotelian causes don't put us on the track of what is meant by "object *a* as the *cause of* desire".

With modern science, let's go to Pisa and the experiments supposedly carried out by Galileo, measuring the speed and acceleration of falling bodies from the top of the tower. It is of little interest to note the material cause in the weight, the formal cause in the trajectory of the fall, the efficient cause in Galileo himself and the final cause as a certain will of the creator. None of this makes sense anymore. Causality was then explained not by the attraction of the earth on the weight falling from the Leaning Tower of Pisa, but by the reciprocal action of the weight on the earth and of the earth on the weight. In other words, the earth falls on the stone just as much as the stone falls on the earth. This first difference from the Aristotelian conception obliges us to think of cause not simply as a cause producing an effect, but as a *reciprocal action*. This is not unrelated to love, which is always reciprocal, and which thus makes it possible for the subjects and objects of love to be created (lovers and beloveds).

In the Aristotelian perspective, causality was valued as a sort of metaphysical shadow of reality, inscribed, for example, in weight or the falling stone. There is no such thing as reality whose cause would be the shadow, its metaphysical duplicate. In his radical critique of transcendental realism, Kant shows that everything that is called an "object" is ultimately nothing more than a *phenomenon* appearing to a subject. Before any object and before any subject, it is the phenomenon that is central, and it is only on the basis of the phenomenon that we can speak of a perceived object and a perceiving subject. The object and the subject are not preliminary and neither can be the cause of the phenomenon, which is primary. At the level of the phenomenon, we have the in-between that occurs before either of the two can appear (as in the case of subjects and objects of love).

Starting from the in-between, from the experience of transference in analysis and the reciprocal love at play there, the whole *Critique of Pure Reason* has to be redone: founded on the in-between, on reciprocal action, on the S_1–S_2 signifying process and not on elements that only come secondarily. In the following year's seminar, Lacan introduced *tyche* in parallel with *automaton*. These two additional accidental Aristotelian causalities (apart from the four fundamental causes) imply this in-between, the encounter, the reciprocal action of two causal series either at a purely objectal deterministic level (the *automaton*, for example), or at a level that leaves room for the choice of two subjects, to go to the agora and meet there by chance, for example (and this will be *tyche*). It will be an encounter that upends the subjects and even makes them appear *anew*.

Freud speaks always of the *causation of* neurosis to express his embarrassment about causality, the multiplicity of aetiological factors and the need to question again and again the very notion of cause, that cannot be reduced to a deterministic cause but always implies questioning the cause.

As a function of the life of the drive itself, the notion of the object is no less problematic. *Instincts and their Vicissitudes* (1915) as well as *Anxiety and Instinctual Life*, chapter 32 of *The New Introductory Lectures on Psychoanalysis* (1932)[2] serve as references for this lesson of the Seminar on *Anxiety*, where, in relation to the drive, Freud distinguishes: (1) the *source*, the place from which it springs (the oral drive comes from the mouth); (2) the *pressure*, the continuous character of the drive that never stops pressing forward; (3) the *aim*, always directed towards satisfaction, which is found within the body and the drive itself; finally (4) the *object*, towards which the drive is exercised. According to Freud, the object is completely random, unimportant, and fundamentally interchangeable; thus when a drive object is missing, we can find a substitute in the same category (one oral object replaces another) or in another category (any frustration can, for example, find a substitute in the oral or sadistic anal sphere, etc.).

But why and in what way does the object impose itself in the functioning of the drive, beyond the contingent and substitutable character of the object? This question introduces Lacan's object *a*: *why is there an object instead of nothing?* Behind the Freudian object of the drive, which in its contingency appears perfectly external to the drive, the object *a* imposes itself in the intimacy of the drive. The question of the object *a* imposes itself as what is internal to even the most external object, to the thing most external to the drive, the object; what is there at the interior of the thing that is most external to the drive, at the interior of the object? It is extimity; it is both exterior and interior. It is an exterior that is inside the most intimate interior, that radical nothingness that is the object *a* in its most rigorous and most important form, that radical nothingness from which the invention of the unconscious and, at the same time, the invention of the subject arises.

From here on, we understand that object *a* is not a phobic object, presenting itself as an external object that is easy to flee from. It is closer to the object of the fetish which serves as a stopper that prevents the mother's castration from being seen. This fetishistic object is the internal, intimate condition for which someone chooses an external object; it is the cause of the choice. The fetish can be understood in common phrases such as "he or she is not my type" where the person in question doesn't have the fetish that determines "my type of man or woman", "she doesn't have blonde hair" or "she doesn't have the right shoes". We understand that the fetish is the cause of desire, the cause of desire that is going to cling wherever it can to an external object.

Far from being the contingent object of the drive, the object *a* is what sustains desire and the libido, the economy of the libido. Can it be situated within the drive or the libido? Lacan rightly criticises the first translation of *Libidohaushalt* (in *Anxiety and Instinctual Life*) as "libidinal content": it is not a question of content (*Libidoinhalt*). Object *a is a* question of *Haus*, house; it is the home economics of the libido, the housekeeping, the maintenance of the libido. For Lacan, the support of the libido.

Now, for Freud, all of the libido is supported *by narcissism*: the libidinal economy is essentially what is played out in the development of the ego. With the development of the ego, we would be back to intentionality, as the articulation of a retention (of what has been played out in the past) and a *protention* (where we could look towards the future with "intention"). No doubt. But this development or intentionality only functions because in the ego ideal, on the side of the future, there is a hole, there is a void, there is *minus phi*. This means that narcissism or the development of the ego cannot in any way be reduced to intentionality. Or again, if the ego ideal is the repetition of the ideal ego it is a *signifying* repetition of the ideal ego (S_1) where S_2 (the ego ideal) is emptied of all the imaginarisation of S_1. In the ego ideal, we find this emptiness, this absolute nothingness where the Other does not respond, we have the evocation of S($Ⱥ$). And it is this absolute nothingness, the vocal form of the object *a*, that serves as the "support of the libido", of the libidinal economy, to invent the subject, a "doing" and a redoing.

Redoing the entire *Critique of Pure Reason* doesn't go without redoing the subject, redoing its emergence from the signifying process, which is the place of the ethical unconscious. The *Critique of Practical Reason* poses the question: what should I do? True human experience does not correspond to the desire to acquire an object that one imagines before oneself, such would be a purely technical or pragmatic doing: the object of such a desire is not the cause of desire, but the goal or end of that desire (relative, in Kant's terminology, to the lower faculty of desiring). The higher faculty of desire consists in inventing the moral law; and the object of such a desire is not before us, it is what drives us to invent. This clarifies Lacan's formula "the object *a* is the cause of desire", where the object *a* is not a phenomenal object, not an ordinary object appearing in sensibility and knowledge, where the cause is not a deterministic cause, but a cause through freedom (the freedom of invention of the unconscious) and where desire is not just any desire, but what Kant called the "higher faculty of desire".

2   Object *a* in the seminar on ethics

Let us again address object *a*, starting with the seminar on *Ethics* and *Kant with Sade* where the reading of Sadean phantasy and sadism is worthwhile in attempting to answer the question: *what must I do?* (Figure 4.1).

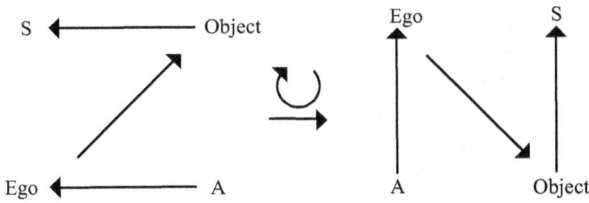

Figure 4.1 From the classic Schema L to the structure of the phantasy (in *Kant with Sade*).

The classic Schema L is shown on the left; turning this figure a quarter of a turn clockwise, gives us the figure on the right, which allows a better idea of where the phantasy lies in *Kant with Sade*.

In both configurations, the diagonal line between the object and the ego orients the ego towards the object: this is the simplified relation of intentionality. But that is not enough, because the object always implies something other than an object upstream of itself, namely the big S, a completely indeterminate subjective side (not the ego), and the ego itself always implies prior to itself the operation of the big Other (the ego is not without the interplay of its development with the big Other). Kantian morality must be read in these two schemas, following the direction of the arrows. However, common sense and an erroneous reading of Kantian morality regularly take the opposite route: we imagine that everything starts with a subject S, who encounters an object and asks himself what he should do; he then finds an answer in the ego and its consciousness of good and evil, which is decided in function of the big Other (the given universal law). Lacan committed this inverted and faulty reading of the Kantian moral law, but he corrects brilliantly by appealing to Sade.[3]

Let us place the components of the Sadean phantasy in the four corners of Schema L: (Figure 4.2).

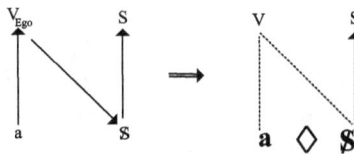

Figure 4.2 From the Sadean phantasy to the usual formula of phantasy.

In the Sadean phantasy (which gives a true reading of Kant), the voice of the tormentor (a) in place of the big Other, supports the will *volonté* of the tormentor's ego in order to address his victim – a completely barred subject in the Sadean phantasy who is valued as an object – to produce an effect on this subject, on this same victim. The complex articulation of the phantasy (which follows the Z of Schema L) is at play in all phantasies, of which we most often retain only the bottom line: a ◊ 𝖲, i.e. the usual formula of the phantasy.

The object *a* (the absolute nothing from which everything starts), the voice, determines the sadistic will. As voice, it aims at introducing, not so much the victim's suffering, but his anxiety. The *cause* of sadistic desire, the object *a,* is what is prior to the sadistic will, and this cause *does not know* what is being sought. It is irreducible to an image, particularly, to the specular image. It cannot be specularised, it cannot be interpreted. From the point of view of positive knowledge, it is zero. The condition of possibility of the sadistic experience serves as the fetishistic condition of the choice of love, it is a fetish; at the same time, it conceals the castration of the mother, the not-knowing of the big Other. But here the fetish does not illuminate a story of love, but of sadism: it is the black fetish, it is darkness, it doesn't know. Object *a* is thus petrified, statufied, in order to hold just this position while not-knowing, but nevertheless determining the whole process.

In the Seuil edition, the cover of the seminar on *Ethics* is illustrated by Man Ray's portrait of the Marquis de Sade where Sade is pictorially composed by a series of stone blocks taken from the ruins of the Bastille, in other words, from the destruction of the incarnation of a ferocious, torturing superego. The vocal object, at the root of both the Sadean phantasy and Kantian morality, is not a consequence of the ferocious superego (as one could read it in Freud). Rather, it presupposes the destruction of the latter superego, to allow a purified superego to emerge, a pure "*Jouis*", to allow the absolute nothing to appear at the heart of the superego and, with it, the opening of *jouissance* and of all creation.

2.1   Sadism and masochism

The masochist is not in any way the sadist's victim or counterpart, even if both sadist and masochist hold the place of *an object*. But while the sadist is characterised primarily by the vocal object, by *the object a*, in its non-exchangeable, non-specularisable, non-explainable function, the masochist inscribes himself in the position of an exchangeable, specularisable, explainable *common object*, he makes himself the object, he makes himself a dog, an object treated as an object on stage.

Both sadism and masochism are played out on stage. Both involve the stage, both involve the big Other and both involve the component of saying. But on this stage, the sadist does not see himself, because he identifies with the non-specularisable object *a* – even if he is on the stage, he escapes awareness and recognition of his function. The masochist, however, is also on stage, but he recognises himself in his identification as an object for the other. "Recognising oneself as an object of desire is always masochistic". *But to so recognise oneself as the object of desire is to not recognise oneself as the objet petit a*; for the object *a* is the cause of desire, not its goal or intention, and it is not for nothing that the object *a* is unknowable as such. To recognise oneself as the object of desire is to recognise oneself as a *recognisable* object of desire. And recognition involves a degradation, an imaginarisation of the object of desire into an ordinary object.

Could we think that masochism is caused by a ferocious superego (whereas sadism involves a *purified* superego)? Man Ray's portraits of Sade (constructed from the ruins of the Bastille prison) highlight two figures of the superego, the superego appearing as ferocious, wicked, terrible (evoked by the Bastille) and the ego ideal, imaginarised in being filled with imperatives coming from society, the family, etc. Additionally, the superego appears as the ideal of the individual (evoked by the Bastille) or, the superego presents itself as radically pure in the form of *Jouis!* (enjoy what? We don't know) and when the ego ideal is emptied of all imaginary, Sade's aim is to make a void of all of the imaginary of society, the family, etc., in order to create and invent a new *jouissance*.

One cannot however simply relate masochism to the figure of a ferocious and malicious superego. Because, if it can be argued that the superego is the *cause* of masochism, *cause* must then be understood in its complexity, as a reciprocal causality, a causality that implies invention, creation, metaphor in the order of desire. This cause must be understood in the order of the object as *the* cause of desire. That the masochist makes himself an ordinary object for the imaginary *jouissance* of the Other does not yet tell us the truth. We shall see later that it consists in provoking the anxiety of the Other.

With the introduction of the object *a* as fundamentally vocal, it becomes clear that it is not a question of making a catalogue of small object *a*'s: oral, anal, phallic, scopic and vocal. For each of these forms, the function escapes and already refers to nothing. With the eye and in the scopic form (the gaze), the equivocation is maximal between what can be seen and known (the eye and the specularisable) and what can neither be seen nor known (the gaze and the non-specularisable). This is why the scopic form, in all its ambiguity, is always present in anxiety. The hole that is there, the frame that is there in the window, in the frame of the painting, of what we can see, and then, when an imaginary object of knowledge that is there, such as the eye, comes to block the place of the gaze: here is the structure of anxiety.

3   Desire and the law: from where does it come?

Not unrelated to the question of ethics linked to the vocal form of object *a*, Lacan regularly quotes verse 7,7 of Saint Paul's Epistle to the Romans: "It was through the Torah that I came to know covetousness". Or again: "It was through the law that I came to know desire". We find the same problematic in Kant: "I can only know the liberty of desire (the higher faculty of desiring), through the intermediary of the moral law". In other words, I can only know autonomy through the question of the moral law. Desire and law are two sides of the same coin, and the law is nothing other than repressed desire.

We can begin by presenting this two-sided surface (desire and law) as the wall of repression, and of original repression in particular. For Freud, the mechanism of original repression involves a counter-investment: to counter the force of investment of a given representation amounts to opposing it with a counter-force that is strictly symmetrical and opposed to it. Regarding the question of maximal hatred, it is enough for the signs of maximal love to oppose it for the hatred to disappear. This structure of original repression persists throughout the history of secondary repression, and is present in the return of the repressed. Of these two sides (investment and counter-investment), one is visible, the counter-investment, the law, the forbidden, while the other remains invisible, the investment, the desire. The very structure of original repression is perfectly illustrated in the clinic: on the one hand, we can *see* the OCD, the prohibitions of the law, etc.; on the other hand, of course, it hides the strength of the desire that lies behind it and that *cannot be seen*.

But why should or would the law repress desire? The myth of Oedipus responds: the father's desire is the law, and the father's desire is expressed as the supreme demand, the supreme commandment: "Thou shalt not desire her who has been the object of my desire". With this law decreed by the father, the desire of the son (the "subject") is restrained by the demand (the supreme commandment) of the father (the Other) and everything seems to be situated in a toric neurotic perspective, where the subject's desire corresponds to the demand of the Other (see the seminar *L'Identification*).

But the commandment is more than a demand. The Oedipal formula indicates that it is the *desire* of the Other that makes the law. This is what the masochist reveals on the stage of the big Other: he has made himself the object of the Other's desire, not the object that causes the Other's desire, but the usual object targeted by the Other's desire, waste, refuse, ordinary object, common object. The usual object is manufactured from scratch by the masochist, like an anal object, like excrement.

But this initial explanation of the origin of the law by the father's demand and desire does not explain the mutation, the transformation, the profound upheaval that was played out with the murder of the father in *Totem and Taboo*. The murder of the father separates two fundamentally heterogeneous types of desire: on the one hand, the desire specific to the father of the primitive horde, a profoundly *naturalistic* desire; on the other hand, the desire of the sons, a *desire* that is *immediately linked to the law*. The father who issues the supreme commandment articulating law and desire is in no way the father of the primitive horde, who would say "you shall not desire those who are objects of my desire". "She who was the object of my desire" is the forbidden mother, who contains within herself the radical lack and castration of the mother, redoubled in the myth by the murder of the father to express the radical non-knowledge S(Ⱥ). There is something quite different starting from this murder of the father: a radical emptiness, a vocal object *a*, an absolute lack of response from the big Other, from any big Other, from any part of the signifying field.

This object *a* as lack is the last irreducible reserve of the libido, the "support of the libido" (*Libidohaushalt*), and this object *a* as absolute lack is inscribed in the structure of the libido as given in Freud's development of narcissism. The true development of the ego must necessarily be understood starting from a fundamental hole at the interior of the ego ideal, the hole of this vocal object *a*.

4   The empty space that allows the transference to be situated

What allows transference to be situated is transference love and the treasure – the *agalma* – that Alcibiades assumes is present in Socrates, the beloved. But the treasure in Socrates does not answer. It is a void, a gaping hole, even though Socrates represents the ideal ego, the specular image that would explain everything for Alcibiades. The *agalma* doesn't respond and nothing is explained. We are right in the middle of the structure of anxiety with its three characteristics: *first*, the question of this void, *second*, the framing, *third*, the object *a* of the phantasy imagined on the stage and coming to fill the void.

With the introduction of the *agalma* – which, in Socrates, does not respond – we have moved from an attempt to explain the law-desire opposition to another way that still does not explain it, but allows it to play out. Initially, the law-desire opposition would be clarified through the intermediary of a consistent big Other, resulting in the imaginary conception of a ferocious superego (as is at play for the masochist). Secondly, there is the question of the fundamental void inherent in the *agalma*, which is the cause of repression, including original repression. In his second theory of anxiety (*Inhibitions, Symptoms and Anxiety*), Freud says that it is anxiety that provokes and causes repression. We can situate this anxiety in the development of the ego, more precisely *in the ego ideal*, which is considered to be S_2 in relation to the ideal ego, S_1. Anxiety is the cause of repression through the intermediary of the ego ideal: the ego represses as a function of the ego ideal. But the ego ideal is profoundly ambiguous: it can be understood either as purely imaginarised and on the side of a ferocious superego, with very strict rules, or as a superego on the side of an opening towards *jouis*, towards *jouissance*. It is therefore because of this equivocal structure inherent in the superego, the ferocious superego or the superego of *jouissance*, that the ego must estimate what should be done. This estimation of the Ego – self-esteem (*Selbstachtung*) – is not a vain and useless self-satisfaction; it is the work of estimating how to do – what must I do? – according to the two possible interpretations of the ego ideal and the superego. The ego estimates what should be done, particularly in the case of repression.

The *agalma* through which Lacan introduced the object *a* implies the whole development of the ego and of love (in its dimension of reciprocal love). And this is how we can, with Hölderlin, answer the question: why did Socrates tolerate Alcibiades and his antics so patiently in *The Banquet*? Hölderlin answers: *Wer das Tiefste gedacht, liebt das Lebendigste*, "He who has thought to the greatest depth loves what is most alive.[4]" Socrates tolerated Alcibiades because of love, Alcibiades' love for Socrates, but also Socrates' love for Alcibiades. This is present in the very structure of transference, which is played out in terms of real, present love. The question of love is the central question of transference. It is based on the greatest depth, the greatest hole, the absolute nothing present in the *agalma*. It is with lack that love is possible. And this is true not only for the analysand, who must be pending (*en souffrance*) so that he may be able to love in analysis, but also able to love the analyst, who, himself, must also be pending, not as someone rich who is able to give positively what he has, such as the right interpretation, but able rather to give *what he does not have*. The lack inherent in object *a* must be there, prior to the reciprocal love at stake in the transference.

5   The young homosexual woman

A Case of Female Homosexuality[5] will serve to illustrate the transference, while introducing the question of acting out and *passage à l'acte*.

Upon the late birth of a little brother when she was sixteen, the young woman must have felt deeply deceived and betrayed by her father. Following this catastrophic disappointment, she changes her sexual orientation. She falls in love with an older woman of dubious reputation and behaves towards her as a knight behaves towards his lady (as in courtly love). This change of sexual orientation is addressed to her father: it is a response to her disappointment, indicating, that in love, "it's not working".

One day in Vienna, the young homosexual woman, accompanied by her "lady", encounters her father, who gives her a furious, disapproving look, full of reproaches against the "lady". Following this sign of her father's disapproval, the young girl throws herself (*niederkommt*) off a bridge onto the railway line. In *niederkommen,* Freud also understands this as a term used for the birth of a child, and Freud can interpret the attempted suicide of throwing oneself onto the railway line as the equivalent of herself being born.

Instead of this interpretation, where the meaning of the suicide attempt is given as equivalent to giving birth (the first conception of the signifier), the same attempt can be understood within the framework of the signifying process and the structure of anxiety: (1) the void of the embarrassing situation, (2) the framing of the scene of the encounter and (3) the emergence of something in this framed emptiness. By hurtling into the void (*passage à l'acte*), the subject is barred, but her act only exists in the aftermath of a position in which she made herself the object of desire for the father (object *a* being present from the outset). The suicidal act is preceded by an initial sequence that serves as an *acting out,* by which means she responds to the frustration she has felt following the birth of her little brother. She responds to her father by engaging in a staging that, on the one hand, does not let go of the *émoi* aroused by the birth of her little brother, in which she felt affected in her life and in her death (third degree of movement) and that, on the other hand, symbolises her affair and her impediment in her idealised relationship with the "lady" (second degree of the difficulty of knowing). She lacks something to express the major difficulty, to express her radical embarrassment (the signifier *en-moins* specific to the *acting out*).

At the second stage, the stage of the *passage à l'acte* when she throws herself onto the railway tracks, she becomes the signifier *en-trop*, embarrassing everyone; she incarnates *plus phi*, announcing the hole *positively*. She is indeed in movement, but the movement of life and death (birth at the risk of death) is here flipped onto a movement *in reaction* to her father's disapproving look and the lady's letting go. She has moved from the third to the second degree of movement (from *émoi* to emotion). At the same time, she maintains the maximum difficulty of knowledge preceding the acting out: she incarnates the *embarrassing* question to the maximum for her father and for the "lady" (at the sight of the father's incensed look, the lady asks her to leave her alone and rejects her). She has turned her *émoi* into emotion and produced the maximum embarrassment: this is *passage à l'acte*.

The transference here is split between acting out and *passage à l'acte*. Freud clearly grasped the embarrassment of the situation, the major difficulty or even impossibility of knowing and unravelling the story (third degree of difficulty); the situation is cluttered with too much meaning. This is what is regularly at play with what the obsessional tells us: the situation is cluttered with too much meaning, but nothing is really mobilised from a movement that implies life and death (third degree of movement) and the movement only exists as a reaction to external events. With these *en-trop* signifiers, we remain in embarrassment, but we don't really move. The same applies to the young homosexual woman who produces too many signifiers: she brings Freud dreams in which she becomes heterosexual again, finds a man, gets married and so on. But Freud doesn't believe it and she doesn't believe it either; it's a staging in emotion, which doesn't mobilise the third degree of movement where her life and death would really be involved. From this point of view, Freud is right: in producing such dreams, she is still in the position of *passage à l'acte*.

The function of the object *a*, insofar as it is the cause of desire, in other words the factor that mobilises desire to the maximum (third degree of movement), is not mobilised in the *passage à l'acte*. Relying on the conviction that his dreams of heterosexuality are lies intended to deceive him, Freud lets her fall, rejects her to leave her in the care of a female colleague. Freud's *passage à l'acte*, who in his embarrassment, lets himself be guided by the emotion triggered by these lying dreams (which themselves have the structure of the patient's *passage à l'acte*). A *passage à l'acte* for a *passage à l'acte*. The initial structure of *acting out*, which preceded the suicidal *passage à l'acte*, had been short-circuited.

The question of object *a*, in its complete structure, brought into play in anxiety (acting out *and passage à l'acte*), could have indicated to him that even if object *a* was not yet fully mobilised in his patient, the question was there and, with it, the question of a reciprocal love that could have developed between Freud and the young homosexual woman.

LESSON 9⁶: TRANSFERENCE IN ACTING OUT AND *PASSAGE À L'ACTE*

1   Signifying division and the end result

On the one hand, the story of the young homosexual woman allows the staging of an *acting out* of her homosexual relationship with the lady to be seen and, on the other hand, the double act of a suicidal patient who lets herself fall and of Freud who lets her fall.

Let us take *acting out* as a staging of the question of the subject with the big Other. How can the subject find room on the stage of the signifier, in the locus of the big Other? Such is the stake in signifying division. To begin with, we have the big Other ("a signifier for another signifier") and in front of this Other, a hypothetical "subject", a subject that exists, only as an idea: how can such a subject come to be? The schema of division has been introduced from the beginning of the Seminar. How can the subject S find its place in the big Other? How can the subject be "represented by a signifier for another signifier"?

First schema of division. The question is *initially* posed in apparently *neurotic* terms: the question of S is intertwined with the question of O, like the two toruses supposed to account for neurosis; subject and Other are supposed to be consistent (imaginary), not fictional. However, the first response is that the Other does not respond, the big A is barred: Ⱥ. If we consider this result for the subject (Ⱥ multiplied by S), we will find that the subject remains deadlocked, it is barred, Ƨ, and it will not find its way into the framework of the subject supposed to know, of self-consciousness, etc. The subject is supposed to be represented by the Other, but it is not represented by the Other. The subject is supposed to be represented by the signifier (S₁): the Other (A) divided by the question of S (first line of division). If the big Other does not answer (Ⱥ, second line on the right), then the subject remains in suspense (Ƨ, second line on the left). Because the question of the subject does not exhaust the Other, there remains the difference between A and Ƨ (A minus Ƨ): there remains the object *a* (third line on the left) where object *a* as remainder is seen as the result of the operation of division (Figure 4.3).

A	S
Ƨ	Ⱥ
a	

Figure 4.3 First schema of the division of the Other (A) by the question of the subject (S).

The first diagram shows how Ƨ and object *a* (second and third lines on the left) are successively engendered by the signifying process. And this engendering only occurs through S₁–S₂ in the second conception of the signifier, where A turns out to be valid as Ⱥ. This is the engendering of the fundamental phantasy, represented by the topology of the cross-cap, as Lacan set out in the seminar on *Identification*. The big Other can be seen as the cross-cap itself, engendered in the functioning of the signifier. If we subtract Ƨ (the Moebius strip) from the big Other (the cross-cap), we are left with the famous "host" or sliver, object *a*. Lacan adds zero to the right of the third line: the result of the division of the object *a* divided by S will always be zero, because the object is non-specularisable and, as a result, escapes.

But this engendering of the Moebius strip (of the Ƨ, of the barred subject) by the interior eight of the signifier *before the* addition of the object *a* is still fundamentally based on the imaginary of the signifier, on the great loop of the interior eight, and not on the signifying S_1–S_2 process that makes the imaginary disappear and *initially* brings the hole to light and object *a* (before the question of the subject). As we have said, in this schema of the division of the big Other by the subject, the first line (A and S) reprises the hypothesis of neurosis: the big Other and the subject are face to face. However, in the two lines that follow in the left-hand column, $\mathcal{S}$ and the object *a* are articulated in the structure of the fundamental phantasy. With this division, we therefore move from the toric and neurotic conception to the practice of the cross-cap and the fundamental phantasy centred on the object *a* (and not on $\mathcal{S}$). To think about desire, we can start from the neurotic opposition between A and S, but the division will lead us to revise the opposition between the Other and the subject and to introduce a new practice on the side of the fundamental phantasy (*a* and $\mathcal{S}$), this being introduced by the structure of the signifier starting from the hole, from the object *a*, and not from $\mathcal{S}$. We thus move on to the second schema of the division of the subject, where the object *a* is visibly the cause of desire and of $\mathcal{S}$ (Figure 4.4 and 4.5).

$$
\begin{array}{c|c}
A & S \\
a & \cancel{A} \\
\mathcal{S} &
\end{array}
$$

Figure 4.4 Second schema of the division of the Other (A) by the question of the subject (S).

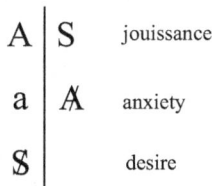

$$
\begin{array}{c|c}
A & S \quad \text{jouissance} \\
a & \cancel{A} \quad \text{anxiety} \\
\mathcal{S} & \quad \text{desire}
\end{array}
$$

Figure 4.5 Second schema of the division of the Other (A) by the question of the subject (S).

Let us now take this schema again with Hamlet and the three stages in mind – the world, the stage and the scene on the stage. The world as such is outside our division. The stage poses the question of *saying* starting from the big Other (Hamlet's father, etc.) and of *finding* the place of the subject (Hamlet, *to be or not to be*) in relation to the big Other: the first line of division of our schema, A and S. The scene on the stage questions the big Other, but it doesn't respond; even if Claudius panics and shows that he is indeed the murderer, the big Other doesn't respond, the impasse remains.

The real answer can *only* come *after the scene on the stage*, after the murder of Polonius (which is still only an *acting out*) and identification with the object *a*, with the object of mourning, Hamlet's identification with Ophelia, allowing him to act. But this "taking action" is not, strictly speaking, a *passage à l'acte* in the sense of avoiding radical movement and *émoi*, because it contains within it the full force of the object *a*, which implies birth and death, life emerging against the backdrop of death. This is what is at stake in Hamlet's final act, who by killing Claudius, avenges his father.

The *passage à l'acte*, in the precise sense of our grid, is always a letting fall, a letting fall of the radicality of movement and exiting from the stage. Embarrassment is clearly there between $ and Ⱥ, the second line of the diagram of division. Added to this is emotion, the disorder of movement, a movement that does anything other than support the question of life against the backdrop of death. The *passage à l'acte*, which would consist of leaving the stage of the tragedy, is not central to the play and only plays a role in the play's side stories (for example, Guildenstern and Rozencrantz). The *passage à l'acte* leaves the scene of the *saying* eventually switching to another piece of destiny, another story.

With the three points of (1) the void that precedes the scene, (2) the framing of the scene within the scene on the stage and (3) the question of the object *a*, in its double value of support of radical movement (the third level of movement) and of the position starting from non-specularisable non-knowledge (third level of difficulty), the structure of anxiety Ⱥ and *a* appears at the heart of the schema of the division of the big Other and the subject. Acting out avoids anxiety by replacing the inventive force of the object *a* with a subject who lets himself fall into a movement of pure reaction. *Acting out* avoids anxiety by remaining on the stage, by supporting the inventive force of the object *a* and in displacing it onto a symbolic stage that demands to be interpreted (the second degree of the difficulty of knowing).

2   Having and being in the development of the ego

Anxiety precedes the constitution of the ego (in narcissism as the development of the ego or in the optical schema). In this way, the anxiety in animals occurs independently of any constitution of the ego. The Freudian hypothesis of anxiety as a signal in the ego must therefore be reviewed (Figure 4.6).

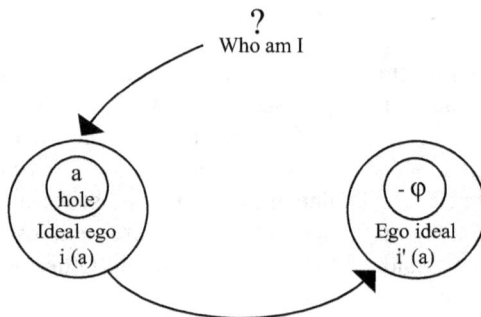

Figure 4.6 New schema of the development of the ego.

Returning to the schema of the development of the ego is to begin with a question: who am I? In other words, how can the subject emerge in the locus of the big Other? A first mythical answer is found, on the side of the past, in the ideal ego that the subject would have been imaginarily (S_1 – unbarred A) and where the mythical subject tries to find something of this ideal ego, on the side of the future, in the ego ideal, the ego ideal this is holed (A barred or S_2 emptied of the imaginary). Of course, the hole in the ego ideal can be filled by a series of identifications, which re-imagine the ego ideal, amounting to returning it to being nothing more than an ideal ego fleshed out by objects to be *imaginarised*. The ideal ego is thus fleshed out by these imaginary identifications, the individual's cards of belonging to such and such a company, bank, political party, social network, etc. The ideal ego is thus fleshed out by these imaginary identifications, the individual's cards of belonging to such and such a club, bank, political party, social network, etc.

How does this kind of identification work, coming as it does to nourish the identity of the ego, presenting itself in fact as an ideal ego? How do certain objects of love (or hate or indifference) become objects of identification? Freud addresses this question in the chapter on identification in his work *Group Psychology and the Analysis of the Ego*. The subject "introjects" a trait of the loved person (of the hated person or of an indifferent person). Dora, for example, introjects her beloved father's cough in order to identify with the law. Without going directly into the signifying process as outlined by Lacan, oral or even cannibalistic introjection, to Freud's eyes, is like a *regression*.

Regression can be presented as follows: the subject had a beloved thing or person; "had" past tense, from the imaginary past, it is of the order of the ideal ego: he had it and he doesn't have it anymore. This may define the objet *a*: "objet *a* is what we had, but no longer have". With this regression, we have already rediscovered the signifying process: "what we had" is the ideal ego charged with the imaginary (S_1) and we no longer have it, it is emptied of all imaginary (S_2).

At this moment, lack (*minus phi*) is established and, while we used to be loved for what we had, we become loving for what we no longer have and are trying to regain. The ego ideal with its hollow, its void, its *minus phi* is put back in place. On the side of having, the ideal ego presents itself as imaginary; on the other side (we no longer have it), the ego ideal presents itself as bereft, and this is where the question of its being arises: what am I? What can I become? But this question finds no response in any knowledge. It has to be invented in the process of love, which consists precisely in "giving what one does not have".

Object *a* is situated in the ambiguity of a small positive a, a+, of "what we h(a)d", and a small negative a, a-, a fundamental *minus phi*, "what we no longer have". And it is on the basis of what we provisionally had (*poros*, what's expedient, wealth) and what we no longer have (*penia*, lack and absence of resources) that the engendering of love can be engaged with. It raises the question of being, but a question of being that has to be invented on the basis of what we no longer have, to be invented in the reciprocal action of love. The one loved at the start, is used here as the initial imaginary material (S_1) from which we can mourn and reveal lack, what we no longer have (S$_2$), in order to invent a new love. The metaphor of love consists precisely in the transformation of the beloved (for what he has) into the lover (with what he no longer has). But the first lover has not, for all that, become a loved one filled with riches; he or she remains fundamentally loving. Love is always reciprocal, that of lovers and of those who are loved who can only give what they don't have (any longer?) and so give themselves the prospect of being and of being reborn. From having to no longer having, in order to become towards the question of being.

From a developmental perspective that is open to being critiqued, object *a* can be evoked in *l'a-voir* (to have it), *a-vant* (before) and *a-vec* (with). This allows us to find a whole panoply of *a*-objects as possessions, as antecedents, as companions. These multiple *a*-objects are supposed to exist in disorder and in chaos, outside the development of the ego, functioning autoerotically where there is no primordial ideal ego, no original narcissism. All these little *a*'s are supposed not to be unified by the spherical mirror and the body is considered to be fragmented. Schizophrenia would thus be explained by these scattered little *a*'s experienced as scattered from before birth, in the mother's body. The question of the ego would be constructed by the spherical mirror, which would bring together all these scattered little *a*'s in the vase of the ideal ego, in i(a), and schizophrenia would be situated before the construction of the ego in the spherical mirror.

But let's note that the development of the ego, inscribed here in the optical schema, is always rightly preceded by a similar process *without the ego's own consciousness*, in other words by a development of the *id*. This allows us to understand anxiety as prior to any question of the ego proper. It is always a movement that is already there. We might therefore understand anxiety as an edge phenomenon in the developmental movement of the ego or of the id. How are we to understand this movement illustrated as the development of the ego and also of the id? Is it based on the positive precedence of various small, scattered *a*'s with the movement coming secondarily? Or, on the contrary, is the developmental movement primary? And the little *a*'s having existence only in function of the process that precedes them.

In the first case, the phenomenon of depersonalisation can be understood on the basis of a former failure in the construction of the ego: the *a*-objects would never have been assembled into a unity by the ideal ego, the objects would have been unsuitable for "ego-isation". In the second case, depersonalisation is a depersonalisation in the process of development (of the ego or the id) *always already underway*. The specular image is always already formed in the mirror (or we have already entered into the process of seeing, knowing, explaining, etc.), but a rupture in this process provokes a non-recognition of the specular image, a depersonalising vacillation. And it is precisely in function of the complete structure of development, which is to say, that there is a vacillation between i'(a), the ego ideal, the empty hollow that cannot be filled and what must be filled in a certain way. A feeling of dispossession arises, not an absence of possession, but a deprivation of possession, a *dés-avoir*, a dispossession. Depersonalisation, dispossession, these phenomena of the double depend on the structure of the fundamental phantasy and the cross-cap (a structure dependent on S_1–S_2), insofar as it always already conditions the relation between i(a) and i'(a). It implies the cut between i(a) and i'(a), or again, the cut that separates the object *a* from i(a), to make it appear cut off from what can be specularised (i(a)) or from the fictional "subject".

The so-called "birth trauma" cannot be placed in a developmental perspective; it is essentially a story of cutting: the cutting of the "new-born" ($ non-specularisable) from its embryonic envelopes (object *a*, non-specularisable). This cut is the fact of the signifying process, in its synchronic structure, which is always assumed to be already present. And in light of this cut, depersonalisation, schizophrenia, etc., can no longer be conceived of as deficits in a primordial positive structure. They depend on the structure of the signifier, on the cut between the ideal ego and the ego ideal, and on the cut between S and the object *a*. This opens up a whole new perspective for theory, but above all for encounters with people said to be depersonalised, dispossessed or generally deficient.

3   Acting out, *passage à l'acte*, the transference

Unlike *passage à l'acte*, acting out consists in not letting fall. To achieve this, acting out remains and clings to the dynamic of the Other and the little *a*. This, says Lacan, creates beings that are "unified", whole and unwavering. A certain type of mother, or even a certain type of parent in general, is characterised by the fact that they will never let their child down. In contrast to this type of person who never lets you down (and who is perpetually in *acting out*), a phallic mother is characterised by the fact that, at some point, she has always already let her child down, either inadvertently, by default, or deliberately. Not to drop the child as an object *a* presupposes the collage of this object *a* with the functioning of the big Other (at the level of a symbolic knowledge, the median degree of the difficulty of knowing), and this collage is not easy to handle. This is because the small *a* (the child) is necessarily taken as positivised in the very structure of the ego ideal (of the parent). The object *a* (the child) then takes its place in a super-egoic function, where the superego appears at its the most ferocious, most unaccommodating, most demanding (rather than the superego as an empty imperative: *jouis!* enjoy!).

With this symbolic commitment to not let drop, *acting out* also presents itself as an entrance on stage with saying (*dire*), with the big Other: it flaunts itself, it shows itself off. But naturally, what is shown isn't it. We have the example of the young homosexual woman's bond with the Lady: something is shown in this bond, but what? This requires interpretation, which is why it shows itself in the locus of the big Other. It is not certain that interpretation is possible (cf. the barred Other). But in any case, it is a demand, a demand that won't give way, as, for example, the *acting out* involving fresh brains on the part of Kris's patient, taken up again by Lacan in *The Direction of the Treatment*. The patient, you recall interrogates himself about what he is, asking essentially, am I a plagiarist or am I not? An intellectual, writing in a field close to psychoanalysis, he wonders whether his articles are pure plagiarism or not, not without hindering his writing process as one might imagine. Kris sees fit to reply, as an impartial judge of the said reality of these writings might do: "No, you are not a plagiarist".

But here comes the analysand's *acting out* (which doesn't let fall the essential part of his questioning): on leaving the session, he goes to check out the menus of restaurants offering fresh brains. Here, the analysand shows something of the scene not letting what he's talking about. But this requires interpretation because the question is not whether his writings are plagiaristic or not. What he shows is brains *that he doesn't eat* ("anorexia regarding the mental"). It is the question of object *a* as the nothing, insofar as it is the origin of creation. Because that is what is not working in his case. Pursuing these culinary fresh brains, he shows the presence of a desire unknown to himself, but also to the analyst, a knowledge that requires interpretation, but a knowledge that has taken the place of the maximum difficulty of knowing (which concerns the unconscious, a not-knowing in its creative power). This maximum difficulty is avoided, the question of *jouissance* for the analysand is avoided, the question of his creation flowing from the *jouissance* of the unconscious is avoided, and everything is transferred to the column of what can be known: the *acting out* demands to be interpreted.

The *symptom* is also the display of an unknown desire concerning the question of object *a*. But it does not yet demand interpretation, in the sense of being set in motion in interpretation. The symptom is not yet addressed to the Other, it is not directly addressed to the analyst as the big Other, it is not yet an *acting out*. It is enough in itself. But why then is the symptom inscribed in the middle of the nine-square grid, that is, at the median (and symbolic) level of the axis of the difficulty of knowing and of the axis of movement? It is because, even if the symptom is a question of *jouissance*, the question of *jouissance* dragging itself along in both axes, the symptom is an *untergebliebene Befriedigung*, it has failed to achieve satisfaction and satisfaction is left in the lurch. In this suspense, the symptom does not demand transference, it does not demand to be radically mobilised, unlike in *acting out*.

Acting out requires transference because it is precisely at the level of *émoi* and therefore of the emergence of the question of life and death, of inventiveness, of creativity, which is absolutely present, and this is why *acting out is* "wild transference". Wild transference is undoubtedly always already there. What can we do about it? To ask the question of transference is to ask the question: what do we do with an *acting out*? How do we respond to the acting out of Kris's patient seeking fresh brains? What could Freud have done with the *acting out of* the young homosexual woman parading herself with her lady, ever before her suicidal act and ever before her deceiving Oedipal dreams?

Phyllis Greenacre envisages three possible responses to *acting out*. *The first* would be to interpret; note that this is the demand inscribed in the *acting out* itself: it asks to be interpreted. It is not obvious that interpretation (in knowledge) is possible, because it would be played out in the first conception of the signifier, and would thereby systematically miss what's at stake, the question of object *a*, what escapes interpretation. *The second* possibility would be to prohibit *acting out*. This should make us smile, Lacan says; the analyst already prohibits so many things, if only by an implicit position, by what he implies in his doing, without realising it himself; we shouldn't now tack on the prohibition of *acting out*. *The third* possibility would be to strengthen the ego. In Greenacre's conception, it would undoubtedly be a question of strengthening the ego through identification with the analyst, where the analyst would serve to plug the hole in the ego ideal, which would prevent any invention by the subject by obstructing the inventive side of the ego ideal, that pushes invention towards the unconscious, the side of the superego as *jouis!*.

In any case, what we can do with acting out is always to resituate it in its place in the structure of the signifying process, which involves both the nine-square grid and the schema of the division of the subject. If interpretation is imposed in a certain way, it will always be directed towards the uninterpretable remainder, the non-specularisable object *a* outside knowledge. If the forbidden is imposed, it will be to make the void between the saids heard. If the reinforcement of the ego is necessary, it will be for the properly inventive side of the unconscious.

With such different structures as *passage à l'acte* and acting out, one of which is to leave the stage and the other to enter or remain on it, the question arises: can we push the reading of the transference in one direction or the other? Freud, with the young homosexual woman, forced what was happening between himself and her in the direction of *acting out*. We could just as easily push *passage à l'acte* to become an *acting out*; wouldn't that cover what Gisela Pankow called a transference graft? Let's return to Freud's *passage à l'acte* with the young homosexual girl. His patient begins to have wonderful dreams where she gets married, where everything is going to be for the best in the best of all possible worlds, she is going to become completely heterosexual. Freud doesn't believe that these dreams tell the truth about this young woman's desire. Nor does she believe it. Freud deduces that the patient has already left the scene, that she has dropped the matter.

So, can the unconscious deceive us? Freud's answers that, in fact, the dream is something other than the unconscious, that the unconscious deserves our full trust, even if dreams can deceive. But why would the dream lie? What causes lies? And children's lies: why do children lie? The lie is impossible to avoid at a certain level, at the level of the saying of the scene: there is always a fundamental slippage between the statement *(l'énoncé)* and the enunciation, which means that we are always in the process of lying, to a greater or lesser extent.

With this question of the deception of dreams and the deception of the unconscious, Freud is embarrassed, and he doesn't really know why. In fact, he is embarrassed because he thinks of the unconscious in terms of a knowledge that would say what is true or false, and he doesn't take into account that the unconscious is above all a non-knowledge that leads to invention. He is embarrassed by the invention of the unconscious based on a nothing that escapes him; he is embarrassed by this hole that nevertheless imposes itself in the lies of his patient's dreams. And he is in emotion because his fidelity to the unconscious is put to the test. Embarrassment plus emotion, Freud rushes towards the *passage à l'acte* that lets her fall. What escapes Freud is the question of the vocal object *a*, the upper line of the graph, the upper line of *jouissance*, which begins with not-knowing, S(Ⱥ).

Notes

1 Lesson of 16 January 1963.
2 Freud Sigmund, "New Introductory Lectures on Psycho-Analysis" in *The Standard Edition of the Complete Psychological Works*, Volume 22, translated and edited by James Strachey, London, Hogarth Press, 1964, p. 81ff.
3 See Christian Fierens, *The Jouissance Principle*, 2022.
4 Quoted by Martin Heidegger in "Que veut dire 'penser'?" in *Essais et conférences*, trans. André Préau, Paris, Galimard, 1958, p. 163.
5 Sigmund Freud, "The Psychogenesis of a Case of Homosexuality in a Woman" (1920), in *The Standard Edition of the Complete Psychological Works,* Volume 18, translated and edited by James Strachey, London, Hogarth Press, 1955, p. 145ff.
6 Lesson of 23 January 1963.

Part Three

The desire of the analyst

Chapter 5

Lack

An introduction to the desire of the analyst

Four types of circle

Four types of circle or closed cut can be inscribed on a surface.

The first is the spherical cut, a simple circle on paper, on a surface. It can be inscribed at any point on any *surface* (sphere, torus, cross-cap, Klein bottle). This circle is always reducible; it can be tightened and reduced to a point: (Figure 5.1).

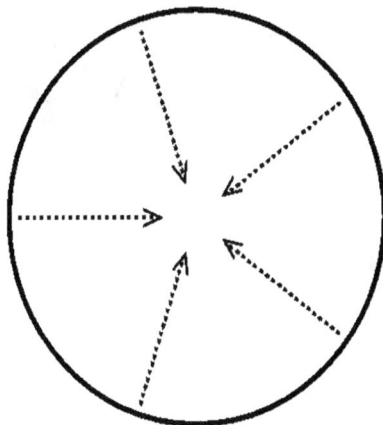

Figure 5.1 The circle can be reduced to a point.

The second and third circles can *only* be inscribed *on the torus* (and Klein bottle). The circle of demand and the circle of desire are irreducible because the body of the torus prevents the circle from being narrowed and reduced: (Figure 5.2).

DOI: 10.4324/9781003477822-8

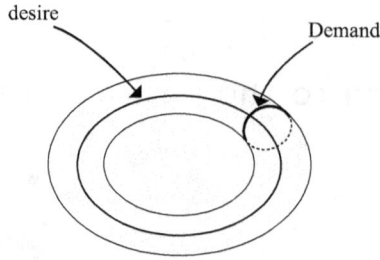

Figure 5.2 A circle of desire and a circle of demand on the torus.

The fourth cut is a *double circle* that is inscribed *only on the cross-cap*. It presupposes the interior eight of the signifier: the large loop of a signifier charged with the imaginary S_1 is repeated in a small mouth emptied of the imaginary S_2. This interior eight automatically generates a Moebius strip and, by closing the edge of the Moebius strip, we produce the cross-cap on which the fourth cut in the interior eight can be inscribed. This interior figure eight is irreducible to the first type of cut. It cannot be reduced to a point. It is impossible to define the central "point" (the little ball) on the figure of the projective plane by a simple circle. Hence, it is not a point. It can only be circumscribed by an *interior eight*, the interior eight of the signifier: (Figure 5.3).

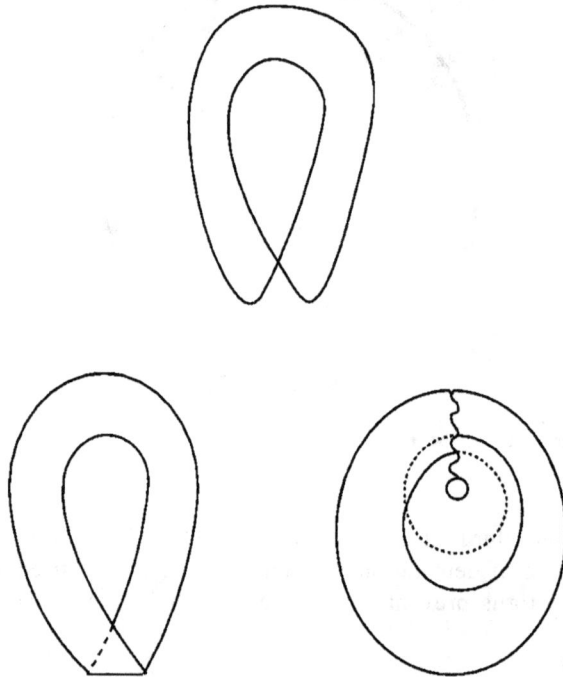

Figure 5.3 Three figures: an interior eight, a Moebius strip and a projective plane (with its "central point").

LESSON 10[1]: LACK, THE TRANSFERENCE AND MOURNING

Lacan's thesis that "anxiety is not without an object" is opposed to the classical thesis that "anxiety is without an object" and can only be explained in terms of three ways of understanding lack.

1   Frustration, deprivation, castration

1.1   First way: the lack in play in anxiety is not frustration (the first type of cut)

In classical logic or purely spherical logic, a third party is excluded. One is either inside the circle or outside it. Anxiety is either without an object or with an object. If Lacan's thesis "anxiety is not without an object" were a thesis of classical or spherical logic, we should be able to conclude: "anxiety therefore has an object" and yes, we know what it is, it is object a except that this object a doesn't exist in classical logic.

We need to understand the phrase "anxiety is not without an object" in another logic which implies two moments or two necessary steps. Firstly: anxiety is without an object. Anxiety is frustrated of an object, of any real object. In clinical practice, there is no real object that is truly the cause of anxiety: even the removal of the phobic object does not make the underlying anxiety disappear. Freud imagined anxiety as anxiety at the loss of a fundamental object: the loss of the breast or a bit of life that allows us to live, the loss of the person who looks after the child, the loss of the penis, the loss of the regard of the loved one, or the loss linked to the superego. But these five objects supposed to be lacking are not concrete objects that it would be enough, in the imagination, to actually replace to make up for their lack. The question of lack is primary, and it cannot be reduced to a possible or real frustration. This is why anxiety is not provoked by the lack of an object, but by the lack of lack (which is in no way a positive object) or again, by the stopper that fills the lack.

1.2   Second way: the lack of lack or privation (second and third types of cut)

The lack of a lack is not equal to the full and "not without" does not mean "with". To explain this, Lacan offers a little apologue. He has bought a book that is missing a certain number of pages; there is a lack in the book. Obviously, making the book disappear (producing the lack of the lack) doesn't allow him to recover the missing pages. The lack is irreducible; there is no negation of the negation that would affirm the positive existence of the object. The very operation of wanting to make the lack disappear redoubles it. In other words, at this level, we have to say that it is true that anxiety is without an object, or better, that the object of anxiety escapes and remains a question. Regarding the object of anxiety still in question there is a corresponding lack of explanation, the lack of pages that would explain anxiety in the field of knowledge remains.

Lack, here irreducible in two different ways, corresponds to the two circles of the neurotic torus, demand and desire. These two irreducibilities can refer to each other indefinitely. In Lacan's little apologue, the lack of images of the missing pages of Lacan's book is, in a way, rescued by the text; the lack of images is explained by the text and, conversely, the lack of text is explained by the images. The irreducibility of demand is circumvented by desire, and the irreducibility of desire is circumvented by demand. Similarly, the irreducibility of transference is explained by counter-transference, and the irreducibility of counter-transference is explained by transference. Desire and demand can be explained by each other, on condition that they are distinguished in two different toruses representing two substantial subjects, the subject and the big Other.

1.3   Third way of addressing the question of the object of anxiety (fourth type of cut)

This is the signifying repetition, in other words the interior eight. Clinically perceptible, when faced with a phobia of flying, we can clearly imagine the object of anxiety: S_1, the airplane. But this repeats, the plane eventually disappearing without the anxiety disappearing. All we have here is a nothing, nothing of a plane (cf. "anxiety is without object"); all we have done here is inscribe the plane in the signifying process: we have not reduced anxiety.

These three ways of questioning the object of anxiety correspond to the three ways of thinking about lack. These are not three different species in the general genre of "lack" (as in classical logic); they are three *ways of approaching* the question of lack. However, we only think of lack in terms of the object: there is no lack without already thinking of the lack of *an object*. Once again, these are not three kinds of object in the set of objects, in the genus object. They are three ways of approaching the object. We can call these three objects the breast, the book and the phallus respectively. These are only provisional names, because the breast can be understood as a phallus and a book. And similarly for the book and the phallus.

To understand them, let us analyse these three lacks in terms of their imaginary, symbolic and real dimensions (Figure 5.4).

	Object	Lack	Agent?
Frustration	R	I	S
Deprivation	S	R	I
Castration	I	S	R

Figure 5.4 Structure of the three lacks (frustration, deprivation, castration).

The first object, the breast, is presented as a real object, in the sense that it is a reality, the rock of a reality, the breast is there before any other thing. From a totally realistic perspective, we think that the breast is a real object and that it can be lacking. Certainly, this reality is systematically called into question in psychoanalytic practice; reality is always constructed of the imaginary and the symbolic; the trap, the trap of realism, would be to believe that this object exists independently of its construction. Since this object is understood as purely real, its lack can only be imaginary. *Frustration* is the imaginary lack of a supposedly real object.

The second object can be represented by a book missing from the library. It is a symbolic object and it is not there in the library, in reality, in the real where it should be. The object of deprivation is a symbolic object (the book) and its lack is inscribed as real (in the library). *Privation* is the real lack of a symbolic object. The "lack of a lack" is thought of as a privation: it is the real lack of a lack that would have symbolic value (and of course, this symbolic lack is not without a third way of thinking about lack: the symbolic lack of an imaginary object).

The third object, the phallus, is the imaginary object par excellence, and if we cut ourselves off from the imaginary, lack acquires a symbolic value. Beyond castration phantasies, the third way of thinking about lack, *castration*, is played out in the signifying process: S_1 is charged with a whole imaginary, and if we manage to lack this imaginary, if we empty S_1 of its imaginary, S_2 appears as symbolic lack. This is castration: the symbolic lack of an imaginary object.

Is there an agent of these different ways of thinking about lack? Let us understand the agent here not as in the Oedipal drama, as the symbolic mother at the level of frustration, the imaginary father at the level of privation, or the real father at the level of castration. Let us understand the agent structurally as that which thinks of lack as frustration, privation or castration, as that which, within us, thinks of lack in such and such a way. With frustration, we place ourselves in a symbolic position in front of a real object and imagine that it is lacking. With privation, we place ourselves in an imaginary position in front of a symbolic object and we realise that it is lacking. With castration, we are in the real in front of an imaginary object and its lack draws us into the symbolic.

The rest of Lesson 10 oscillates between the two latter ways of approaching lack and the object, where, regarding privation, the analyst is in an imaginary position or, regarding castration, in a real position. Independent of our analytic approach, we systematically exclude the first way of thinking of lack as frustration, ruling out the trap of realism from the outset where objects are taken for real objects. On the one hand, Margaret Little's article, *The Analyst's Total Response to his Patient's Needs (1957)*, examines *privation*, where a symbolic object is actually missing. Here, where a missing signifier exists, the question of *acting out* is central, demanding interpretation. On the other hand, on the side of *castration,* the imaginary object constituted by the two intertwined toruses of demand and desire (the neurotic theory as phallus) must come to be lacking in order to give this lack a symbolic value, thereby making room for the signifying process (interior eight, Moebius strip, cross-cap and object *a*). Let's start with castration, which allows us to better situate privation.

2   Castration and the cross-cap

On the cover of the Seuil edition, tiny ants scamper across the surface of a Moebius strip. The strip is not specularisable; each insect can believe that there is a reverse side of the surface on which it is trotting. For it to understand that the surface has only one and the same side, the surface simply needs a marking on one side of the surface (and not on the other). With this marking, after one traversal of the strip, the ant will be able to know that it has already passed that way, but, "on the other side", so to speak and conclude that this other side proves to be in perfect continuity with the first side. This makes for only one surface to the Moebius strip. This marking on a bilateral surface is not present on the Moebius strip. But it is there in the little bilateral piece that corresponds to object *a* (the small central piece in the drawing above with the so-called central "point" in the middle, comprising two clearly separated faces).

We can represent these two sides of object *a* as absence and presence, as nothing and something. And the insect, as it travels along the Moebian strip, can detect: "Now I'm on the side of nothing" or "on the side of something". The object *a*, where the two sides of presence and absence are separated, offers no "short-circuit" for passing "from one side to the other". Passage is only possible through the Moebius strip itself. But it is only by means of the marking, at play in the object *a* where the two sides are distinguished, that the insect can notice that after a certain time it is indeed on the other side of where it was, a turn before. But it is a missing piece, we've drawn it on the diagram, but it is fundamentally absent, it is not specularisable. So we have to understand that the insect turns in a short-circuit and the short-circuit is the Moebius strip, the Moebius strip that turns in a short-circuit on itself while avoiding the central and absent part[2].

With this structure of the Moebius strip and its complement of the object *a*, we could imagine having everything, structure, the projective plane, the phantasy, $ \mathcal{S} \lozenge a $. But object *a* is essentially *lack*, even if it can be drawn topologically. Object *a is* lacking, not just for the ant, but for anyone. The projective plane remains in suspense, an unrealised hope, because object *a* is never given. And it is a lack that no symbol can make complete (not even the little coin Lacan drew in the centre of the cross-cap). "Without symbol" does not mean "without signifier", because this lack is an integral part of the structure of the signifier in its unachievable process. This lack is in no way a privation, since we can make up for the privation and fill it by putting a symbol back in its place, by putting the book back in its place. In the meantime, the little ant continues its Moebian circle in short-circuit, and the barred subject with it.

The object *a*, this part lacking to the projective plane of the cross-cap, is an irreducible lack, of a different irreducibility to that of demand and desire, because it has no symbol. It is a radical lack that we can try to circumvent. In the very effort to circumvent it, we highlight not the central point that would assign it a place, but the "point lacking a signifier". We can understand it as "the missing point" and not as "the lack of signifier". The central point of the cross-cap is missing because it is not a point (it is impossible to identify this point with a spherical circle). Every attempt to encircle it leads to revolving around it *in an interior eight that is specific to the signifier*: it is the essence of the signifier that is at stake here. Object *a* in its radicality (the vocal form of object *a*) is in no way the imaginary matter of sound, of analogue or digital sound. It is in no way the imaginary material of any signifier (S_1), and we must be wary of the term *matérialité*, which can too easily lead us to think of the signifier in terms of an imaginary materiality (S_1) rather than in terms of the real of the emptiness of any imaginary (S_2).

But the two conceptions of the signifier always work in concert. On the one hand (second conception), the signifying process seeks to erase the trace, S_1 presents itself as an (imaginary) trace and, in S_2, the trace is erased. On the other hand (first conception), the more we try to erase the trace in order to produce S_2, the more the trace insists as signifier S_1. One modality of the signifier continually insists on zero (the S_2), and the other is the continual return of the trace (S_1). These two conceptions correspond to the two modalities in which the object *a* can appear in its relation to the Other. One presents itself as S_1, as a trace, and the other as S_2, as the real, the hole.

The function of anxiety combines these two modes. Anxiety is always the signal of these two faces of object *a*: on the one hand, it presents itself as something, as a trace; on the other, it presents itself as an absolute nothing. Anxiety thus presents itself in two opposing aspects and both nonetheless articulated by the signifier: at times anxiety can be accentuated as the anxiety of the real, *Hilflosigkeit*, the most original danger, the most destructive, danger in the face of absolute nothingness; and at times it is presented as the anxiety about something, anxiety in the face of relatively minimal dangers that it would be possible to avoid or circumvent (as in phobia). Anxiety thus circulates between anxiety about something and anxiety about the absolute nothing. It is this circuit that is at play in the contradictory positions "anxiety is without an object" and "anxiety is not without an object". This circuit is the interior eight circuit of the signifying process: S_1 it's something, the trace, and S_2, like the erasure of the trace, nothing. It suffices to connect the two loops of the interior eight by crossbeams of resonance between the two loops, to generate the Moebius strip, which is completed by the bilateral pellet that is the object *a*, in order to form the cross-cap. By generating these two pieces of surface (the surface of $, the Moebius strip, which is non-specularisable and has only one face, and object *a*, which is non-specularisable and has two faces), the signifying process also brings about two ways of practising the psychoanalytic discourse in the handling of transference.

3   Two ways to practise the transference

Firstly, on the side of S, the transference would amount to the constant reversal of the Moebius strip; everything is continually reversed into its opposite and is constantly presented as the job of negation and reversal into its opposite. All this escapes to the specular image and the coherence of explanations in general; the

Moebius strip is "unspecularisable". But it is a short-circuit, because this perpetual movement systematically avoids the other way of practising the psychoanalytic discourse. The second way of practising psychoanalysis: from the side of the object *a*, the other surface of psychoanalytic discourse, consists in taking charge of object *a* in its absence. The object *a* in its lack is a call to creativity. The lack proper to the object *a* must be understood according to the third way of understanding lack, that is, on the side of "castration". This way of taking charge of the non-specularisable, unexplainable object *a*, of taking charge of absolute lack, is the opening to the creativity that, for the subject, restores access to the world by recreating it.

These two ways of practising psychoanalysis can be explained by means of the structure of the fundamental phantasy, emerging from the signifying process and represented in the topology of the cross-cap. How is the relation to phantasy established, on the one hand, in neurosis and, on the other, in perversion and psychosis?

In the seminar on *Identification*, neurosis, psychosis and perversion, all three appeared as *normal* structures of the human being, that is, as responding to the structure of the cross-cap. This normality of the signifying process engendering the cross-cap is fundamental for all three, for the pervert, for the psychotic and for the neurotic. The difference between neurosis, psychosis and perversion is merely a matter of accentuation, insofar as each of the three pathologies insists on and consists in imaginarising one of the three components of the fundamental phantasy and of the cross-cap. The pervert gives all imaginary importance to the object *a* or the *phallus*, which is in it as the so-called central "point". The psychotic gives all imaginary importance to the S and the *body* that represents it. The neurotic gives all imaginary importance to the signifying cut, S_1–S_2, represented by the lozenge at the *big Other*, locus of this cut.

In *the case of perversion or psychosis*, where object *a* or $\mathcal{S}$ is already imaginarised, the handling of the transference will consist in the analyst himself taking charge of the object *a*, not as imaginarised, but as a foreign body, as a radical lack. Here we find the structure of the psychoanalytic discourse, where object *a* is in the place of the semblance and addresses the question of the barred subject $\mathcal{S}$ to eventually produce an S_1, any S_1, as a product left in suspense (in the place of truth as the zero degree of knowledge in the analytic discourse and in suspense of not having an answer on the side of knowledge). In perversion and psychosis, the analyst takes upon himself the burden of this object *a*, as an absolute nothing that can set in motion the phallic imaginarisation of perversion and the corporeal imaginarisation of psychosis.

In *neurosis*, it is the signifier that takes on all its importance, and the big Other takes on an entirely imaginary consistency. The hole, the void (*minus phi*) inherent in the ego ideal, i'(a), is filled by the imaginary product of the signifier, that is, by the "phantasy" – to be understood here as the *phantasy imaginarised* in neurosis and not the fundamental phantasy that arises directly from the signifying process. Yes, the object *a* appears in the transference. And with it comes the question of the authenticity of the analyst, that is, the place of the analyst as imaginarised in the fantasy. The analyst must withdraw from this imaginarisation, because the real object *a* is not specularisable, one might say, is never on stage. Here, the analyst has no choice but to support the movement of the signifier and its consequences in the continual reversals characteristic of the Moebius strip. Because playing the card of object *a* as an absolute nothing serves only to feed the neurotic phantasy of creation. The neurotic takes the stage, but we must not forget the object *a*, not as the imaginary phantasy that would fill the space of the ego ideal and make it explicable (that it would be specularisable). For this, it is better to rely on the non-specularisable of the Moebius strip, which mobilises the non-specularisable object *a*.

Neurosis directly introduces the question of *acting out*, which requires interpretation. The analyst must respond. And the analysand would expect the answer at the imaginary level of the phantasy and the two intertwined toruses where the desire of the analyst (big Other) corresponds and responds to the demand of the analysand (subject). This is the demand of the *acting out* addressed to the analyst. It is this structure (neurotic and toric) that is Margaret Little's central issue with her patients: whatever their diagnosis, Margaret Little, according to Lacan, is dealing with only one type of patient, with only one thing: an *acting out* that truly poses the question of transference.

To situate the transferential and counter-transferential relationship in *acting out*, it is useful to remember an always reciprocated love and the transition from object love to identification in the mourning process.

4   Love, the mourning of having and the mourning of being

The question of *I* – who am I? What am I worth? – finds an answer in the past, on the side of the *ideal ego,* to then project it into the future in an attempt to rediscover this ideal ego in the form of the *ego ideal* with a void in the middle.

We can first understand love as having: I love an object of love and I want to incorporate it. I love chocolate and I want to incorporate it. If I don't have it, I just have to mourn it. The first level would be the loss of having this loved object, the loss of the object of love in general appearing as the loss of having the loved person, ("I had a friend", "I had a lover", "I had a partner", and "I no longer have him/her"). But, the loss of the *having* of this loved person comes, at the same time, to highlight the incomplete development of the ego, the emptiness of the ideal ego. "I've lost my friend, what will become of me?"

Instead of having the other and having lost him or her on the side of having, the person we are mourning questions our becoming; it is a mourning at the level of what we can be. Hence, the mourning that first appeared as mourning for having now presents itself as a hole carved out at the level of being, of becoming, of the development of the ego: a hole has opened up at the level of the ego ideal. And it is with this mourning in being that the whole development of the libido and love is played out. Love is always reciprocal, and each of the two lovers gives what he does not have, his hole in the ego ideal, to support the development of the ego and give consistency to the becoming of the lovers.

We are here at a second level of mourning based on love, *as a support for identification*, where the two lacks of being of the two subjects at stake in reciprocal love come into play. Here, it is no longer "I've lost what I had", but "I was his lack", "I was in this process of becoming, in this process of lack with the person who has disappeared, but I didn't know it". Of course, it is a mourning that reopens the hollow at the heart of the ego ideal.

These two levels locatable in mourning, at the levels of having and of being, can be heard in the expression *he is not without having it* and *she is not without being it*: in what is played out at the level of *having* on the "masculine" side and at the level of *being* on the "feminine" side. It is obvious that the place of the analyst is to be "his or her lack, lack of *being*". It is truly there, says Lacan, "that we can be what is most precious, most indispensable for the analysand".

This lack of having and being can be understood in the dialectic of demand, on the side of having, and of desire, on the side of being, and of their articulation in the two toruses. *Acting out* presents itself as a demand for interpretation, or even the demand to have the interpretation, to which the analyst's desire should correspond. The analyst does *not have* the interpretation, and it is, in this way that he can give the hole *in his being* (*minus phi*) that energises the developmental movement of the ego.

From this structure of love and mourning, centred on the development of the ego and the signifying process, we can approach two little vignettes presented by Lacan in this session.

The first vignette is that of an analysand who has done very well on a radio programme on a subject close to the analyst's heart and who arrives at his session all depressed. And the analyst gives the following interpretation: "you spoke very well, I see you all depressed, you're probably afraid of having hurt my feelings by encroaching on my turf". From the perspective of transference-countertransference, the interpretation reveals an anomaly in the supposed structure of two neurotic toruses: the patient's wish to make a successful broadcast and to be happy about it does not correspond to the desire of the analyst. Should the two toruses be readjusted? The broadcast in question had in fact revived the feeling of mourning for the death of his mother, who had not been able to witness her son's success. By establishing her interpretation of a neurotic structure, the analyst had made herself deaf to the love affair between the analysand and his mother, a reciprocal love in which the lack of both served to give what one does not have. Mourning – ignored by the analyst – was inserted into the hollow of the ego ideal, perhaps to relaunch it in its inventiveness.

The second vignette (another case of Margaret Little's) was taken up by Aulagnier in the lesson of 27 February. The patient suffers from kleptomania and does not talk about her thefts. The analyst tried time and again to interpret; in vain, nothing budges, until the day the patient arrives at her session distraught, in mourning for a friend of her parents, a person of apparently little importance to her. The analysis seems to be able to move forward at last with the question of grief and *lack on both* sides. On the one hand, the analyst misses all her interpretations; on the other, the patient is in mourning. The analyst again attempts some interpretations to explain the bereavement, possibly in the transference, but to no avail. The analyst concludes by admitting that she is at a loss, that she no longer understands anything, that it hurts her to see her patient in such pain, and so on. In short, she's at her wits' end. This admission by the analyst is a major turning point in the treatment: now the analysand has become a lack for someone, a lack for the analyst. And at the same time, of course, there is the lack of the analyst. The lack of the patient for the analyst and the lack of the analyst for the patient, this lack is on the part of both. The fundamental $S(\bar{A})$ at the moment of mourning brings the process of identification back into play with the hole inside i'(a). Clearly a cut, it must be understood as the cut between S_1 and S_2, S_1 serving as all the attempts at interpretation, and S_2 as lack. It is the cut in the interior eight (the fourth cut after the spherical cut and after the cuts of demand and desire)

Two further examples of the cut can be understood with the same patient and the same analyst, Margaret Little. Firstly, the analysand kept talking to her about money matters involving her mother, little problems that seemed to be going nowhere, and the analyst cut her off: "Stop talking about money, you're boring me, I can't take it anymore". Secondly, the analyst has changed her furniture and after a day of comments from her patients, the analyst cuts the analysand off straightaway: "think what you like about my furniture, I couldn't care less". Two cuts in the signifying chain highlight lack and the cessation of possible responses: a real mourning. Now, the patient's father had died, but there had been no mourning, because this admired father did things so well that it was completely impossible for her to have been a lack for her father. As for his mother, she was an extension of her, like a piece of furniture, an instrument: no lack there either. Her kleptomania was a perpetual *acting out*, consisting of saying: here on stage is a delightful, stolen object, to tell you that there is another object, the object *a*, a lack, the real lack that deserves to be isolated for a moment, isolated, that is, not directly in relation to S. It is the lack recognised as fundamental in mourning on the side of being. With this lack, with this hole in i'(a), the subject is made anxious, while object *a* becomes lacking.

LESSON 11[3]: PSYCHOANALYSIS: SCIENCE OR CREATION?

In his absence, while Lacan was away on winter sports, session eleven was chaired by Vladimir Granoff, who presented an article by Barbara Low before giving the floor to François Perrier, who presented an article by Thomas Szasz. The opposition between these two types of analyst is radical, between the feminine creativity of Barbara Low and the masculine scientificity of Thomas Szasz.

Barbara Low (already cited by Freud in "Beyond the Pleasure Principle" 1920) had early on introduced the "Nirvana Principle", which could easily be correlated with the creative and inventive side of the *jouissance* principle (as opposed to the knowledge of a supposedly scientific psychoanalysis). Barbara Low's article studied by Granoff, "The Psychological Compensations of the Analyst" (1935) deals with the desire of the analyst and the analyst's psychological engagement in the treatment, because the analyst's job necessarily entails three types of privation. *Firstly,* on the narcissistic side, the analyst does not promote his own narcissism. *Secondly,* on the intellectual side, attempts at interpretation provide little certainty. *Thirdly,* on the side of the superego, the analyst has to suppress many of the tendencies aroused in the treatment. Where can the analyst find compensations, reparations for these wounds?

Barbara Low presents the analyst as if he were playing out the scene of the analysand's life on the stage of analysis. As we saw with Hamlet, the scene on the stage is not enough to sustain Hamlet's action. It is only on the basis of Ophelia's mourning and the highlighting of this nothingness, this annihilation at play in mourning, that this creative power can emerge, which allows Hamlet to avenge his father at the end of the play. The analyst's compensation, which enables him to sustain the analysis despite the privations inherent in the job, is a creative activity beyond the stage on the stage. This creation is very much present in Freud's joy at invention and in communicating it to the reader; it is also very much present in Ferenczi's (who introduced Barbara Low to analysis). The desire of the analyst is sustained in the shared, fraternal joy of invention and creation.

On the contrary, Lucia Tower's 1956 article *Counter-transference* presents the case of an extremely annoying woman, who is insulting to the analyst and puts her through the wringer. The analyst, fed up to the gills, decides one day to leave her office twenty minutes before her appointment with the patient to go and enjoy a delicious meal. Returning late for the patient's session, she learns that the patient has left in a huff. To the analyst's astonishment, the patient returned at the next session and told her: "Frankly, I can't blame you".

Had the analyst committed a *passage à l'acte* or an acting out? This can be interpreted in terms of its consequence: it works (and is an acting out) or it breaks (and it is a *passage à l'acte*). It is the very structure of the analyst's doing that is in question. On the one hand, the analyst's embarrassment is maximal and she reacts emotionally: this is a *passage à l'acte*. On the other hand, the analyst doesn't give in on *jouissance* (her own *jouissance*, in particular), the only thing capable of sustaining the third stage of the axis of movement, *émoi*; her action is an *acting out* that requires interpretation on the *part of the patient. Passage à l'acte* or acting out? Which, we don't need to decide in order to support the question of creation raised in terms of the desire of the analyst, her curiosity and interest in the invention and creation that can and must take place in analysis.

Thomas Szasz's position as an analyst is totally different: "I have the right to see what it's all about, you have to tell me what it's all about, because you need me because of my knowledge, I'm the one who has the scientific rigour you're looking for and it's with this scientific rigour that you're going to come out of this". Barbara Low accorded little importance to knowledge, relying far more on the not-knowing that opened to invention and creation, on the side of the principle of *jouissance*. Thomas Szasz explicitly relies on knowledge, the search for interpretations and explanation, based on the pleasure principle and the reality principle.

Szasz refers to Freud's metaphor of analysis as a game of chess. Taking all the rules into account, the aim of the game is to checkmate the king. The whole framework of the treatment, as a game, is already determined by the rules and, according to Szasz, psychoanalysis consists of getting the analysand to fit into the already established mechanics of the standard analysis, the "standard treatment". As in the game of chess, in analysis, the two players – analysand and analyst – would already have to be of comparable strength, with a certain symmetry between them: this we understand in the neurotic symmetry of the two intertwined toruses.

For Barbara Low, the "counter-transference" is an integral part of the analytic process where the question of the desire of the analyst is central, not in the neurotic and toric conception in which the desire of the analyst would correspond to the demand of the analysand, but in the creative movement of the analysand and the analyst, that is, in the topology of the cross-cap or projective plane. In Barbara Low's work, the symmetry of the chess game and the two intertwined toruses, gives way to the creative power inherent in the principle of *jouissance*. This is why it would be more appropriate to speak of "the desire of the analyst" rather than "counter-transference". For Szasz, counter-transference is merely an artefact that can and must be dealt with, with and within knowledge.

LESSON 12[4]: THE DESIRE OF THE ANALYST, THE LAW AND OBJECT *a*

The expression "the desire of the analyst" refers to what, in the analyst, supports and is situated in the process of the signifier within the topology of the cross-cap, whereas "counter-transference" is easily situated "in the mirror" in relation to "transference" in a toric and neurotic topology. On either side, what is the analyst's participation in the analysis?

1   Demand, desire and the law

The question of the analyst's participation is introduced by acting out, insofar as an acting out demands the reaction or participation of the analyst, who may respond in a variety of ways, by an interpretation, by an absence of interpretation, by an acting out or by a *passage à l'acte* (for example, Freud's *passage à l'acte* with the young homosexual woman). Acting out and *passage à l'acte* frame anxiety in the nine-box grid constructed with the two axes of movement and of difficulty of knowledge.

To understand the analyst's part as "counter-transference" dependent on a return of the repressed in the analyst (who has not been sufficiently "analysed") necessarily amounts to situating the whole affair in knowledge, an interpretation to be pursued and so on. We thereby fall back into the first conception of the signifier, while losing the vigour of the signifying process. The only way of correctly posing the question of the analyst's part in the analysis is the *desire* of the analyst', with all the ambiguity of what is meant by "desire". Desire comes into play in two oppositions: desire and demand on the one hand, desire and the law on the other. The "desire of the analyst" is thus immediately caught up in the ambiguity of its opposition to either demand or the law.

As we have seen, the opposition of desire and demand is first situated in the neurotic structure, with the two intertwined toruses. Demand, including the impossible demand for love, awaits a response, and this response might be given at the level of the desire of the Other. In this sense, the demand of the analysand (particularly in acting out) would be answered by the "desire of the analyst", the desire to give an interpretation in and with his knowledge (cf. Szasz). But this desire/demand opposition – centred on the analyst as supposed to know – must be set in tension with the other bipolarity, that of desire and the law.

Now, the pairing of desire and the law can itself be understood in two ways. Firstly *starting from the law*, as a commandment, as a supreme demand, we return to the opposition between desire and demand and to the neurotic structure: the big Other, the father, demands, commands, enacts the law: "you shall not desire she who has been the object of my desire", with this law-demand providing the framework for desire – or *at the start of desire*, more precisely *with the cause of desire*. Thus, in Hamlet, desire is not framed in the scene or the scene on the stage, but in its dependence on object *a*, lack and the mourning introduced by Ophelia. In this first case ("you shall not desire she who has been the object of my desire"), desire is presented as the primary substance of the law, as the raw material that the law would come to shape, where there is no natural desire, given as a raw material. Secondly, starting from the *cause* of desire, desire is presented as secondary, and the law is seen from the point of view of this cause and with it, as the freedom to invent. Here, the law is not given by a big and consistent Other; the law creates itself from the vocal object *a*, from the *nihil negativum* (this is the whole sense of the autonomy of Kantian moral law); similarly, it creates itself from the voice of the tormentor (in the Sadean phantasy).[5]

In all cases, desire presents itself as the will to enjoy. It is fundamentally foolish to present analysis as an operation aimed at cutting off *jouissance*. What must first be done is to grasp the *jouissance* in its principle and not reduce it to more or less unbridled extreme pleasures. *In perversion*, desire is given as what makes the law; the law is subverted. The Sadean character creates the law. But in fact, he remains fundamentally restrained by the hypothesis of a consistent Other who suspends the creation of the law and stops the subject on the path to *jouissance* ("The Supreme Being is restored in Evil Action[6]"). From the outset, *the neurotic* remains subject to the Other; he needs to pass through the institution of the law itself; he can only desire subject to the law, subject to its conditions. This law is constantly called into play and questioned in hysteria, desire remaining unsatisfied (including the desire of the analyst). This law presents itself as knowledge of the precondition of desire in obsessional neurosis, desire there appearing as impossible (including the desire of the analyst, which is in no way reducible to knowledge).

2   Anxiety to situate the desire of the analyst

The desire of the analyst has been approached from the side of perversion and from the side of the transference neurosis. It is too easy to rely on transference to question the desire of the analyst. Let us now take up the question again, starting from anxiety itself, which insinuates itself into the gap between desire and *jouissance*, insofar as all desire is always the will to jouissance. Pure anxiety, so-called "anxiety neurosis" is not a transference neurosis (it is not a phobia). It is an actual neurosis, supposedly caused by an overflow of libido automatically transforming itself into anxiety, according to Freud's first theory of anxiety. Regardless of this naturalistic assumption that libido transforms into anxiety, anxiety neurosis serves to address anxiety independently of the characters involved in the transference, particularly, the subject in its dependence on the Other. This is because anxiety is regularly defended by the ever-greater accentuation of the "autonomy of the moral law", to be understood as the accentuation of the subject's independence in relation to the big Other.

The expression "autonomy of the moral law" might bring to mind Kant and a misreading of Kantian morality that we have already denounced (a subject, faced with a concrete example as an object, questions his ego to find out where the Good is and finds the answer in a universal moral law that he finds or chooses on his own, autonomously). This reading of the moral law avoids the question of anxiety. However, a careful reading of the *Critique of Practical Reason* shows that the said "autonomy" is not that of a prior subject, but that it is the self-engendering of the law, in the locus of the Other, we would say: the autonomous law is fundamentally heteronomous in the sense that it depends on *something other* than any self-consciousness or any constituted subject. It arises from the unconscious, from the Other, and it is in this that the unconscious is essentially ethical. Not without anxiety.

Anxiety must be related to the ethical unconscious or to what we might call the heteronomous autonomy of the law. The pervert avoids this anxiety-provoking autonomy by claiming to found the law on the subject, the neurotic by imagining that the founder of the law is the father as the consistent Other. But the law is founded neither by the subject himself, nor by the consistent Other; it emerges from the signifying process and the real at work. The big Other on which the law depends can only be of the order of the real, the real, intimate to each of us.

We have seen how the real of *minus phi* at the heart of the ego ideal controls repression (how anxiety provokes and determines repression, according to Freud's second theory of anxiety). From this point on, repression can no longer be reduced to a bilateral surface, vice versa, back and forth, investment and counter-investment, love and hate, desire and law. And the desire of the analyst can no longer be understood as the other side of the law (of the law of analysis). Everything must be understood on the *basis of anxiety*. It arises from the real of $S(\cancel{A})$, from the question of the signifier and the trace. And it is from there that we must specify the desire of the analyst. S_1 is the trace, S_2 the erasure of the trace, and it is in the erasure of the trace that anxiety and repression are situated. But traces are not erased and there is not only the real of S(A̶), but also the real of the failure of the passage from trace to signifier: the trace insists and returns in the real, *underlined* insofar as it has returned from the signifier S$_2$ (in the return of the repressed). The real thus returns the subject to the pure trace (which does not pass to S$_2$). But if the real abolishes the passage S$_1$–S$_2$, it also abolishes the subject; for the subject is represented by S$_1$ only for S$_2$.

The real abolishes the subject, and we might think that the big Other takes up all the space; as in the position of the masochist who devotes himself to being the common object (the dog) for the *jouissance* of the Other who enjoys. The perverse in general is looking for something on the side of the *jouissance* of the Other. The masochist may believe and allow others to believe that he is devoted to the *jouissance* of the Other, but in fact he is looking for the *anxiety* of the Other. By presenting himself as the dog for the Other, he appeals to the Other and his anxiety, he plays the common object that fills the hole, the plug in the void of the Other.

Anxiety is central in the desire of the analyst. But it is not without the displacement that takes place from Freud to Lacan. For Freud, anxiety is a signal in the ego; it signals the danger for the ego of losing the object, the object of care, the person giving care, the phallus, the gaze or the superego. It is a danger situated within the psychic apparatus. For Lacan, with the cross-cap, there is no longer any interior, the psychic apparatus becomes the Moebius strip, we are in the third form of lack and the fourth form of cut. And the danger is no longer of losing the positivised object, but of losing the lack, as is the case in the real of the return of the repressed, where the signifying process is lost in the insistence and highlighting of the trace.

"Anxiety is the manifestation of the desire of the Other", Lacan had said already in the seminar *Identification*. This does not mean that a great personified Other desires me, the subject (as would be seen in the face-to-face between the two neurotic toruses). If anxiety arises in the place of the Ego, that is, in the development of the Ego, it is to signal something other than the Ego already present, something where I am completely in question, where I am lost. It is not that the ego is afraid of being killed, it is that the ego can only become from its loss, from the hole in the ideal ego and the ego ideal. In other words, the desire of the Other is in no way Hegelian desire: I am not caught up in a dialectic of master and slave self-consciousness. It's not a question of recognition. The desire of the Other is the desire of the barred Other: d(A̶), as Lacan wrote in the second lesson of the Seminar. The big Other neither recognises nor ignores me. On the contrary, the very root of my own desire lies in the object *a* that escapes, that cannot be specularised. Anxiety, including the anxiety of the Other – with this genitive that can be subjective *and* objective, prior as it is to any subject and object, prior to S and A, prior to the neurotic torus – depends on *jouissance*.

The desire of the Other insofar as it is dependent neither on the personified Other (the Other is barred) nor on a prior subject (I am lost) is on the side of love. Reciprocal love is to be understood here as the movement of libido from which the lover and the beloved, the subject and the object, which appear only as consequences of love, can emerge. Reciprocal love does not come from persons, it is persons who come from it insofar as it is this emergence of creation proper to *jouissance* (the mythical level where the question of the appearance of the subject in the field of the Other is posed, cf. the schema of division.

As long as we don't understand that desire – including the desire of the analyst – depends on *jouissance*, in this game of reciprocal love where things emerge, we will remain stuck on normative values dependent on the characters in play, the personified Other, the subject supposedly already there, Oedipal characters. With this in mind, Freud's article *On the Universal Tendency to Debasement in the Sphere of Love* (1912) analyses the love life of certain men who need to belittle women, to consider them prostitutes, whores, etc., in order to be sexually powerful. These men are still encumbered by the big Other personified in their mother, and they can only manage by dividing the libido addressed to this big Other into a tender current (for the mother) and a sexual current (for the debased woman). But by confining this story to the framework of the Oedipus Complex, Freud himself also remains within a perspective of love and desire that is added to actors supposed to precede love and desire. Now, the desire of the Other (which invokes anxiety) is the desire of the barred Other, beginning with S($\bar{A}$), creating and inventing analyst and analysand alike according to the principle of *jouissance* proper to the unconscious.

The desire of the analyst is not an avatar of Oedipal desire determined by individuals. It starts with the line of *jouissance* and the S($\bar{A}$), letting d($\bar{A}$) come into play and specifically allowing for invention, which starts from this zero point of the object *a*.

Notes

1 Lesson of 30 January 1963.
2 Lacan's expression is ambiguous here, and the Seuil edition presents the short-circuit that would allow the insect to pass to the other side as objet *a*, the small central piece. It is easy to see that object *a*, which has two sides, is not a short-circuit that allows the insect to pass from one side to the other. It's the Moebius strip that is a short-circuit: by turning endlessly on itself, it short-circuits and avoids object *a*.
3 Lesson of 20 February 1963. This lesson is not included in the Seuil edition.
4 Lesson of 27 February 1963. Chapter XI in the Seuil edition.
5 Christian Fierens, *The Jouissance Principle*, London, Routlege, 2022.
6 Jacques Lacan, "Kant avec Sade" in *Écrits*, *Écrits, The First Complet Edition in English,* translated by B. Fink in collaboration with H. Fink and R. Grigg. New York, W.W. Norton & Company, 2006, p. 790.

Chapter 6

Anxiety and the desire of the analyst

Setting out the theory, the concepts, the signifier, the desire of the analyst, etc., puts in place clear-cut oppositions: thus, the first conception of the signifier is opposed to the second; "counter-transference" is opposed to the desire of the analyst; *passage à l'acte* is opposed to acting out; knowledge is opposed to non-knowledge, and so on. We might think that, consequently, psychoanalytic practice will, at all times, have to position itself on one side or the other of these oppositions. While these distinctions must be clearly posed, they are not like classes that would allow such and such a practice or even this or that moment in practice to be classified. For each time, these clearly separated concepts must be part of the same structure in motion and each of the opposites is only as good as the passage to its opposite.

Thus, to conceive of the signifier, the understanding of S_1–S_2 implies both the opposition of S_1 and S_2, and the movement from one to the other: we represent S_1–S_2 as an interior eight, where S_1 would be the large loop and S_2 the small loop, generating a Moebius strip, the object a, the cross-cap. At the same time, however, a new opposition arises: the topology of the cross-cap (corresponding to the second conception of the signifier) is opposed to the topology of the two intertwined toruses (corresponding to the first conception of the signifier).

Obviously, we never have a pure cross-cap in practice. The highlighting of S_1–S_2 does not go hand in hand with a disdainful or arrogant disregard for a practice that leaves room for an interpretation on the imaginary side, with meaning; it aims at indicating a possible and necessary displacement to get out of a practice that would only be focused on imaginary interpretation, on meaning and on *knowledge*. This displacement never takes place once and for all, because whatever the emphasis on *doing*, opened up by the vocal object a, the question of knowledge (and non-knowledge) never ceases to arise: "knowing how to do it". The two conceptions of the signifier are always intertwined, articulated, in the same listening structure, where we are constantly moving from knowing to not-knowing, and from not-knowing to a certain kind of knowing. All oppositions depend on a movement that doesn't cease to run through them. We are always in a general structure, a topology in movement, where these concepts take their vigour from an infinite questioning. Anxiety itself only exists in this complex movement in which we think

DOI: 10.4324/9781003477822-9

and experience concepts and conceptions in their movement and articulation with other concepts and conceptions.

LESSON 13[1]: ANXIETY AND THE IN-BETWEEN

1   Anxiety, fear, fright...

We have been able to accentuate the difference between anxiety and fear as these relate to the object – "anxiety is without an object", "fear has an object" –wherein the subjective position likewise differs, inadequate on the one hand and adequate on the other. Fear in the face of external danger would prompt an appropriate response to that danger, although paralysing fears would not, and, despite their difference, fear is also related to anxiety. Let us also add fright where the positions of the subject and object vacillate. All these categorisations are eminently questionable. Such phenomena cannot be isolated definitively: there is no such thing as pure anxiety, pure fear or pure fright. Relations are built in every concrete situation, and the distinctions between fear, anxiety and fright cannot be used to classify the different affects or reactions we encounter in reality, but rather to understand what is at play in all three. The differences between anxiety, fear and fright are intended to sharpen our listening and our response to them.

We say "fear is the fear of an *object*" and "anxiety is *without an object*". Phobia reshuffles this classification: phobia is anxiety that has found its object, the phobic object, the wolf, for example. It has transformed anxiety into fear (fear of the wolf). "Anxiety is without an object"? Lacan *replies* "anxiety is not without an object". This does not equate to the object of fear, the phobic object. It is precisely on the basis of the absence of an object, of something in suspense, that a passage is made, not towards the determination of a given object, but towards the *question of* the object, towards object *a*. Object *a* presents itself firstly as lack ("*without* object"), and this lack is not simply to be understood in the sense of privation, as we have seen, but in the sense of *castration*, in the sense of the interior eight, with the real introduced through S_1–S_2, S_2 as something that completely escapes us, the zero degree of knowledge.

The subject, which seemed primordial in fear and anxiety, is itself called into question in fright. In a short story by Chekhov, a man recounts three frights he had experienced in his past. *Firstly,* in the distance, in a winter landscape, he saw a mysterious flame inexplicably beginning to burn on the unreachable floor of a bell tower. The subject was in no danger in this case. *Secondly*, he saw a ghostly carriage speeding by on the horizon. Again, the subject is in no danger here. *Thirdly*, he saw something totally mysterious behind a dog, but the dog was not menacing remaining at a distance. Once again, the subject was in no danger. Each time the subject is neither concerned nor interested. The only thing that is reported, each time, is an inexplicable and mysterious fact. Not-knowing?

If Lacan takes this short story of Chekhov's, suggested to him by Pierre Kaufmann, it is to emphasise the inexplicable, the mysterious, the pure *real*, *independently of* a threatening *object* or an involved *subject*. It is the *real* that is at stake, which has nothing to do with the reality of the danger attached to fear, nor with the prior position of an anxiety already attributable to a substantial subject.

The real may well already risk being occluded by a certain presentation of anxiety. So we could say that anxiety, like fear, presupposes a subject's relation to something that affects him, concerns him and puts him in danger. The danger would be external to the subject in fear and internal in anxiety. When the internal danger is projected or carried over to the outside, anxiety is transformed into fear and becomes a phobia. The phobia would commence with an impulsive anxiety, with an internal danger; and then, a mythopoeic process would relate this internal danger to an external danger, the fear of a wolf outside, for example.

But what is the danger internal to anxiety? The danger in anxiety, unlike the danger in fear, is always linked to the function of a structure that is threatened and must be preserved and supported. What is this structure? We can immediately think that it is the structure of the subject and that it implies everything that has been said about privation and castration, about the topology of the two intertwined toruses and the cross-cap (with object *a* at the centre and the Moebius strip representing the barred subject). It would be this subjective structure that is threatened. But it would be saying too much to centre the said structure *on the subject*. Because it is short of the question of the subject that something is threatened on the opaque side, on the side of the real *before any accomplished subjectivation*. Hence the usefulness of Chekhov's novella: anxiety presupposes the real, the real starting from very beginning of the principle preliminary to the question of the subject, which is the *jouissance* principle.

2   The division of the big Other by the question of the subject

It is not possible to think of anxiety outside the structure of the real, insofar as it is given in the signifying division, and of the polarity in the conception of the signifier. The real is implied, on the one hand, between the signifier understood from a signifying chain leading to a hermeneutic interpretation, and on the other hand, the signifier understood as S_1–S_2, directly implying the S_2 emptied of all imaginary, from which an invention can arise, the invention of metaphor. The establishment of anxiety thus presupposes the division of the big Other by the *question of* the subject, with the appearance of the object *a* as a consequence. The signal of anxiety draws attention to the fact that the structure of the division of the big Other by the question of the subject (first line) is threatened, and always is so.

Let us start with the first diagram of the division of the signifier (Figure 6.1).

A	S
$\cancel{S}$	$\cancel{A}$
a	

Figure 6.1 First schema of the division of the big Other (A) by the subject (S).

In this schema, the division is like a mathematical division. The big Other (A) is the numerator, the number to be divided by the denominator (S). The quotient, the result, is that the big Other is divided or barred: $\bar{A}$. $\bar{A}$ multiplied by S gives $\bar{S}$, which corresponds to the part of A that has been divided. There remains a part of A that has not been divided: this is the remainder, the object a as remainder, which is not divisible by the subject. This first schema of division seems more "logical" than the second, and would suit the Hegelian conception of desire in the dialectic of master and slave, as we saw earlier.

Despite the resemblances, the second schema functions in a completely different way, irreducible to the arithmetical operation of division, making explicit the structure of the signifier understood on the basis of the second conception of the signifier "a signifier S_1 is what represents the subject for another signifier S_2", where S_2 is emptied of all imaginary: (Figure 6.2).

$$
\begin{array}{c|c|l}
A & S & \text{jouissance} \\[2mm]
a & \bar{A} & \text{anxiety} \\[2mm]
\bar{S} & & \text{desire}
\end{array}
$$

Figure 6.2 Second schema of the division of the big Other (A) by the subject (S).

In this diagram, we can distinguish three levels that are different from each other, but at the same time interact within *the same structure.*

The *first level, the upper level* called *"jouissance"*, poses the question of the subject (S) in relation to the signifier (A). The big Other is supposed to contain the primary species of the signifier, the place where the treasury of signifiers is assembled: *all these signifiers are on the side of S_1.* The question arises: how can a subject S appear in this sea of S_1 signifiers? It should be noted that the subject does not exist at this point, emerging only by responding to this question. This is the starting point of the narcissistic *question*: the ego is not given, it exists only in its development. We can, no doubt, choose a series of S_1 signifiers (with their signifieds) to characterise the individual in terms of sex, religion, country, profession and a thousand more or less insignificant details. These so-called signifiers are no more than traces, serving as indices or labels to characterise the individual, and they can be combined to form the mosaic of the ideal ego, the specular image, i(a). Structure here is reduced to "signifiers that partially represent the subject", to traces: "the traces (S_1) represent the individual". We don't have the subject as such; instead, we only have the identification of an individual, which conceals the question that remains unanswered: how can a subject *invent itself* in the place of the big Other? This is the question of *jouissance*, which only appears in the ethical dimension of allowing the law to emerge (the law of the ethical unconscious), of allowing it to be invented from S_2, from the radical nothing (*nihil negativum*).

The *second level, the middle level* named "*anxiety*", is the lived consequence of the first. If the subject is not the individual indicated by traces (S_1), it will not find an answer in the infinite sea of S_1's encountered in the Other (A). In place of the subject's question (S), the answer *that there is no answer on the side of the Other* is necessary: $\cancel{A}$. No need to swallow the whole sea of signifiers, just one suffices to let the non-response of the Other play itself out. By passing from any S_1 to its repetition, which empties it of all imaginary, S_2 emerges as the signifier of $\cancel{A}$: S($\cancel{A}$). And now we can say that the subject is represented by a signifier (S_1 in the big Other) for another signifier S_2, which is the signifier of the absence of response in A, that is S($\cancel{A}$).

These three terms, A, S and $\cancel{A}$, introduce the difference between a given, questioned, responding A and an ($\cancel{A}$), A barred with no response, except that the big Other does not respond ($\cancel{A}$). This can be read in the development of the ego and the schema of narcissism. The unbarred big Other provides the S_1's that make up the ideal ego. But at the moment when any signifier making up the ideal Ego is repeated to serve as a focal point, it is emptied of all imaginary and the ego ideal, which serves as the reprise of the ideal Ego, is fundamentally perforated, including, by right, S($\cancel{A}$); *minus phi* is the radical absence of this phallus of the supposedly all-powerful Other. But what becomes of the Other? Admittedly, it is absent at the level of the response expected by the subject's question. But it persists as unusable waste for the question of the subject: something or nothing, inescapable, inexplicable, unspecifiable. *Anxiety* is precisely the confrontation of $\cancel{A}$ and *a*, specific to this second stage. It is fundamentally outside the subject, like Chekhov's terrors evoked at the beginning of the lesson: the Other does not respond and what remains is the object *a*, incomprehensible, irreducible to any specular image or interpretation.

The *third level, the lower level* called "desire", is merely the "end" of the journey of the question of the subject in the locus of the Other, an end that never ends: infinite metonymy. In the end, the subject is nothing more than this journey along a Moebius strip, where it turns around unceasingly, in a movement of permanent contradiction, carried along by the Moebius strip. The $\cancel{S}$, the continual turning around of the ant in its journey along the Moebius strip, only occurs subsequent to anxiety or of the object *a* confronted with the A. The object *a* (second level of the division) is indeed the cause of the desire of $\cancel{S}$ (third level of the division).

3   Illustrations of the division

3.1   Oedipus and "Totem and Taboo"

What is the place of the subject in the field of the Other? What is man in the field of the big Other that is the Sphinx? We are indeed at the first upper, and mythical, level of *jouissance*: where to find S in A? Oedipus was able to answer the Sphinx: "the animal that walks on all fours in the morning, on two legs at midday and on three legs at night, that's man!" But that's not the point. Yes, he has understood what man is and he ascends the throne of Thebes, marries the queen and so on. But the question of the subject?

All is well until the plague ravages Thebes. The soothsayer Tiresias is consulted about the causes of the plague. At first, Tiresias refuses to answer: this is a figure of the big Other supposed to know who is barred, but it's only a first figure. When the soothsayer finally reveals Oedipus' double crime, the whole system of the big Other on which the kingdom of Thebes was built collapses; the whole field of the big Other collapses with the revelation of the murder of the father and the incest with the mother ($\bar{A}$). This is the second level of *anxiety*. Horrified by what he has just seen, Oedipus now tears out his own eyes, instruments for seeing and knowing, instruments serving the subject supposed to know and the big Other. He sees his own eyes torn out on the ground, the wretched remains of a big Other unable to succeed. In this maximal anxiety, his gouged-out eyes take the place of the big Other as object a in its original structure (something or nothing? seeing / not seeing). His own eyes, Oedipus is not without seeing then. He sees them and they are plucked out at the same time; he sees and he is blind. This is the very mechanism of the interior eight: the most imaginary "seeing" (S_1) is reduced to its simplest expression, to zero, to blindness (S_2), but at the same time, this is seeing in its most inventive form. It is at this point that Oedipus becomes truly seeing. He sees the future destiny of Athens. This is the power of vision that emerges from blindness. The seeing of the blind man, Oedipus takes up the very structure already at play in the story of Tiresias, who himself had surprised Athena in the bath (A and S at the level of enjoyment); "to punish him", Athena took away his sight ($\bar{A}$) while giving him the gaze (a) that belongs to the diviner who sees the most important things.

We can apply the same schema to the father of the primal horde (*Totem and Taboo*). Again, at the upper level of *jouissance* (A and S), we remain in a purely mythical story, where the big unbarred Other, the all-powerful father can enjoy, where he has the enjoyment of all the women; in this context, the question of the subject arises with the sons, who are there as subjects that still do not exist. How could a subject manage to exist in relation to this father, the great all-powerful Other? The answer to the myth is obvious, and we move on to the second median level of *anxiety*: it's the killing of the father of the horde ($\bar{A}$). And in place of what dictated the law of his omnipotence (A) comes the object a, the voice from which emerges the properly moral law and the superego (in its two forms, on the one hand a ferocious superego and on the other, the superego of *jouissance*, of a *jouissance* that exceeds myth to be the invention of law).

The big Other is there, it functions, even if everything can be called into question. *Cogito ergo sum*: there Descartes will find the subject and its certainty at the first upper level of *jouissance*. But this is a purely mythical response, because the subject is precisely not where it thinks: "I am where I do not think" and where the big Other does not respond to the subject. With the barred big Other, we are confronted with the certainty of anxiety (the second middle level), and the certainty of the *Cogito ergo sum* is no more than a facade of certainty, a defence, based on the certainty of anxiety and designed to evade it. Where is the object a?

3.2   Object a on a silver platter?

Can object *a* be seen? Can we give an image of it, a "specular image"? Two paintings by Zurbarán seem to answer this question affirmatively. Saint Lucia (*lux*, light), patron saint of all those who need to be able to see better (the sighted, the visually impaired, ophthalmologists, etc.), presents her own eyes, out of their sockets, placed on a silver platter. Saint Agatha (*agathos*, the good) presents her own breasts, ripped off by her torturers, placed on a similar tray. It is easy to say that the breasts and the eyes, two objects of desire, are here recognisable as the scopic and oral forms of Lacan's object *a*.

But are they the cause of desire? Do they provoke desire? In any case, we should note that the objects presented in these paintings do not cause us *anxiety*, at most a slight disgust or a feeling of strangeness evoked by the scenography of the painting. This is because we are not implicated: as unconcerned spectators, we are neither martyrs nor executioners. With these paintings, we are not caught up in the question of *jouissance* (the first upper level of division): how can the subject come to exist in the field of the Other? And if these objects evoke no anxiety (the second middle level), they can't be the cause of desire either (the third lower level). In short, for us, these tableaux are outside the circuit of signifying division.

For the subject to be affected at the level of anxiety, anxiety must be understood as dependent on the first level (*jouissance*). For the non-response of the Other, $\mathcal{A}$ to really concern us, it has to emerge from the signifying operation where the "subject", who does not exist, asks the question: how can I come into being in the place of the signifier? The answer will always be: by hollowing out S_1 so that it becomes S_2 without any imaginary, with a big Other that doesn't respond.

The story of the martyrs Saint Lucia and Saint Agatha is about God's non-response and their testimony of Christian life, which is not without a certain masochism.

3.3   Obvious jouissance and anxiety hidden in masochism

The neurotic, who always tries not to be too affected, is hardly suited to highlighting anxiety where the real object *a* is encountered.

Taking our support from masochism, which first presents itself at the upper level of the division of the subject: the masochist presents himself as an object for the *jouissance* of the Other: a dog, a human wreck, an object, mistreated, more or less, to serve the *jouissance* of the Other. At first glance, the masochist would not but be situated simply at the upper level of *jouissance*: A facing S. But each of these three levels does not exist independently of the other two. And if the masochist *presents himself* as a mere object for the Other's enjoyment, it is not without hiding something else deeper within himself. What the masochist seeks in this staging of the object for the Other's enjoyment is what is below him, a subject as common object (and that is that the big Other cannot respond to it) and it is what is beneath A, i.e. what remains of it, the object *a*. The object *a* here is far from being presented on a silver platter, but it has the value of being only what remains of the Other from the moment when the Other is at a loss; object *a* concerns the Other and provokes his anxiety. The anxiety of the Other is the masochist's aim, an aim hidden by the common object.

We find this masochistic structure in the Christian myth, the myth of Christ. Let us begin with the upper level of jouissance: man presents himself as a simple object for the jouissance of the big Other, for God: A–S. But God does not respond: A̸; so, we move on to anxiety, the middle level, the anxiety of Christ who, in his Passion, assumes the anxiety of Job, left without a response from his God: "Why have you forsaken me?" Why don't you answer? As a good masochist, Christ aims to provoke the anxiety of the Other, the anxiety of God. But God has no soul and therefore cannot be touched by anxiety. This leaves Christ with the only possibility of assuming divinity himself, of making himself the soul of God in order to bear God's anxiety, in the second person of the Trinity.

In his presentation as a simple object, the masochist pushes *from the outset* from the upper level of *jouissance* (but this remains imaginary). We must start from A and S, in other words the signifier S_1–S_2, which opens up the question of *jouissance* and the topology of the interior eight, the Moebius strip, the cross-cap, and then come to the second level of hidden anxiety and the hidden object *a*, hidden and yet sought out in masochism. In sadism, the position of object *a* is not hidden and the victim's anxiety is clearly sought.

3.4   Visible anxiety in the sadistic scenario

Unlike the masochist, the sadist seems to want to first bring the second middle level into play: *anxiety*. Like the masochist, the sadist aims to provoke anxiety. In one case, it is the anxiety of the Other (possibly the anxiety of God), in the other it is the anxiety of the other (the anxiety of his victim). The sadist targets his victim's anxiety rather than his pain. The story of Epictetus, a Stoic slave, is eloquent in this respect: his leg was tortured by his master, who eventually broke it. Epictetus says to his master: "I told you, you would end up breaking it". Whatever the slave's pain and stoicism, this line completely dismantles the Master's sadistic intent (who was supposed to want to provoke the slave's anxiety rather than his pain).

In the sadistic scenario, the object *a* is directly there and aims at arousing the anxiety of the other. With the masochist, this is not the case, and object *a* remains hidden behind the common object. In *Juliette,* the sadist announces: "I had", cries the tormentor, "the skin of the cunt". Surprisingly, the Seuil version transcribes: "I had the cries of the tormenter, I had the skin of the cunt". Even if inaccurate, this wording is of interest to us. Firstly, "I had the skin of the cunt". Turning this sliver inside out, like turning a glove inside out, what the tormentor is seeking is the other side of the subject. And the other side of the subject (the other side of the cross-cap) is object *a*, the supplement to the subject $\cancel{S}$ that forms the cross-cap, a supplement that cannot be specularised (like the subject's Moebius strip), that cannot be explained. It is a moment that is totally impenetrable by the subject himself. But what is the structure of this skin of the cunt, of this object *a*?

With this false (and happily so) transcription by Seuil, "I had the cries of the tormentor", the object *a* is not simply the object *a* located in the victim, *it is also located in the tormentor*, it is the cry, the *voice of* the tormentor. The object *a* is not locatable once and for all in this or that person, victim or tormentor. Before any subject, before any person, it is in the voice, in the cry, which enacts its own law, which invents its own sadistic law in the autonomy *of the law*, not the autonomy of the subject, but in the autonomy of the unconscious and conditioned by the barred Other. We are, of course, already at the second level of anxiety.

The big Other certainly intervenes at the upper level of *jouissance,* but in its *place* (not the place of any subject) from the outset, comes the object *a* (the voice of the tormentor) and the anxiety that depends on it. The sadist's operation is related to God, to the big Other, recalling that Sade regularly quotes "the Supreme Being in Evil Action". The supreme Being is the big Other, which we first assume to be a substantial subject. But why "in malice"? It is to empty the big Other of its substance and make room for the vocal object *a* in the emptied place of the Other, and to invent something beyond good and evil. It is to counter the good being, to offer him an anti-hero, something to counteract him, and above all to open up invention, creation, beyond good and evil. The vocal object *a* in the place of the big Other is the reading of Sadean phantasy (Figure 6.4) within the framework of Schema L (Figure 6.3).

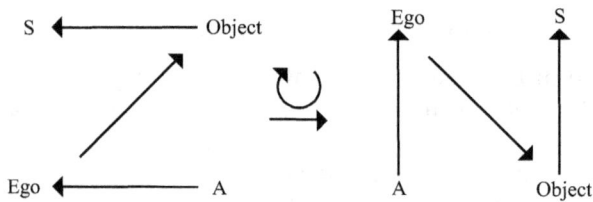

Figure 6.3 From the classic Schema L to the structure of the phantasy (in *Kant with Sade*).

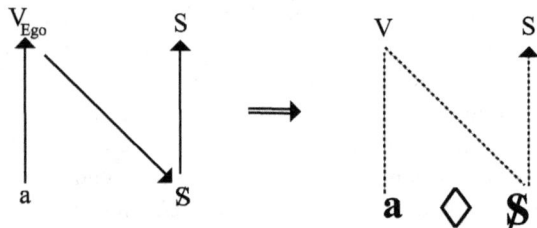

Figure 6.4 From the Sadean phantasy to the usual formula of phantasy.

The path of the zigzag arrows starts from the vocal object *a* in place of the Other (1), going then to the ego or the will V to decide good and evil (2) then to the object or subject $ victimised by the sadist (3) and ending with the purified subject S (4).

In this schema we can read the three levels of the division of the subject. The upper level of *jouissance* (position 1) is represented by the Other (which Other is only of interest in relation to S, hence A–S), but it is already occupied by the object *a* in order to unfold the schema; the middle level of anxiety (positions 2 and 3) is represented by the oblique line linking the sadistic ego to the object or victim, in whom the tormentor wants to provoke anxiety; the lower level of desire (position 4), which gives rise to the subject S, who, in fact, remains a subject barred by his dependence on the sadistic process.

The left side of the sadistic diagram (which corresponds to the lower part of Schema L) concerns the sadistic tormentor and the right side (the upper part of the L diagram) the tortured victim. On the left side: the shamelessness or impudence of the sadistic character and on the right side: the modesty of the victim. Shamelessness and modesty are absolutely interconnected; one cannot exist without the other. It's an "amboception"[2]: the sadist's object *a* (the voice, the tormentor's scream) remains attached to the victim's object *a* (the skin of the cunt) and the will is attached in anxiety to the object that is the victim. The conjunction of one side and the other in the same structure is maximal, because one cannot exist without the other. The object *a* is not at all a particular object, that can be snatched up and its possession noted "I got the skin of the cunt"; it only exists as such attached to the voice in anxiety.

4   The in-between of object *a* or the issue of *minus phi*

In the schema of division, object *a* is situated at the middle level, in-between, astride the level of *jouissance* and the level of desire. Can we conceive of object *a* as receiving from both sides? Like an amboceptor, receiving from both the side of jouissance and of desire?

For amboception to occur, we generally assume that two things exist beforehand and that for interaction to take place between them, a third thing is necessary which takes part in each of the first two: for an antigen to act on an antibody, the interaction of an amboceptor which attaches itself to both is necessary. In the Sadean schema, we assume two prior things, the sadist and his victim, and then an "amboceptor" between them, made of shamelessness and modesty, or again, the amboceptor object *a* made of the sadist's shameless voice and the victim's shameful piece of skin.

Amboception is evident with the first form of object *a*. The breast is amboceptive between mother and infant. Does it belong to the mother who suckles or to the child who sucks? The cut or separation between the two is twofold: in one, the breast is exhausted of the living forces coming from the mother (a source of *anxiety for the mother*); in the other, the child sees the nipple slipping away (sustaining *desire on the part of the child*). The whole of the placenta, its envelopes, umbilical cord, etc., is also an amboceptor between mother and child; at birth, it is cut differently for the mother and the child: the mother is severed from the placenta (this is "delivery"), but the child is severed at the other end (this is the cutting of the umbilical cord). Each time, there is a double separation: separation from the mother and separation from the child. And each time, it is the separation of the object a – se-paration (from the Latin *se-parere* to engender oneself) on both sides, it is the child who engenders itself in its own se-paration and it is the mother who engenders herself on her own. In other words, two prior things did not exist before, but are engendered in the separation.

Can we see the male sex (*plus phi*) as an amboceptor, as an organ of linkage that receives information from both sides, the male and the female? In insects, the sting – the egg-laying and attacking organ – acts as an amboceptor between the two specimens. Can we inscribe phallic *jouissance* at the site of this amboceptor, on the model of the insect's sting? *Jouissance* would thus essentially be in the copulation between male and female. It would be the consequence of the amboception between two individuals. Lacan notes that we know nothing of the *jouissance* of the cockroach. In other words, if these insects do indeed *copulate* through the amboceptor that is the sting, there is nothing to suggest that there is any *jouissance* there. Enjoyment cannot be reduced to copulation, to the organ of copulation, to the amboceptor, to the sting, to *plus phi*. It is located elsewhere: in the schema of division, it is at the first upper level, it is *prior to* any amboception.

The amboceptor (or *plus phi*) is an easy object for imagining the relationship. But it is an imaginary object. What is of interest about this object is its lack, which has a symbolic value. Castration is the symbolic lack of an imaginary object. The imaginary object in castration is the tumescent organ, the tumescence of *plus phi*, and the lack of tumescence is detumescence. In castration, we have the passage from an S_1 signifier, charged, tumescent with the imaginary, to an S_2 signifier, detumescent with no imaginary. We find again the image of the interior eight with a large tumescent loop and a small detumescent loop. Detumescence is what is important, it is S_2, not in any supposedly natural order of positive things like the phallus *plus phi* or the insect's sting.

The *primordial* importance of *minus phi* (in relation to *plus phi*) or of *detumescence* in relation to tumescence, is illustrated in coitus interruptus, seen as the interruption of complete coitus, the interruption of the process of detumescence that follows the tumescence of the organ. The instrument of *jouissance* that brought castration into play, or the passage from a signifier phallus inflated with the imaginary (*plus phi*, S_1) to a signifier phallus with no signified, deflated of all imaginary (*minus phi*, S_2), is suddenly stripped of its function of *jouissance*, of its S_1–S_2 function. It remains there in all the positivity and massiveness of *plus phi*, whatever happens to it afterwards. This is what triggers the anxiety that follows coitus interruptus. Where lack, detumescence, the true function of *minus phi* (S_2) should have arisen, the hole is plugged by the positive instrumentality of the organ (and ejaculation outside the circuit of S_1–S_2 does nothing to change this instrumentalisation). Anxiety insists precisely where true castration (the symbolic lack of an imaginary object, also to be understood as S_1–S_2) is short-circuited by the positivity of the object. The object a, summoned in anxiety, thus always accentuates the primordial negativity of the object against all positivisation.

The point of cleavage between *jouissance* and desire is anxiety that insist where the signifying process already present at the level of *jouissance* risks not being respected. Yes, mythical *jouissance* involves the Other, the signifier and the subject. But the important thing (and this is what anxiety insists on) is that the *Other* does not answer the question of the subject ($\cancel{A}$) and that, in place of the Other comes an object *a*, not in a positivised form (*plus phi*), but in a *primordially* negativised one (*minus phi*). With the barred big Other, comes the death of the imaginary and then, opposite, the affirmation of this irreducible object *a*. The importance of this *minus phi* (as opposed to *plus phi*) cannot be overestimated, for it is on the basis of castration that we must understand and reposition object *a* in its proper function. It is said to be a "partial object", a positive object bringing partial satisfaction to desire, but its function is, on the contrary, the *cause of* desire. It is this causation of desire that the neurotic discards; the neurotic's phantasy, in fact, fills in the question of engagement starting from the void, from the "cause of desire", with the idea of a partial object that can perhaps be understood in the dynamics of amboception, that is, as an object that would make a connection between two actual people.

The positivisation of object *a* may still be at play when a subject *must objectively* hand in a copy of his essay or his exam in a hurry. The process of invention is short-circuited and replaced by the positivised object *a* that is torn from it. The *jouissance* at stake in this process of invention is perhaps replaced by an ejaculation, but it is anxiety that imposes itself, that insists on A and the negativised object *a*, minus phi.

LESSON 14[3]: DESIRE IN QUESTION BY AND WITH *MINUS PHI*

1   The question and the teacher

What is the desire of the teacher? This is a question not unrelated to the question of the desire of the analyst. On both sides, it's a *real question,* a question that can't be suppressed by a closing answer: the big Other doesn't respond, knowledge fails. In other words, for both teacher and psychoanalyst, lack is central. For the teacher, however (and this brings Hegel and absolute knowledge to mind), the answer is supposedly already written down, and the teacher, concerned with connecting and anxious to avoid any gaps, simply cuts out pieces of the written word to reassemble them in his collages. We can imagine teachers tending to become professors (towards knowledge without lack) and professors who orient themselves towards teaching (towards the question and a lack of knowledge). What is important is to start from lack in order to sustain the liveliness of the question: the barred Other ensuring desire for both the teacher and the analyst.

Regardless of a certain tendency to regard philosophy as the practice of the professor, we must recognise that the question of philosophy in itself is never closed and is continually relaunched. Read Kant and the "discipline of pure reason" in the "theory of method" at the very end of *The Critique of Pure Reason*. Read Nietzsche and his aphorisms. Read Heidegger, who regularly insists on the unending process and tireless questioning of all concepts, being and time first and foremost.

The same applies to the whole field of psychoanalysis. The question – the question as question – is explicitly articulated in "Subversion of the Subject and the Dialectic of Desire", notably in the graph. Stated as *Che vuoi?*, it is made explicit by relying first on the so-called signifier stage: the message as question waits to be interpreted at the level of the big Other, who could thus erase the question, but above all the question is supported at the so-called *jouissance* stage, at the unconscious level, where the big Other does not answer and never will: S($\bar{A}$). This is the stage of the question that never ceases and that opens up a place of continual invention (starting in particular from the vocal object *a*). ($\bar{A}$) in the face of the non-specularisable object *a*: this is the anxiety inherent in teaching. It is as a teacher and not as a professor that Lacan introduces the object *a*.

2   Resuming the question: the primacy of *minus phi*

Here Lacan revisits the essentials of the previous lesson, but always emphasising the question. If there is a haste, an undeniable haste in Lacan's exposition, it is not to find the conclusive answer, but to reinvent the question and sustain it. The question was first posed as that of the division of the signifier (upper level of jouissance); the non-response to the question was written as not-knowing $\bar{A}$ in the face of the object *a* point of invention (middle level: anxiety). Anxiety, in the end, says that the subject's satisfaction is always a false lead. The dream as a wish fulfilment is a false lead; something fundamentally hidden and fundamentally disguised always remains.

With inescapable lack at the heart of the real question (which remains unanswered) and taking anxiety into account (the second level of signifying division), the question of the phallus can no longer be centred on the tumescent, erect ("phallocentric") phallus; it is *primarily* the failure, the radical lack, or the worn out, detumescent state of the said "phallus" (*minus phi*) that predominates in *jouissance*, in anxiety, the positive phallus appearing only as a constructed element of the phantasy for a certain form of desire. This highlighting of the primacy of *minus phi* indicates, at the same time, that object *a* cannot be grasped by any positive form, such as imagined in Zurbarán's paintings (Lucia's eyes are *not* the scopic object and Agatha's breasts are *not* the oral object).

The primordial highlighting of *minus phi* and of the negative, unrepresentable, unspecularisable character of the object is neither solely nor primarily a theoretical affair. Practice depends on it, and the question of the end of an analysis is illuminated by it; if *minus phi* is central and primary, and will remain so, the analyst cannot imagine, still less promise, still less achieve an end of analysis as something positive. The desire of the analyst cannot be focused on *plus phi*, as it was for Freud. In *Analysis Terminable and Interminable*, Freud describes how his analyses systematically stumbled on the bedrock of castration (*gewachsenen Fels*). On the one hand, the woman remains dissatisfied; she does not receive the penis, the interpretation or any other substitute that would give her *plus phi*; she has no reason to stop her analysis: "analysis interminable". On the other hand, the man, who possesses the penis or *plus phi* to begin with, ends his analysis prematurely because of anxiety and the threat of castration; his *plus phi* is threatened by the power of the analyst; he has every reason to stop his analysis as soon as possible: "analysis terminable".

On condition that it is understood in its primordially negative aspect (all that is at stake in the accentuation of *minus phi*), Lacan's object *a* goes beyond not only Freud's impasse and immobilisation concerning the ending or not of analysis, but also, and at the same time, any practice focused on the acquisition of positive knowledge. And anxiety implies the two functions of non-knowledge (Ⱥ) and invention (object *a, minus phi*), which correspond to the two extreme (real) positions on the axis of the difficulty of knowing (the big Other barred) and on the axis of movement (movement of creation and invention, starting from the object *a* negativised).

With masochism and sadism, Lacan had shown the necessary place of anxiety in the division between *jouissance* and desire. The division of the subject is fundamentally a question, not a response. We need to take up *jouissance,* anxiety and desire again in the form of a question, avoiding the stopper of knowledge (Hegel's supposed "absolute knowledge"?), and avoiding *plus phi*. Aphorisms are presented as answers, but they hide, conserve and elevate the fundamental questioning.

3   Aphorisms on *jouissance*, anxiety and desire

Aphorisms conceal undertones and can also produce misunderstandings. On the one hand, the real is always implied in them; the real of saying "remains forgotten behind what is said in what is heard". Aphorisms should make it possible to approach the real in the saying (the real of movement and the real of the difficulty of knowing in anxiety). On the other hand, misunderstanding occurs as soon as they serve as imaginary answers to imaginary questions. So, the inevitable misunderstandings between man and woman should refer back to the real of the encounter and continue to raise questions. And aphorisms would not be necessary to drown out everyone's difficulties with a general formula of defeatist consolation such as "there is no sexual relation". A misunderstanding is a certain failure if it remains only in the imaginary face-to-face, where we think and practice from a completely imaginary *plus phi*. *Jouissance* itself is a misunderstanding while it remains oriented towards a positive phallus (phallic jouissance), towards a positive meaning (joui-sens) or towards an unbarred big Other (*jouissance* of the Other).[4] But *jouissance* in the schema of division is nothing other than a question: how can a subject begin to exist in the place of the signifier? It is a question that continues to accompany us throughout the structure (unless there's a misunderstanding... which still continues to relaunch the question, if we're willing to hear it).

The four aphorisms proposed by Lacan consist in overturning and renouncing the preconceived order concerning *jouissance*, anxiety and desire, by starting from the point of view of the man, the male, in particular. And it is not a question of now introducing a new order (which will always end up being preconceived): it is a question of sustaining the question. The four aphorisms take up the schema of division of the subject with its three levels, jouissance, anxiety and desire, but, in this version, adding love in place of anxiety.

1   *The first aphorism* references the descent of *jouissance*, its incarnation – *"Only love permits jouissance to condescend to desire"* – and reads the division of the subject *in a descending sense* (from the upper level of *jouissance* to the lower level of desire). The means of descending from *jouissance* to desire had been previously indicated in the diagram as anxiety. Why and how does love replace anxiety here? And what happens to anxiety in this substitution? The answer will be given in the fourth aphorism (not without reopening the question).

2   *The second aphorism* is the aphorism of the sublimation of desire: *"Love is the sublimation of desire"* – and reads the schema of the division of the subject *in an upward direction*: we ascend from the lower level of desire to the upper level... of *jouissance*, which is un-named, but which focuses the movement. Love is defined positively, but *where* does this "sublimation" go?

3   *The third aphorism* is the aphorism of the *minus phi* in the desiring male. It starts decidedly from the lower level (desire) and is formulated from the androcentric point of view, starting from male desire: "To *propose myself as desiring is to propose myself as lacking (a). And in this way, I open myself to the jouissance of my being"*. The aphorism starts from masculine desire, while immediately specifying that it is lack: *minus phi*, the only thing that can be proposed in order to provoke desire, it is the object-*cause* of desire as *minus phi* and not the object as the *aim* of desire *plus phi*. By this path = *minus phi*, "I open up to *jouissance"*, at the upper level, "of my being", not only will the partner be able to enjoy me, but it is only there that I can be, that is to say, that I can pose the question of my being as subject (S) in the field of the signifier (A). This third aphorism may resonate with the desire of the analyst: to propose oneself as lacking (a), as the semblance of object *a*, in the discourse of the analyst, with all the consequences in terms of the opening up of *jouissance*. This is undoubtedly still too masculine a way of conceiving analysis, and Lacan will go on in subsequent lessons to evoke the feminine way of practising analysis.

4   *The fourth aphorism* is the aphorism of the woman reduced to a positive object *a* (*plus phi*) by the man. It again takes up a masculine point of view, and deals with what a man might expect from a woman: *"Any demand for (a) on the path to encountering a woman,* woman on the side of *jouissance, can only trigger the anxiety of the Other, in this way, precisely, that I make it more than a, that my desire a-ises it"*. In the masculine way of encountering a woman on the basis of the lack of (a), on the basis of *minus phi*, desire can only appear as a demand for something that would fill the hole, as a positivised object *a*. The woman – who is in the position of A barred – is thus confronted with what I take her to be, i.e. a positivised object *a*. This is the anxiety of the Other; it signals that the question of *jouissance* (implying the barred big Other and the object *a* as minus phi) has been badly managed or short-circuited.

How can we bring primary jouissance back into play? The first aphorism gives the answer (which reopens the question) through love: "Only love…". And we can reread the rest of these four aphorisms in circuit. The place of anxiety is indeed there (indicated in the fourth aphorism), but where it is made acceptable and even profitable by the substitution, the placing of the question of love in the place of anxiety.

4 Woman, *jouissance, minus phi*

The man for the woman

These aphorisms have an air of preaching, of sermonising about them, which Lacan readily acknowledges: "As you can see I'm not afraid of the ridiculous". This ridiculousness is linked to the masculine perspective of the circuit of the four aphorisms. And Lacan proposes to take a few more small steps in the schema of division, a few more steps *outside the male perspective.*

The woman is essentially in the place of *jouissance.* And the first aphorism can now be reinterpreted in terms of her, for her: the woman's *jouissance* condescends to the man's desire through love. The woman's *jouissance,* that is, the *jouissance* that the woman wants to experience with the man, condescends to desire, but not without arousing the man's anxiety. For it is not possible to pass to desire without the question of anxiety, namely *a* as *minus phi* and barred A. This implies that the woman "resents (wants?) my being",[5] "wants to castrate me", that is, wants to destroy the positive substance of what I think I am. It is only from this fundamental lack of being that love is possible.

Freud characterised woman by her lack of a penis, which determines their unquenchable craving for it: *Penisneid.* Lacan's responds categorically "the woman lacks nothing". Regarding the object of desire, the woman lacks nothing, because the object *that causes* desire is not the positivised phallus, it is *minus phi,* which is at the centre of castration and anxiety. And if the phallus presents itself as tumescence and detumescence, as what inflates and deflates, the crucial point that could come to be missing is not *plus phi,* but the negative side, the *minus phi,* detumescence, the emptying of all imaginary in the signifying process. On this *all-important* negative side, on the side of *minus phi,* the woman is undoubtedly at an advantage, and *jouissance* is her business from the outset.

Notes

1 Lesson of 6 March 1963. Chapter XII of the Seuil edition.
2 Lacan Jacques, *La Troisième,* Paris, Navarin, 2021, p. 772.
3 Lesson of 13 March 1963. Chapter XIII of the Seuil edition.
4 *Jouissance* is regularly reduced to this triad, which is certainly present in the drawing given by Lacan himself at the end of "La troisième" (Paris, Navarrin, 2021, p. 41), whereas the writing of the same text also refers to the *jouissance* of the body, the *jouissance* of life and, implicitly, the *jouissance* of death.
5 La femme "en veut à mon être".

Part Four

Minus phi and object *a*

Chapter 7

Minus phi and the desire of a female analyst

The four aphorisms of Lesson 14 are founded on the division of the big Other by the question of the subject: how can the subject – who does not exist – manage to find himself in the signifier, in the big Other? This is the first line of division, the line of *jouissance*. The second line gives a "response": namely, the big Other does not respond (on the subject's side) and the big Other is replaced by the non-specularisable object *a*; this is the line of anxiety. Finally, on the third line, the line of desire, the barred subject turns and turns again and again around his question as if on a Moebius strip.

The first aphorism (only love permits *jouissance* to condescend to desire) descends from the line of *jouissance* to the line of desire through the intermediary of the ladder that is love, which allows us to leap over anxiety (the intermediate line) and span the abyss, the gap between *jouissance* and desire. The second aphorism (love is the sublimation of desire) starts from the lower line of desire to rise and sublimate desire. It is the same ladder of love that is called upon for the upward path from desire to *jouissance* over the abyss of anxiety. The third and fourth aphorisms are situated in a masculine perspective, which Lacan had already surpassed at the end of the last session by introducing what the Other wants, what the woman wants. What the woman wants concerns the level of *jouissance* and not simply that of desire. Not without giving rise to anxiety.

The woman's perspective, centred first and foremost on *jouissance* (and not on desire), at the same time mobilises the very principle of the functioning of the unconscious (the principle of *jouissance*). The question of what a woman wants goes hand in hand with the very practice of psychoanalysis centred on the principle of *jouissance*. It is not surprising, therefore, to note with Lacan that a woman analyst enjoys greater freedom in her way of being an analyst. The analyst must always have a feminine side.

LESSON 15[1]: *MINUS PHI* AND ENJOYMENT

1 The place of *jouissance* in the ethics

Seminar X on *Anxiety* can be situated only in its dependence on the field of *jouissance*, a field highlighted in Seminar VII on *Ethics*, which directly follows on from

DOI: 10.4324/9781003477822-11

Seminar VI on *Desire*, where the primacy of *jouissance* has already been pressed home. Now we have the sequence *jouissance*, anxiety, desire.

Let us briefly recall how *jouissance* is introduced in the *Ethics* and developed in *Kant with Sade*. Kantian morality (*Groundwork for the Metaphysics of Morals* and *The Critique of Practical Reason*) is the first ethics in Western philosophy not driven by the search for happiness or pleasure in reality. In other words, it is the first ethics that does not function according to the pleasure principle and its acolyte, the reality principle. With the ethics of the unconscious, which takes over from Kant's revolution in ethics, another principle will have to be taken into account, beyond the pleasure principle: the principle of *jouissance*.

With this new ethics, the moral law is presented as *absolutely* unconditional, independent of any condition of the subject. It does not start from an Ideal; it does not start from a determined goal to be reached; it does not start from a God or some other big Other who would dictate the law; it does not even start from a subject, who is always conditional. The moral law thus starts from itself, it is *autonomous*, creating itself as its own law (1); from there on and according to itself, *good and evil* can appear (2); the rule of good and evil will *subsequently* be posed *in reality* (3) and one *finishes up* producing a *subject*, a moral subject purified by the law (4). It is difficult to imagine the starting point of all this (1), the purified starting point that is absolutely unconditional, autonomous, independent of everything in the sea of subjects and objects, ideals and gods that occupy our world.

With psychoanalysis, we have to recognise something that presents itself as absolutely unconditional, independent of any condition of the subject. This is what Freud called the unconscious, which we can recognise as the Other (1): we cannot avoid it, we can try to repress it, but it comes back as the return of the repressed; correlatively, with its own imperative, unconditional law, the unconscious invents, creates a new universe. It is only *after* and in relation to the movement of this law's emergence that there comes the question of the ego to judge what is good or bad for actions: is it good or bad relative to the inventive force of the unconscious? This is the real work of the ego's self-esteem (*Selbstachtung*) based on the unconditioned imperative of the unconscious (2) and it is only in a third stage that all this inventive work of the unconscious can find application in examples, in the reality of objects (3). Finally – and only in a fourth and final stage – can the process that has begun in the unconscious bring a subject into existence as its effect (4). With these four stages, we have described the emergence of the subject (S) in the place of the unconscious controlled by the signifier (A). This four-stage journey – describing what is at stake in the division starting from *jouissance* – goes through a schema Z, in which we recognise Lacan's Schema L as well as the subject of *jouissance* in the Sadean phantasy[2]: (Figure 7.1).

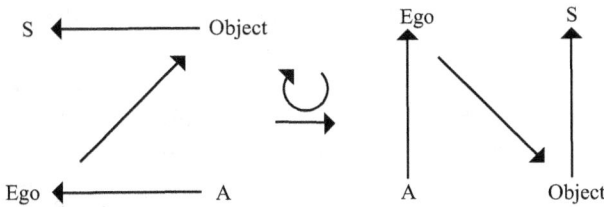

Figure 7.1 From the classic Schema L to the structure of the phantasy (in *Kant with Sade*).

More often than not, Kant is not read as he should be. Lacan himself catches himself reading Kant the wrong way round: all we have to do is follow the arrows backwards in the diagram above, i.e. starting from a given subject (4), confronted by objects, objective situations, examples, etc. (3) who poses the question to the ego of where good is, where evil is (2), and finally finding the answer in a universal law already given in a big Other who knows (1). This ordinary reading by Lacan is of little importance, until he adds "…with Sade", who gives the truth of Kant by showing the path of *jouissance* in the right direction: creation, the emergence of a law (1) which secondarily decides on good and evil (2) which then applies to objective situations e.g. to the victims (3), and which finally has a subject effect (4).

With the moral law (Kant's in the *Critique of Practical Reason*) and with the ethical unconscious (introduced by Lacan from the Seminar on *Ethics* onwards), the field of *jouissance* is introduced. This field of *jouissance* does not consist in offering a field where a given subject might be able to enjoy the Other and with the Other. The question is rather how a subject that is not given, that does not exist, can emerge from the signifying process, how a subject invents himself and comes to be, only at the *end of the process* prior to which he did not exist. This is *jouissance*, the invention of oneself.[3]

2 Enjoyment (*minus phi*) and desire (*plus phi*)

Jouissance first implicates the big Other. Desire first implicates the big Other. And yet *jouissance* and desire can in no way be confused and are even opposed by the function of the big Other, which function is completely different on both sides.

The big Other is fundamentally barred in the question of *jouissance* (contrary to the Hegelian presentation of desire in the master slave dialectic) and fundamentally unbarred in relation to desire; there is a great risk attached to understanding desire in the Hegelian perspective of self-consciousness, in other words, of the subject supposed to know. This is the very reason we must start from *jouissance* in the schema of division in order to situate desire.

At the level of desire, the big Other first appears as personalised, posing the question to me, subject: what do you want? *Che vuoi?* In this face-off, where A and S oppose and articulate each other in the figure of two entwined toruses, where the demand of one corresponds to the desire of the other, desire appears as fundamentally normative, introducing an intimate correspondence between desire and the law: desire is the law, and the law is repressed desire. Thereby, desire, modelled on an Other who appears as normative, must correspond to the demand of this Other, who enacts the prohibition of incest and the prohibition of the murder of the father.

However, such is not the centre of the Other. Starting from *jouissance* and the Other as the field of the signifier from which the subject might emerge, the Other is fundamentally barred (as written in the schema of division at the middle level of anxiety). The centre of the Other is essentially perforated, neither responding nor asking for anything.

As a direct consequence of the gap between the approach to desire through the law (the unbarred Other) and the approach to desire through *jouissance* (the barred Other), the superego *in itself* must be conceived of in two radically different ways, two conceptions that are always present, and more or less visible in any appearance of the superego: *firstly*, the ferocious superego, normative for desire, corresponding to the prohibitions of incest and murder, etc., and dependent on a big personalised Other who demands and prohibits in the structuring of desire and the law; secondly, the superego of *jouissance*, which does only one thing: open *jouissance* "Jouis", and the space for creation and invention on the basis of the signifier and the unconscious "j'ouïs".

For Freud, desire is normative, but not without consequences, altogether clear in practice. In *Contributions to the Psychology of Love* (1910–1912), Freud dwells on the "universal tendency to debasement in the sphere of love". Almost inevitably, man, the male, in his sexual practice, is divided between two currents, the tender current corresponding to the impulses of self-preservation and the properly sexual current. Either he needs two women, one to love tenderly and one to desire sexually, the mother and the whore; or he stays with one and the same woman, but, to enjoy her sexually, he needs to debase her. According to the Freudian interpretation, this degradation depends on the Oedipus and the related prohibition of incest: "you shall not desire the woman who was the object of my desire". Since the chosen woman is necessarily a substitute for the mother, there remains the solution of repression, which consists of incestuous sexual tendencies with opposing purified and tender love, in other words, elevating and sublimating one half (and loving it tenderly) and degrading the other half (and demeaning it violently). In any case, it's not that: woman is not the personified sublime Other (still in the perspective of the great positivised Other of desire), nor can she be reduced to an object, to a positivised object *a* (cf. the fourth aphorism). Woman's anxiety responds to and questions this double reduction according to Oedipal normativity. The seminar *Anxiety* is a radical questioning of a psychoanalysis centred on desire and the law represented by the Other personified in the father.

As we saw above, the same precedence of a big Other who knows and imposes his phallic law *plus phi* leads to the impasses encountered by Freud regarding the end of analysis. One could say that the *gewachsenen Fels* the solid rock of castration upon which, at the end of the treatment, Freud confessed in *Analysis Terminable and Interminable*, his analyses regularly stumbled, this rock has grown like a plant. This rock, the stone of scandal, in fact consists of Freud's own phallocentric – *plus phi* – conception. On the woman's side, *plus phi* is still not there, the woman lacks a penis and the analyst will never fully satisfy her, it will never be enough. On the man's side, *plus phi* is always there and always under the threat of possible castration by the analyst, who would present himself as the big Other who knows: analysis must end as quickly as possible.

By *first* giving primordial prominence to *jouissance* and *minus phi*, Lacan completely displaces Freudian analysis, centred on desire and the law, as managed by the Oedipus complex and the castration complex.

The woman is superior to the man in the domain of *jouissance* because she does not have to go through object *a* as positively conceived. Being from the outset with *minus phi*, she does not need to pass through the negation of the phallus, through the negation of *plus phi*; she does not need to pass through the castration complex (symbolic lack of an imaginary object that is *plus phi*).

Jean Allouch regularly speaks of the "two analytics of sex"[4] that he believes Lacan draws from; the first corresponds to an approach to sexuality through the object *a*, the second is centred on "there is no sexual relation". In fact, this is fundamentally a question, *on the one hand*, of an analytic deduced from the positivity of the object *a*, from *plus phi*, including the lack of *plus phi*, castration (a "first analytic of sex" centred on desire) and, *on the other hand*, of an analytic starting from *minus phi*, which is made explicit in all the negative formulae like "there is no sexual relation", "woman does not exist", etc. (This "second analytic of sex" corresponds from the outset to *jouissance*). It should be noted, however, that object *a*, despite its positivations on the *plus phi* side, must fundamentally be situated first and always at the level of *jouissance*; this is the whole importance of first introducing the object *a* as a vocal object, *nihil negativum*, through the ethics of the unconscious.

The schema of division justly highlights the primacy of *jouissance* and *minus phi*. There, as a result of the first level of *jouissance*, object *a* appears, at the next level down, comes the level of anxiety. It is neither the object targeted by desire, neither waste product nor irreducible remainder of the process of desire. It is prior to desire insofar as it is *first and foremost* negative, *minus phi* originating in *jouissance*. The Other's desire is indeed there, but it is directly dependent on *jouissance*, the passage from big Other to barred big Other already having taken place before any articulation of desire, before the opposition of the Other and the Subject (in neurotic and toric topology), before the opposition of desire and the law. The transition from the big Other to the barred big Other takes place within the signifying process, in the transition from the first to the second conception of the signifier (cf. the interior eight, Moebius strip and cross-cap).

The comparison between woman's and man's *jouissance* highlights the abyss that separates *jouissance* (on the woman's side) from desire (on the man's side). We know the story of Tiresias, the transgender man who went from male to female and female to male, experiencing *jouissance* on both sides. Having seen what should not be seen, namely Athena's nakedness (what cannot be seen or known), he was blinded, though not without becoming a seer, a diviner, a savant of essential things that cannot be seen (such as *jouissance*). In another story, where he had again seen what should not be seen, disturbing the mating of snakes, he had questioned the phallus (phi: plus or minus?) and had become a woman, not without opening up the question of *jouissance*. Where is *jouissance* greater? Tiresias's verdict is clear: a woman's *jouissance* is far more important than a man's; for a man is always initially in a relation to desire, with object *a* initially positivised (*plus phi*).

3   Man's misdirection

We have seen *object a* as the object that falls, the object that becomes lacking; satisfaction is therefore never complete. We have seen Saint Agatha's breasts, represented by Zurbarán as positive objects, torn away and presented on a platter and, similarly, Saint Lucy's eyes in another painting. Positively, these objects are there before they are ripped away, before they are lacking. We saw these objects in the context of castration: the positive presence of an imaginary object followed by its symbolic lack.

From the point of view of the creativity of the ethical unconscious, a completely different dynamic takes hold: one that starts from an absolute nothing. It is starting from the totally negative value of object *a* – at stake with the vocal object *a* in the ethics of the unconscious – that the liveliness of all creation and invention can be played out. This is the question of *jouissance*, which does not involve the presupposition of a *plus phi* prior to negation (as the castration complex is generally understood in a masculine sense).

We have to think in a contrary fashion to any imagined positivity, as represented in Zurbarán's paintings. Unfortunately, we are used to understanding the positive as always coming first, the positive imagined as *plus phi*. *Minus phi* would then simply be the result of the subtraction of this original *plus phi*. This is what we see in Zurbarán's two paintings: the subtraction of an original positive object. Even in Hegel, where negativity is completely central, positivity, the full, the "something" would be primary, according to Lacan. Sartre himself is here characterised by his "marvellous talent for misdirection", misdirection consisting in first giving oneself a positive reality and then moving on to lack or negation. This is Freud's phallic theory: the boy has a phallus originally thought of as positive (*plus phi*) and he risks losing it secondarily with the threat of castration. In the girl, it's the same thing except that castration has already taken place.

To express this supposedly primary positivity that makes a secondary hole, Lacan again quotes Sartre: a child on the beach sticks his finger in the sand, thereby sticking a positive phallus in mother earth and making a hole in it. Lacan is quick to see this as a typically Oedipal phantasy, and, what's more, a phantasy of the impotent. The law of the father forbids incestuous desire for the mother, which is therefore repressed. The return of repressed desire occurs in the displacement of the image of the little child sticking a finger in the sand. Impotence – dictated by the prohibition of incest – is overcome, so to speak, by a displacement onto the beach and into the sand. The little boy sticking his finger into the hole of the mother is a typical phantasy of the impotent.

But at the same time, woman and all sexuality is demeaned ("On the Universal Tendency to Debasement in the Sphere of Love[5]"). It is in relation to the positivisation of the phallus that one's love life is debased, at the same time as impotence with the woman who is loved, asserts itself. The child or adult is impotent with the woman who is identified with the mother. All this depends on a specifically masculine way of thinking of the castration complex from *plus phi*. Phallic positivity pervades Sartre's conception of the world: again on the beach, we come across little molluscs called razor-shells ("knives"), which have a whole series of appendages that are like little phalluses. They bear witness to the fact that the world in general is made up of phallic positivities. The world and the psychic structure would essentially be made, *wesentlich,* of phallic substances: "for all x phi of x". This conception is based on "essence" as the primary substance made explicit by the phallic symbol.

Could we now conceive of Lacan's real on this model of positivity, of fullness, of the omnipresent *plus phi*? "The real is always full"? The phrase could sound like a Lacanian aphorism, a good-natured Lacanianism. But Lacan said nothing of the sort. This is not what we encounter in our experience. What needs to be said is that "nothing is missing from the real". This is in no way equivalent to the phrase "the real is always full". "To the real, nothing is lacking" means that we don't have the real as something primarily positive that lacks something secondarily. *Jouissance* lacks nothing; the woman lacks nothing; the real lacks nothing. These phrases indicate that we must not think in terms of an imaginary positivity (*plus phi*) that might be missing from *jouissance*, woman or the real. In each case, this positivity is absent from the outset and, consequently, there is no castration that can secondarily subtract it. We're not in the dialectic of desire, castration, the object that's missing, and so on. From the outset, we are confronted with the void, with lack before any object of lack.

4   The feminine void and desire as market value for *jouissance*

The void, lack before any object of lack, the hollow of the vase before the vase itself, are fundamental not only for woman, but for the history of mankind and civilisation. All pots made by *homo faber* differ, even if they all appear similar; because what makes and what is made by the pot is the void, and the void is never the same. The pot realises the signifying process itself: it appears as rich in everything imaginary that it could be filled with (S_1), but it is only as good as its emptiness (S_2), emptiness as the locus of invention, of creation. And creation is always different, contingent, even if the S_1–S_2 structure is given as necessary. Even if its structure is necessary, it is always contingent, always different which is precisely what psychoanalysis is all about. The criterion for recognising the presence of an established civilisation is that archaeological digs unearth pots, vases and ceramics. These objects bear witness to the fact that the invention specific to the mechanism of the signifier was already at work there.

A case of one of Lacan's analysands illustrates the woman's relationship to signifying division and the primordial place of *jouissance* and *minus phi*. Her husband has been neglecting her for a little too long; yet she should be relieved, given her husband's lifelong relative awkwardness. The woman comments: "It doesn't matter if he desires me; as long as he doesn't desire others". Is this a distancing from desire, in favour of *jouissance*? Lacan recounts a temporary symptom that arose during her analysis: a vaginal swelling, a tumescence that is not unpleasant when she sees a moving object appear, a car, any other object that surprises her. A little later, this symptom is clearly linked to the transference: "the appearance of any object obliges me to evoke you, Monsieur Lacan, as a witness, not to seek your approval, simply your gaze". The associations immediately lead her to the title of a play she had become acquainted with in her adolescence: *Je vivrai un grand amour* (Steve Passeur, 1935–1947). The great love is addressed to the analyst; according to Lacan's first aphorism, it is he alone who allows *jouissance* to condescend to desire. But her *own first* great love had been a student for whom, in a correspondence, she had invented a tissue of lies built around what she wanted to be in his eyes. This is a correspondence in the full sense of the word, a correspondence of desire to desire, as in the structure of the two entwined toruses. On the contrary, she says, she always strives to be true with her analyst; the two great loves go in opposite directions, where, with the student it was all about lies and with Lacan she strives to be truthful. With the student, on the one hand, the correspondence of the desire of one with the desire of the Other takes the place of love (the first great love) and it is a tissue of lies. With Lacan, on the other hand, things are not primarily at the level of desire and true love is otherwise situated (striving to be true on the side of jouissance?). "It doesn't matter whether he desires me or not"; that's not the question, provided that desire for others doesn't take the place of *jouissance*. The "great love", stretched between the first great love, which revolved around the deceptive correspondence of desires, and the great transferential love with Lacan, opens on the question of *jouissance*. She remains however in-between the levels of desire and *jouissance*, as evidenced by her "only word in bad taste", when she says "I'm remote-controlled", meaning "I'm dependent on the man's desire instead of placing myself in the field of *jouissance*".

The feminine vase is entirely self-sufficient. If it is to be filled foolishly with whatever, the presence of the object filling the vase is surplus. From the outset, the empty vase is immediately placed in pure *jouissance* and the rest is accessory. The position is completely different for the man, for whom the woman, according to the biblical myth, is only the man's rib, the man's lost object.

When Kierkegaard says that the woman is more open to anxiety than the man, this anxiety is not castration anxiety, it is not the anxiety of being deprived of the instrument of power in all its forms. For the woman, anxiety is linked to the infinite possibilities that remain undetermined on the side of desire. Object *a* – the cause of desire – is not fundamentally determined (as it might still appear in its oral, anal or scopic expressions), it is indeterminate because it is the locus of invention, of creation, opening up indeterminate possibilities of desire: desire is suspended from jouissance.

The myth of original sin is a masculine myth: the serpent comes as a positive phallus that presents itself as the tempter (*plus phi*). But Lacan modifies the myth – surreptitiously, but very clearly – because he erases the snake from it: woman tempts herself by tempting the other, and to tempt the other, Lacan says, any pretext will do. The woman can take any object to tempt the man, an apple, for example. She needs no positivity, neither that of the phallus, nor that of the snake, nor that of the apple.

If the fish has nothing to do with an apple, the apple – whatever void, this *minus phi* – will do perfectly well to try and catch the fish that is Adam the man, always in search of his own phallic fish (*plus phi*). But what is the woman trying to catch in the man? Not the phallic fish that interests man, but desire of man as desire *of the Other,* that is, *his desire insofar as it is dependent on jouissance.* Desire for the woman thus serves only as a commodity, a commodity for bringing *jouissance* into play. At that level, we can see that desire is close to a capitalist conception, it is quoted on the market, it has a price, and this price will also determine the value of love, on the scale that relies at its summit on *jouissance.*

Lacan says here that love is an "idealisation of desire", whereas in the previous session, the second aphorism holds that: "love is the sublimation of desire". There is a fundamental difference between the *idealisation of* desire and the *sublimation of* desire. In idealisation, desire takes on a market value and this value is augmented, idealised; here, we're in the capitalist perspective of valuing, putting a price on desire and love, an essentially masculine perspective. In sublimation, the transition is to something quite different, to the zero of S_2, and to the start of invention and creation. Here, desire is not given a rating or a value; it undergoes a metamorphosis towards *jouissance.*

If desire is nothing more than a commodity to play the game of *jouissance*, it is understandable that the woman in general attaches little importance to the fact that her man's desire is more or less sick, or even impotent. The rating of desire is of little importance, contrary to what the man thinks, because the woman is situated at the level of *jouissance*, where desire is secondary and only a commodity for involving the other.

If the woman is thus centred on the question of *jouissance*, should we not compare her to the masochist who makes herself a mere object (dog, etc.) for the enjoyment of the Other? Should we not rightly speak of "feminine masochism"? Yes, *jouissance* is invoked every time. As for the rest, the structures diverge fundamentally: masochism makes itself an object, which is not the case for women; and behind her dedication to the *jouissance* of the Other, what the masochist seeks is to arouse the anxiety of the Other. The woman does not make herself an object, the woman's aim is not to arouse the anxiety of the Other, but the desire of the Other *for jouissance.*

So-called "female masochism" is simply a male phantasy through which the man tries to support his own structure of desire: the woman would make herself an object, object *a* positivised, *plus phi*, an *a*-isation for *jouissance* in the sense of orgasm, the man's *jouissance*. For men, enjoyment depends on the question of the object as a condition of desire. We find this perspective in Freud's reading of desire, in his "*Contributions to the Psychology of Love, A Special Type of Object*

Choice made by Men, On the Universal Tendency to Debasement in the Sphere of Love", "The Taboo of Virginity" but also in *"Fetishism"* where the fetishist object is the *sine qua non* of desire. If the man sees the object as the condition of desire, we can ask ourselves the following question: isn't the formula that equates *object a* with the *cause of desire* essentially a structurally *fetishist* formula from a *masculine* perspective? From a feminine point of view, wouldn't we have to consider that object *a* is directly engaged with the question of *jouissance*? This would be the fourth face of object *a*, the vocal face where the properly *vocal* object *a*, the *cause of* desire is necessarily an invention, and implies the freedom of the unconscious.

For the woman, the desire of the Other, when she tempts Adam, is the means for her *jouissance* to take hold, which is primary. By summoning the desire of the Other for *jouissance* in this way, the fact that the man might well reduce woman to being no more than a positivised object *a*, an object (the male phantasy of female masochism for example), is left in the shade. The imposture of the man who reduces the woman to being nothing more than a positivised object *a*, the imposture that objectifies, *a*-ises the woman, can nevertheless be blatant and can indeed trigger anxiety in the woman.

This masculine imposture differs radically from the feminine masquerade, which plays on the man's desire – like Lacan's analysand with her first great love woven of lies to make a desire correspond to another desire. In the woman's masquerade, primary *jouissance* must first be to find an object; and the woman knows full well that the masquerade of desire has value only as a measure of her *jouissance*, of the question of *jouissance*. The woman may thus disregard this question of desire, whereas the man cannot disregard this misunderstanding, the misunderstanding of desire hooked on as it is to the question of the positivised object *a*; this is because the man is necessarily held by the question of pricing, of giving a price, he remains in this quantifiable side, in an absolutely quantitative logic; "for all x phi of x": this remains the primary, quantitative, quantifiable formula of desire for the man.

5   Don Juan, the desire of the female analyst as a feminine dream

The latter part of Lesson 15 returns us to the examination of Lucia Tower's article, *"Counter-transference"*, which will enlighten us on the desire of the analyst in its dependence on primordial *jouissance*, that is, in its dependence on the *minus phi,* fundamental to the feminine position. The desire of the analyst in general is thus illuminated by a woman analyst, because the woman analyst has something freer in the way she conducts analyses. This freedom is the freedom of *jouissance* proper to the unconscious, the freedom to let the unconscious create and invent.

As a preamble to Lucia Tower's article, let us set out the framework within which the *desire* of the female analyst presents itself. In other words, how does a woman, starting from the question of *jouissance*, come to embody this question of *jouissance* in her desire and her desire with a man? This question, which

Lacan proposes as an introduction to the reading of Lucia Tower's article, already indicates the orientation of the reading Lacan proposes for it, namely, in a continuation of the schema of division (jouissance, anxiety, desire). This preamble is Don Juan and it is a feminine *"dream"*. And what we understand by *"dream"* (Lacan does not say "phantasy" here) is a wish fulfilment, the fulfilment of desire, the incarnation in desire of something that starts from the ethereal level of *jouissance*. Don Juan is the story of the first aphorism: "Only love allows *jouissance* to condescend to desire", and it is a woman's dream, fundamental for a woman analyst and, through her, for any analyst who wants to conduct his or her analyses with a little more freedom.

How is Don Juan constructed? Firstly, Don Juan is not a real person; he is a man perfectly equal to himself, flawless and without castration, to whom absolutely nothing is lacking. He resonates with the myth of the uncastrated father, the father of the primal horde; he is a figure of the big Other who is not barred. Secondly, Don Juan is a purely feminine image; this does not contradict the first point: on the contrary, it is the establishment of a big mythical Other at the level of *jouissance*. Thirdly, following Rank here, Don Juan is someone who, in his actions, gives his all, his soul, but without ever losing it. With "all his soul", Don Juan summons the object *a*, and object *a* presents itself as the absolute object, which does not mean the positivised object *a*, but on the contrary, the object *a* with its unconditional, imperative, irresistible character, in other words the vocal object *a* (*minus phi* and not *plus phi*).

Lacan makes Don Juan resonate with the practice of *droit du seigneur*, of priests deflowering young girls, with all the figures of the uncastrated father. But that doesn't make him an ideal of masculinity for men (*plus phi*). On the contrary, Don Juan is inscribed in the feminine perspective of a pure uncastrated female image (primordial *minus phi*). Don Juan is outside, below and beyond any threat of castration: the relation of the man's castration with his object is completely absent. If the imposture – typically masculine – is preserved and even accentuated in the myth of Don Juan, its function is to sustain the space of *jouissance* in the repetition of conquests. No emphasis is ever placed on his behaviour in relation to one or other woman.

The figure of Don Juan does not inspire desire; Don Juan does not even have desire as such. But he does exude an *odor di femina*, already evoked in the seminar on *La Lettre Volée*'.[6] Don Juan is feminised insofar as he is the bearer of the stolen and fleeting letter in the field of *jouissance*. Don Juan is therefore not at all a fearful character for women, and if his conquests multiply, they only serve as points in support of the purloining of the letter in the field of *jouissance*.

5.1   Don Juan and Lucia Tower

In her article *Counter-transference*, Lucia Tower "has two men", two men undergoing analysis. How is she going to manage with these two men? What is her desire? Is it imbued with the myth of Don Juan? These questions are not explicitly posed in the seminar, but the question insists: what is the desire of the female analyst? These two men undergoing analysis suffer from anxiety neurosis. Note that anxiety neurosis is not a transference neurosis (it is not a phobia), it is an *actual* neurosis, characterised by the actual insistence of anxiety. In the schema of division, the question of anxiety arises from *jouissance.*

These two men have aggressive tendencies with their respective wives and have a penchant for the other sex left and right. Nothing out of the ordinary. The remarkable fact is that their wives each think that their man is too submissive, not hostile enough, not male enough. These men are not the true Don Juan. And the women are frustrated.

We get to the heart of the matter with Lucia Tower's questioning of her desire. Lucia Tower has her own little idea about the man, about the woman and about each of the two men in their relationships. Lucia Tower feels protective of one analysand and of the wife of the second analysand. She is protective. But fundamentally, these two men tire her, going on and on, telling and retelling the same uninteresting stories again and again She indeed tries one or other Oedipal interpretation in the transference: "the first patient uses his conflicts with his wife to attract the attention of his analyst and to get the attention he never got from his mother". Nothing changes in the boring course of these analyses.

Everything changes with a dream of her own. In this dream, the wife of the first analysand, the wife whom Lucia Tower had been protecting against her husband, shows herself to be cooperative in the analysis, siding with the analyst in order to move the analysis forward. The dream leads Lucia Tower to revise the opinion she had formed of this man, which corresponded to his wife's opinion of him. Deep down, the analysand is not as adrift as one might think; he is capable of taking himself for a man. But what is a man? Does the feminine dream of Don Juan underlie the analyst's thoughts following her own dream? The analyst has completely revised her opinion and her position in relation to this analysand, who has now taken on a new consistency and now expresses grievances in the transference, which are followed by a storm of depressive movements and naked rage. The analyst interprets: "this is phallic sadism couched in oral language".

That may be so. But what is important is what happened first on the side of the desire of the analyst. She drew this storm on herself from the moment her desire became interested in this dream. It is the analyst's dream that gets things moving and that can be connected with Don Juan as the dream of a woman. From this the desire of the analyst, the analysand and everything that revolves around his case ends up completely invading the analyst's mental space, who can only think of this man during her other analyses. Amusingly, says Lacan, these obsessive thoughts about this analysand disappear when she goes on holiday. She is no longer interested, because everything revolved around a purely mythical position, evoked on this occasion by the analysand: the story of a man who is a real man, the story of Don Juan.

LESSON 16[7]: OBJECT *a* STARTING FROM THE WOMAN

1   The desire of Lucia tower, analyst

Lacan resumes his study of Lucia Tower's paper. It is through the rectification of the analyst's position, it is through putting the desire of the analyst in question on the basis of *jouissance* (Don Juan) that the desire of the analysand is restored. Before her dream, that is, before the desire of the analyst was brought into play, Lucia Tower was thinking vicariously in the place of the analysand's wife whose concern was that her man was not really a man. We can legitimately assume that the analysand's current anxiety depended in part on being trapped by this. After the analyst's dream, the question of what a man is, the myth of Don Juan, turns out to be a woman's dream, a woman's desire dependent on the question of *jouissance*. With this readjustment, the analysand is returned to his own question, the question of the man's desire and the object *a* on which it depends and which can be distanced from the myth of Don Juan.

But Lucia Tower does not have the full measure of the dream of Don Juan or of a man, truly a man well established in *jouissance*. She is still in a confrontation in which she imagines that her analysand is a phallic sadist, while she herself would be more masochistic than she thought. But no, she is not a masochist, she is not taking the place of an object that satisfies the *jouissance* of the Other, in order to arouse the anxiety of the Other. She was caught in a structure of entanglement of what her analysand was supposed to be with what she herself dreamt of as a man, a real man. And this structure of toric and neurotic entanglement is unravelled by the revelation of her own desire as analyst and woman. And the desire of the analysand, freed from this entanglement, can now open up: what he is looking for is no longer anyone's business but his own.

The analysand can now mourn the loss of his partner, who is supposed to know what he should be. He is no longer obliged to be trapped by the phantasy or the dream of his analyst and his wife about the Don Juan that he should be. This mourning allows him to find the place of invention on his own side, the place of creation starting from castration as S_1–S_2, with the interior eight, with the force of creation inherent in the cross-cap. The Oedipus ceases to be the tragedy of a magnificent *plus phi* that one will sooner or later have to lose if one hasn't already lost it, according to a conception of castration that presupposes the positivity of the phallus in the first place. Now we laugh about it, and it becomes a comedy in which desire and the law turn each other over.

The law is nothing other than repressed desire. Desire and law are the same thing on both sides. But the front, the first appearance of the thing, is not desire; it is the law. "It was only through the law that I discovered covetousness, desire", says Saint Paul to the Romans (7:7). But the law first presents itself as the failure of the law, namely as guilt. It is the experience of guilt (law) that leads to the discovery of freedom (desire). Guilt is not guilt for a peccadillo or even for a major crime.

Guilt is fundamentally disproportionate, fault stems from the fact that the action lies outside all the measures given by laws as regulations. "Out of proportion" is also what characterises the moral law with its categorical imperative and the unconscious, which does not think, calculate or judge. This immediately brings us back to the upper level of the schema of division, without which the couple of desire and the law is not possible. We are in the invention starting from *minus phi* and no longer in castration starting from *plus phi*.

2   Woman and *minus phi* (non-specularisable)

Resonating with the myth of Don Juan and the dream of the analyst Lucia Tower, the shackles in which the analyst's desire was caught were untied. The analysand is freed from what had bound him to a certain expectation. But why? The next step consists in shifting the question of object *a* and understanding it no longer in terms of the man's desire conceived in a masculine way based on a preliminary *plus phi*, but in function of *jouissance*, in function of the woman's desire conceived in a feminine way, based on the upper level of jouissance and a preliminary *minus phi*. This further step, at the same time, moves the practice of analysis from the first to the second conception of the signifier.

Lacan quotes the *Book of Proverbs*, in which Solomon gives voice to wisdom. Here are the two verses quoted: "Three things are too astonishing for me; and four, which are impenetrable: the track (*la route*) of the eagle in the sky, the track of the serpent on the rock, the track of the ship at the heart of the sea, the track of the man in the young girl"[8]. The first three are astonishing, being essentially routes, wakes, we could say drifts, drifts that are played out in the three elements of the sky (the eagle), the earth (the snake) and the sea (the ship), at every attempt they are difficult to pin down. These routes are astonishing, difficult, but possible to know in a certain sense, (in our grid we are in the middle of the axis of the difficulty of knowing). But the fourth remains impenetrable – *penitus ignoro*, I am profoundly ignorant of it, it is a radical Not-knowing – and this impenetrability has an impact on the other three: "yes, four, which are impenetrable".

With these questions of the track and drift, we hear the constitutive drift of desire, which presents itself as metonymical. It is difficult, however, to think of the fourth route as a metonymical drift of desire, given its impenetrable nature. What is it about? Straightaway, let us leave aside the perverse deviations that occasion the indelible mark on a young adolescent barely out of childhood: the mark left by an exhibitionist, the mark of rape or any other sexual assault on the emerging puberty of a little girl. It is not a question here of trauma, but of something profoundly structural (independent of more or less traumatic contingent circumstances), which is nonetheless very important in the case of proven trauma. But the point here is absolutely general.

At the level of the fourth track, there is no trace whatsoever, which is why it is impenetrable. Regarding the man's drift towards a young teenage girl, there is no trace. There is the erasure of the trace, the very characteristic of the signifying process itself (second conception of the signifier): S$_2$ is defined as empty of all imaginary, that is, without trace. The young woman, the young adolescent is in radical lack, without trace of man, not surrounded by something that could be withdrawn from her, not surrounded by the oral object, by a deprivation, by a castration, she is in a place of radical lack, of fundamental dissatisfaction that is completely independent of the phallus (even if secondarily, after this first moment of emerging sexuality, the constitution of the object of desire in all its complexity will come). We are at the opposite end of any specification of the young girl as castrated, as subject to the desire for the penis. From the start, it is an absolute nothingness, *minus phi*, impenetrable, "non-specularisable", that is involved as soon as the signifying process begins at the upper level of jouissance. The young girl's dissatisfaction comes first, before any question of castration, and it is only secondarily that she becomes interested in the phallic object and eventually in castration. Ernest Jones is quite right: women can *only* be phallic *secondarily*; they are "deutero-phallic".

You might think that the first three routes are astonishing and penetrable, comprehensible. The fourth now allows us glimpse that all four are impenetrable or incomprehensible. Similarly, we might think that the three forms of object *a* (oral, anal, scopic) are astonishing and penetrable (specularisable). The fourth – *minus phi* – suggests that they are *all* fundamentally impenetrable (non-specularisable). The young woman is essentially the guardian of the fact that the object *a* is not first and foremost a positive object (*plus phi*), that it is first and foremost an emptiness independent of any withdrawal from any whole, independent of castration. It is this radical *minus phi* that Isis seeks in the imaginary form of Osiris' lost limb. It is this radical *minus phi* that is sought by Teresa of Avila, a "rough fucker" in her search for *jouissance*. It was this radical *minus phi* that Marguerite-Marie Alacoque sought in the graphic form of the Sacred Heart (nothing to do with erotomania, lovers of priests, etc., which could easily be explained by penis envy, Freud's *Penisneid*... although this kind of facile explanation should also be reviewed).

The primordial importance of *minus phi*, this fundamentally empty object *a* that is not the result of deprivation, frustration or castration, is further demonstrated in an English film[9] about the mirror stage in girls and boys. For the little girl, on seeing her sex, there is the nothing, a moment of vertigo, the first nothing (*minus phi*) that has not been preceded by a little something (capturing the ultimate nothing which refers to the non-specularisable character of object *a*). For the little boy, it is quite different; there's the little something (*plus phi*), the little tap, the little penis, problematic because it doesn't compare well with his big brother's or his father's; in addition, this little tap does as it pleases, remaining largely uncontrollable. From this *plus phi*, you can play the game of addition and subtraction and so on. Assumed to come first, it is the male homosexual's game of lose-lose-win.

In the woman, object *a* arises from the first radical nothing. At the same time, it is from this radical *minus phi* that we can and must reread the whole conception of object *a* in general ("yes, four which are impenetrable"). Not only does this *minus phi* radically go beyond the Freudian conception of desire centred on the phallus and castration, but at the same time, it opens up a new way of practising analysis, on the side of the invention promoted by the ethical unconscious rather than on the side of the translation of the unconscious in the knowledge of interpretation. Object *a* is the cause of desire, not as a deterministic cause, but as a cause of creation and invention (object *a* as glimpsed by the woman).

3   What is a vase?

Minus phi, is to talk about the vase. *Plus phi*: the vase is filled with contents, all of which recalls the story of the mustard pot: half-empty, half-full, it depends.

But why put something in the pot? Why mustard, when we could be satisfied with an empty pot, *minus phi*? Lacan's answer follows the movement of the woman: he is interested in the positive object *a* because the woman is also interested in the object *a* as *plus phi*. It is not only silence, not-saying and not-knowing that characterise her, the object *of desire* (and not just the emptiness of jouissance) must also be constituted for her. And this constitution of the object of desire is played out in the woman's speech. "It so happens that women speak. One may regret it, but it's a fact". Is this just primary misogyny? On the contrary, women, in their speech, they *also* participate in the construction of a positivised object *a*, of *plus phi*. One may regret that they do not confine themselves to the main thing, to silence, and to bringing the empty vessel, *minus phi* into play. But it is a fact that must be taken into account: women are not altogether *pas toute* in *jouissance*.

"Women, we are told, are primarily weavers, while men are certainly potters". This would attribute the topology of knots to the woman and the topology of surfaces to the man. But let us leave the weaver and look at the potter. He is the man, the *homo faber*, who certainly positively makes the pot, to put objects into it (not necessarily object *a*!). Fabrication is still seen from the side of the *plus phi*. Yet, it is its emptiness that makes up the soul of the pot, and it is emptiness that enables *homo faber* to become what he is. The emptiness of the vase is essentially feminine, radical nothingness. Naturally, if the woman presents herself as a vase, the man may think that it is to hold within it the object of his desire for her (*Penisneid*) – all part of the man's (and Freud's) phantasy. King Solomon's fourth example, bringing us back to the absence of any trace of the man in the young adolescent, corrects this phantasy. The vase does not contain the man's sex and remains fundamentally empty.

However, this emptiness is rich in the power of invention and creation that it allows. The vase and the uterus may contain an egg, a spermatozoon and maternity, objects bearing witness to what is at stake in *minus phi*, namely the starting point for the invention and creation specific to the unconscious, by whose yardstick all these stories of man and *plus phi* "become slightly redundant".

Therefore, one must distinguish between two opposing ways of conceiving of a vase: according to the masculine model, a vase is a surface, a curved, spherical surface suited to containing the *plus phi*, while, a vase is its void in the signifying process S_1–S_2 (a cross-cap or a projective plane) according to the feminine model. *According to the masculine model*, the vase is for filling, just as girls are for boys; the vase is constructed by the evacuation of the object (castration of *plus phi*) and it asks only to recover what it has lost, to fill itself with the lost phallus. In this sense, the vase presents a simple circular orifice through which the phallus *plus phi* object can enter and exit. *According to the feminine model*, from the point of view of analysis and its unconscious structure in invention and creation, it is the signifying process S_1–S_2 that gives rise to the surface of the cross-cap or projective plane.

However, these two models (masculine and feminine) do not divide vases into two types. They are two ways of comprehending the vase, the hollow, the void, the lack of object that is at stake. They imply two opposing ways of understanding the signifier, of making the unconscious speak and of practising psychoanalysis. And yet these opposing ways are not systematically exclusive. How can we move from one way to the other, from the (primary) feminine model to the masculine model, and *vice versa*?

It is easy to reduce a cross-cap, or more precisely a projective plane, into a vase: it suffices to practise a cut that strictly follows the line of penetration of the cross-cap or projective plane (a double cut in fact, as the scissors cuts the two parts of the surface that interpenetrate). This cut was explicitly mentioned at the end of Lesson 7, as the cut of the self-intersection of the cross-cap: (Figure 7.2).

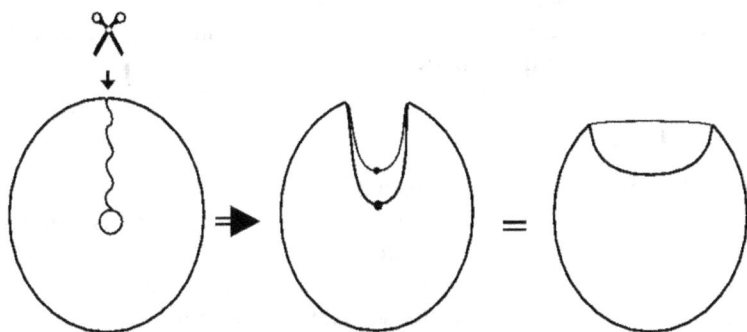

Figure 7.2 The cut of the self-intersection of the cross-cap.

If we simply close the resulting hole, we form a sphere.

But if we join the opposite points of the edge of the vase (which will mean a reversal of the surface), we reform the original cross-cap or projective plane[10]: (Figure 7.3).

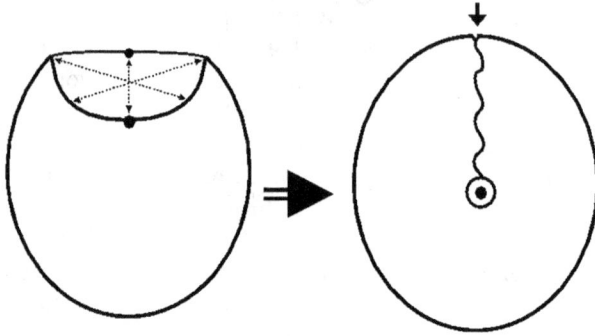

Figure 7.3 Joining the opposite points of the edge of a vase to form a projective plane.

In the masculine view of the spherical vase, object *a* (*plus phi*) is either inside or outside. But what counts is the transformation of the cross-cap into a vase (with the scissors) and of the vase into a cross-cap (by joining the opposite points of the edge of the vase). The cross-cap functions essentially from *minus phi*, in other words around the "central point" of the cross-cap, which is in fact a "point" that is not a point since it is impossible to surround it by a strictly circular (sufficiently small) neighbourhood. This structure of transformation, which implies *plus phi* and *minus phi*, tells us that we will never be done with *plus phi*, even if it is *minus phi* that controls the whole structure (each little piece of the cross-cap can function as a little vase, a little diverticulum of the cross-cap). "Anxiety is not without an object", would allow us think in a masculine way, that we have taken the object in question from the vase. But this object is not what is decanted. It first appears only with the structure of the signifier and *jouissance*, as something completely beyond what we can see, know and master in a spherical logic.

4   Circumcision

Coming to the end of the lesson, the study of circumcision should now show its value, independent of the castration of a so-called primordial phallus (*plus phi*). Let us situate circumcision in the story of Moses.

In *Moses and Monotheism*[11] (1939), Freud puts forward the thesis of an Egyptian Moses, a close disciple of the pharaoh Akhenaten, of the 18th dynasty, priest of the sun god Aten and staunch defender of monotheism as promoted by Akhenaten. After the fall of Akhenaten in the 14th century BC, Moses the Egyptian priest brought the Israelites with him, rescued them from slavery and fled Egypt to re-found monotheism. En route, Moses is assassinated. The Israelites, faithful to Egyptian monotheism, merged at Kadesh with the Midianites, worshippers of Yahweh, the god of volcanoes. This alliance between two peoples is also evoked in the story of Dinah (Genesis 30, 21): Dinah the Israelite can only be given to a man from Shechem on condition that the men of Shechem undergo circumcision.

Circumcision is the foundation of the covenant; it is a very ancient practice, dating back to the tomb of Saqqarah, the tomb of a so-called circumcising physician of the 24th century BC (a millennium before Akhenaten); circumcision is depicted there as being performed with a flint knife: we are in the Neolithic period.

If Lacan insists on the very ancient practice of circumcision and its importance for the alliance between two peoples, it is an attempt to show that it depends on a normalisation of desire and has nothing to do with castration. The prepuce is in no way the substitute for a positivised phallus, which would eventually be subject to castration, it is object *a* that can be said to be engendered by the cut in the interior eight of the cross-cap, it is the central pellet which Lacan calls in an earlier lesson "this little host that I give you" insofar as it is separated *sé-parée* from the barred subject, $.

Circumcision might appear to be a masculine ritual. To show that it is essentially linked to the law and guilt, Lacan cites the episode of Sephora[12], Moses' wife, who circumcised their son. Moses had killed an Egyptian who had hit an Israelite. To punish him for this sin, God attacked Moses and wanted to kill him. Sephora circumcised their son and touched Moses with the bloody foreskin, thus protecting Moses once and for all from God's wrath. This foreskin is the object *a* of law and desire, dependent on the signifying process and not on a prior positivised phallus. It is object *a* that is not dependent on castration and is directly engaged with the question of *jouissance*.

Notes

1 Lesson of 20 March 1963. Chapter XIV of the Seuil edition.

2 Jacques Lacan, *Kant avec Sade*, in *Écrits, The First Complet Edition in English,* translated by B. Fink in collaboration with H. Fink and R. Grigg. New York, W.W. Norton & Company, 2006, pp. 774–775.

3 This field of enjoyment can be read as Samuel Beckett's journey of self-invention. See Marie Iemma-Jejcic, *Le métier d'être homme. Samuel Beckett, l'invention de soi-même*, Louvain-la-Neuve, EME, Lire en psychanalyse, 2021.

4 http://www.jeanallouch.com/pdf/383.

5 Sigmund Freud, *The Standard Edition of the Complete Psychological Works*, Volume 11, translated and edited by James Strachey, London, Hogarth Press, 1957, p. 177ff.

6 Jacques Lacan, "Le séminaire sur le 'lettre volée'" in Seuil (Ed.) *Écrits*, Paris, Seuil, 1975, p. 35.

7 Lesson of 27 March 1963. Chapter XV in the Seuil edition.

8 *Book of Proverbs* (30, 18–19), in *La Bible*, trans. Chouraqui, Paris, Seuil, 1975, p. 1275.

9 Shown at the end of a meeting of the *Societé Psychanalytique de Paris* when Lacan was still a member

10 The Seuil edition and Staferla's website offer here the construction of a Klein bottle, which is not mentioned in the context and which unnecessarily distracts from the much simpler point directly at stake in the seminar.

11 Sigmund Freud, *The Standard Edition of the Complete Psychological Works*, Volume 23, translated and edited by James Strachey, London, Hogarth Press, 1964, p. 7ff.

12 *Exodus*, 4, 25.

Chapter 8

Minus phi and the scopic object

The question of *jouissance* arises before desire; it conditions it. It imposes itself before any bearer of desire. It brings together the unconscious and a certain way of dealing with counter-transference or, more precisely, transference. Women are more directly in tune with the question of *jouissance* (*minus phi*), while men are more deeply involved in questions of desire and castration (*plus phi*). This is why, says Lacan, women analysts can practise analysis with greater freedom, particularly in the transferential relationship. Thus, in the seminar on anxiety, the question of the analyst's desire is approached preferentially from the perspective of women analysts.

If "only love – (love in the transference) – allows jouissance to condescend to desire", shouldn't we say that the question of the "desire of the analyst" becomes in fact the question of jouissance? To arrive at an effect at the level of desire, shouldn't we rather speak of the "*jouissance* of the analyst", and situate ourselves first of all on the basis of *jouissance* through the intermediary of transference love?

At the upper level of jouissance (that of the principle of jouissance), the subject does not exist. The subject analyst has no place. In the expression "the desire of the analyst", it is the analyst himself who must occupy himself with the place where he is *already* engaged, namely with his desire. He will have to question his desire in relation to the upper level of *jouissance* (which engages the pre-subjective question of the unconscious) and not in relation to his personal *jouissance* or his pleasure.

Jouissance is introduced, as a principle, at the first level of the schema of division: how can the subject come to be in the big Other? A mythical question as we have seen, because the subject does not yet exist and the big Other only indicates the field of the signifier. As soon as we situate ourselves from the outset in desire, starting from desire without taking division into account, *jouissance* presents itself in a lowered, degraded form: orgasm, addictions, the *jouissance* of the symptom, even "the *jouissance* of the analyst". These degraded *jouissances* are simply the return of the primordial question of *jouissance*: how can the subject *come* into being in the big Other?

DOI: 10.4324/9781003477822-12

LESSON 17¹: OBJECTALITY AND THE SCOPIC OBJECT

1   The path of the Freudian message is objectality or object *a*

Whatever about *jouissance*, *desire* is the basis, the goal and the aim of the practice and theory of the specifically *Freudian* message. After a trip to Japan and an interruption of the seminar for more than a month, Lacan resumed his questioning from the point of view of desire rather than *jouissance*. Drawing on the Buddhism that had occupied him while there, this questioning of desire was from the perspective of the division of the subject, involving, in particular, the dialectic of anxiety.

One might think that the Freudian message begins at *plus phi* and passes through castration anxiety, itself commanding repression and so on. Right from the start of the lesson, Lacan distances himself from this primacy of *plus phi* and castration, to once again emphasise circumcision, not as a substitute for castration, and clearly on the side of *minus phi* (cf. Moses' *wife*, Sephora, who touches Moses with their son's bloody foreskin to protect him from Yahweh's wrath).

Lacan's underlying thesis is clear: the *path* through which the Freudian message passes is not *plus phi* and castration. The path – we could say the *Tao* – the path along which the Freudian message travels presupposes a *place* (a topology) that is "ultra-subjective". This is not to be understood as engaging with a multitude of characters, but, on the contrary, engaging with the *question of* the subject, i.e. from the first level of division. In other words, the central desire in the Freudian message moves forward without immediately relying on the desire of the subject and the desire of the Other, but to be understood as the pure function of desire, a function purified of particular subjectivations. Desire descends ("condescends") from jouissance via the path of anxiety, via the place where object *a* is formed, the object of all objects, the object that explains *what an object is*.

To follow the Freudian path, according to Lacan, it is therefore crucial to clearly distinguish between the *objectivity of objects* in general and the objectality that focuses on the question of what makes an object an object, *the objectality of the object a* underlying all objects.

The objectivity of objects in general is the point of view of scientific thought and of common thought, which depend on it. It is correlated with logical formalism: with objects fitting into the boxes of formal logic (the universal, particular, affirmative and negative propositions of Apuleius' square).

Objectality – what makes the object an object or the *object a* – is characterised, says Lacan, by the "pathos of the cut". By "pathos", we mean both bodily *suffering* – we are the victims or the aftermath of the cut – and the structural *insistence* of the cut. The "cut" is illuminated here by the critique of logical formalism, which is inherent in the customary objectivity of objects in general.

Lacan associates this logical formalism with Kant's *Critique of Pure Reason*. This association we must critique, not so much for the sake of historical accuracy, but above all because this critique will enable us to better put Lacan's precise argument in relation to objectality and the path of the Freudian message in place. Kant's logic, in the *Critique of Pure Reason*, "transcendental logic", is constructed from the categories of judgement. It is *logical* in the way of formal logic, which formalises its grip on the object through what is at stake in a judgement, a statement, a proposition. Formally, a judgement is characterised by its quantity (quantitatively, the grammatical subject is either universal or particular), by its quality (qualitatively, the judgement is affirmative or negative), by its relation (in the relation, there is a substance which does not move and a change which implies cause and effect), by its modality (modally, the judgement is expressed as a simple possibility or as a reality). Explained in this way, the four categories of quantity, quality, relation and modality are purely *formal*. And if Kant were to confine himself to this exposition of the categories, Lacan would be quite right to equate transcendental logic with logical formalism.

But Kant's transcendental logic is not only logical and formal. It is also *transcendental*, and this is Kant's great innovation in the *Critique of Pure Reason*. As *transcendental*, logic doesn't just fit simple objects into their formal conceptual boxes, it makes the structure of the object, it fabricates what makes the object the object (and this ties in with the question of objectality). Kant constructs a transcendental logic in which it is a question of fabricating the object in its logic, and not simply of placing the object in a certain box of formal logic. This transcendental logic is inherent in every object insofar as every object is constructed in its appearance, as a phenomenon.

For the object to be truly constructed as an object in the phenomenon (for objectality), the two dimensions of each category that occur in formal logic are no longer sufficient. Kant introduces a third dimension into each category, the most important, fundamental dimension for the construction of the object. In the case of *quantity*, for example, the quantity of a judgement is not simply universal or particular but it can also be *singular*. The singular object is made precisely outside purely formal logic; we might add here that it is made in the field of the *pas-tout*, the not-all, that is, not in the all and not in the particular that depends on it. On the side of *quality*, a judgement is not simply affirmative or negative, but it can also be *infinite*, because it establishes a *cut*, a delimitation between a finite domain and an infinite domain; with the judgement "bees are non-humans", I establish a cut between the finite domain of "humans" and the infinite domain of "non-humans". This question of the cut comes up again in this lesson. The category of *relation* cannot be grasped simply on the side of substance (which does not move) and its accidents, or only on the side of cause and its effects (which would explain what moves), because the object itself is made only in a *reciprocal action* in which every object depends on other objects. Finally, on the side of *modality*, the object is not simply possible or real; in its making, it appears as necessary (we would say in the necessity of invention, always in a contingent way, starting from the unconscious).

For each of the four categories, the third dimension (singularity, cut, reciprocal action, necessity) is fundamental each time in distinguishing very clearly between formal logic and Kant's transcendental logic, insofar as the latter takes its objectality, in other words, the making of the object as an object, into account. And this is the way that is required to receive Freud's message.

1.1 Causality in question

Lacan dwells at greater length on the second dimension of the category of relation: the cause, that which would explain any change. It should be noted from the outset that the cause escapes logical formalism. A formal logical demonstration does not address the question of cause. If the demonstration of the Pythagorean theorem leads to the conclusion of what had to be demonstrated (the square of the hypotenuse is equal to the sum of the squares of the other two sides of a right-angled triangle), we can never say that the demonstration is the cause of the result of what had to be demonstrated. Logical reasonings are not causal; they remain purely formal.

However, to get to know, to know something, the function of knowledge always implies the question: what is the cause? Psychotherapeutic practice necessarily asks the question: what is the cause, what is the aetiology of the symptomatology, so that we can apply the appropriate treatment? In psychoanalysis, the search for the cause of the symptom or illness is a poor way to start, particularly because the cause remains in the second dimension of the relationship and avoids the third. Freud was forced to realise the difficulty introduced by the term "cause" and to speak of *causation* rather than cause: the causal schema had to be called into question.

Throughout Western philosophy, the question of cause has been central. Among physicists, Thales of Miletus, for example, believed that the cause of the entire universe was to be found in water. Plato thought he could find the cause of things in ideas, and ultimately in the cause of ideas, the idea of all ideas, *agathon* (the good). For Aristotle, the first cause was hidden in the immobile prime mover that would explain everything. For Leibniz, the cause is affirmed by the principle of sufficient reason: anything that exists must have a sufficient cause. However, as Lacan observes, the cause has always proved insufficient, never determined, never achieved.

Are we finally going to see Lacan appear like Zorro to finally find a sufficient cause, completed in the form of object *a*, the true ultimate cause, which would come to fill in the void of logical formalism? In a certain way, yes: object *a*, cause of desire, is indeed this ultimate cause. But it only exists insofar as it is constituted by the work of the signifier, and not once and for all. The object *a* has to be made and remade. The necessity of doing so is akin to the question in Kant's transcendental logic of the constitution of the object in general (with the help of the third dimensions of each category). Nothing is achieved in waiting and hoping to encounter the *ready-made* object by chance. It must always be constituted anew in our practice by the S_1–S_2 signifying process (interior eight, Moebius strip, cross-cap, object *a*). It can only be produced by starting with an S_1, a signifier full of the imaginary, which is repeated in an S_2, a signifier having lost all imaginary.

The object *a*, constituted by the work of the signifier, is at the same time the authentic support of any function of the cause, what we can know and not know at the same time as what sustains the doing outside of the doing of pure reaction. On the one hand, we have deterministic cause in the order of knowledge – if we know the cause, we know the effect and on the other hand, we have causality that we might call freedom, that is to say, causality of the order of the emergence of the unconscious, which does not respond to deterministic causality, and which corresponds to something of the order of an unconscious doing, of the order of the ethics proper to the unconscious. It must be done and this refers back to the question of the principle of *jouissance*.

2   The body and object *a*

Lacan insists on saying that the object *a*, as the fragment that emerges from the signifying process, is the body: "*desire remains desire of the body of the other*", he says, "*and nothing but that*". That object *a* cannot be grasped by logical formalism is emphasised in the body, in that the body is not an ordinary object that can be secondarily encircled or squeezed into logical boxes – it is *constituted by the signifier*. There has to be an act of production of this body, of this object *a*. This can be heard very clearly and very sensitively in the bodily encounter between the analysand and the analyst. This bodily encounter is not the encounter of two bodies reduced and understood at the level of the banality of physiology or of the body that is materially there; such a reduction rather creates a feeling of unease or inadequacy. The bodily encounter of the analysand-analyst is the encounter at the level of the constitution of something, at the very moment of analysis, through the S_1–S_2 signifier: something happens and is created regarding a signifier, first with a meaning and then with what no longer means anything – thereby allowing an encounter at the level of the body, as invention, as creation. The presence of the analyst does not consist in the analyst being materially present in the same place as the analysand; it consists in a presence that from the outset fabricates something in the understanding of the signifier, with an openness to a replication, an immediate replication that is always there in one form or another. This is what happened in Lacan's practice: he very clearly sought the proximity of the body with his analysands, not for the pleasure of a physiological proximity, but to be precisely in this movement of the constitution of the body and the question of the object *a*.

How can we specify this body and object *a*? Lacan had hoped to find support in a work dealing with the metaphorical use of body parts in Hebrew[2]; work that does not deal at all with either the male sexual organ or the foreskin, but whose metaphorical use is nonetheless obvious. Lacan takes up the question of the body in its *objectality*, as constituting every relationship to any object by way of the signifying process: the body is what *does* something, and we can understand this *doing* broadly enough to include the two sides of the cause, the deterministic cause and the inventive cause, through freedom. On the deterministic side, my arm is supposed to be determined in its movements and actions by my intentions (a supposition called into question in hysteria to be addressed later). On the inventive side of the cause, how the mystic Marguerite Alacoque mobilises the heart, not as a simple affair of the heart as we might say, but the heart as guts *(la tripe)*, the Sacred Heart, as this would count as a real invention of the ethical unconscious.

These two aspects of the cause respond, in different and opposite ways, to the question: what should I do? How does *doing* work? On the one hand, the *doing* of the body functions in a deterministic way (the arm). On the other, the body in its *doing* functions with an inventive edge, with its guts (the Sacred Heart). As for the unnamed parts of the body in Edouard Dhorme's book (the male sexual organ and the foreskin), they are essentially inscribed in a doing, in an act on the side of the freedom of invention of the unconscious. The foreskin, representing the object *a* and *minus phi*, is not a metaphorical substitute for the male sexual organ. It stands for the non-specularisable, unnamed, unnameable, uninterpretable object *a,* and it exists only in relation to the signifying process S_1–S_2; whereby we pass from a possible interpretation, S_1, to a void, a nothing that is no longer interpretable, an S_2, a signifier without meaning. The question of the non-specularisable object concerns the question of this causality of invention, of freedom that imposes itself, and is inscribed in the body as "the causal guts".

We regularly think and talk about the body from an objective medical perspective. Fortunately, some people remind us of its objectality: these are the hysterics, who forget and erase a part of the body, either in an anaesthesia or in a paralysis, indicating that the body implies something quite different from the deterministic mechanism of objectivity. Despite the warnings of the hysterics, we remain suffused by a knowledge modelled on logical formalism, and we remain caught up in the preconceived idea (even in psychoanalysis) according to which knowledge is to know and interpret as much as possible. We still think that if we could arrive at an interpretation of the unconscious in its formations, we could really push forward in analysis.

Lacan radically challenges the objectivity of knowing, seeming as it does to be devoid of all feeling and supposed to be independent of it. But in order to know, we need to know the cause, and the cause completely challenges this assumption. It is precisely the cause that is called into question in the endless series of whys of the child's quest for knowledge. These whys necessarily lead to the impossibility of finding the cause, an impasse that obliges us to step away from pure objectivity. The same applies to the whys of the analysand in search of the cause of his symptoms and of other elements of his history.

The question of the whys and the impossibility of finding the ultimate cause are played out in the structure of the S_1–S_2 signifier. The whys can undoubtedly be answered to a certain extent, and an interpretation then given (according to the first conception of the signifier: the signifier has a meaning), and we encounter things full of meanings (S_1) in the course of an analysis. But at the *same time,* listening as the signifier shuttles between S_1 and S_2, between an S_1 signifier that has a meaning and the same signifier that ultimately has none, these beautiful signifiers may only be screens hiding the void, the radical absence of any meaning (S_2). The shuttle between S_1 and S_2 returns us to the two loops of an interior eight, the back and forth, forming a Moebius strip (which closes in a cross-cap or projective plane).

With the question of cause and of whys, we have plunged knowledge back into the structure of the signifier: in the same way, we have plunged knowledge back into the structure of the cross-cap or projective plane, which is nothing other than the closure of the Moebius strip. On the projective plane, we can practise a double cut around the central point, this cut separating the Moebius strip, S (the unilateral, non-specularisable surface) from the rest, the famous host that Lacan says he gave us, the object a (the bilateral, non-specularisable surface). Such is the structure of the fundamental phantasm (S cut of a), which is not a simple object that can be studied scientifically, but, a making, a way of making the signifier (Figure 8.1).

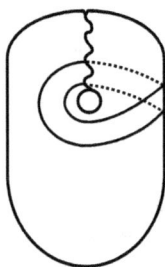

Figure 8.1 A Moebius strip on a projective plane.

The phantasy in its structure, is regularly approached as knowledge that can be reversed and turned around (a child is being beaten, I am beaten, etc.). This structural reversal can be represented as a Moebius strip. With such an understanding, something has disappeared from the structure of the *fundamental phantasy* and this is the object a. Phantasy *as knowledge* implies the aphanisis of the object a and its properly creative and inventive importance.

This creative issue in object a can be seen in the essentialist proof of the existence of God. I have the idea of an infinite God; this idea cannot come from me, who am finite; it comes from an infinite thing, therefore God exists. The proof can be found in Saint Anselm and in Descartes, among others. Kant severely critiqued this proof of God's existence, which, by treating existence as a quality that God cannot lack (since he has all qualities to the maximum degree), moves from a possible existence to an existence affirmed as real. *Wishful thinking*, we would say today to characterise and dismantle the essentialist proof of God's existence: it is not because my *desire* seeks the immeasurable infinite that the infinite exists.

Yet Lacan maintains the truth of this proof of the existence of God, not because of desire, but *because of the mechanism of the signifier* (first at the level of *jouissance*). Everything I can imagine in my finite world is of the order of S_1. If, from this imaginable finite world that is S_1, I withdraw all meaning, then I produce an unimaginable and infinite S_2. Lacan's proof of the existence of God is essentially an example of the S_1–S_2 signifier process: S_1 as a signifier full of meanings, proper to the human or finite being, S_2 as an empty signifier, unrepresentable, outside all signification, proper to the divine and infinite being. Proof corresponds to the structure of the signifier in its creative, inventive form.

Perhaps proof corresponds to desire, but this desire only comes into play here in its creative, inventive force, and depends fundamentally on the formation of the object *a* in the signifying process. The proof of God's existence is therefore a certainty, the certainty of the structure of the S_1–S_2 signifier – and this certainty is the shadow of another certainty: that of anxiety.

God takes shape in the signifying process. In all objectivity, therefore, the existence of God is not founded; it is played out wholly in objectality, in the faith resulting from the signifying process that commands faith accorded to Plato's Good, to Aristotle's immobile motor, to Leibniz's sufficient reason, and so on. The God of the philosophers, whatever it may seem, is not without faith, and commitment to it is undoubtedly not objectively founded. But to again return to the opposition between objectivity and objectality, faith is objectally founded, that is to say, it is founded in a subjective commitment, we could say a holding as true, based on the structure of object *a*, the object of anxiety and invention.

3   The primacy of object *a*

The function of phantasy in knowing is reduced to S and object *a* disappears (aphanisis of the object *a*). What is now the place of object *a*, in function, not of the phantasy as commonly understood, but of the *fundamental* phantasy insofar as it engages the signifying process in a corporal history? The question is one of structure, not in a phenomenological sense, not in the sense of *The Structure of Behaviour* or *The Phenomenology of Perception,* to quote the titles of two works by Merleau-Ponty. It is not an analysis of the intentionality of a subject confronted with an object, or an analysis of the articulation of body and mind (*body-mind*). Nor, says Lacan, is it the transcendental analytic of Kant.[3] Nor is it the signifier as inscribed in a signifying chain. It is the engagement of man, who is certainly born into the signifying chain, but who, from then on, finds himself essentially engaged in the S_1–S_2 process and set in motion again by the opening up of the question of object *a*.

It is on the basis of the signifying process that a part of the body is preferred, *qua* as a part of the body *without* signification; and this gives its full sense to Lacan's emphasis on the foreskin and circumcision. In Shakespeare's tragedy, *The Merchant of Venice,* it is the pound of flesh that the Jewish usurer Shylock, could demand from the said merchant Antonio, should the latter fail to repay his loan on time. Recalling the plot of the tragedy, Bassiano wants to win the beautiful Portia, but not having sufficient money for a dowry, he asks his friend Antonio, the "merchant of Venice", to advance it to him. Antonio, a wealthy merchant, is awaiting the return of his ships, which will bring him lots of money from the New World; in the meantime, he asks Shylock to lend him the sum requested by his friend. Shylock agrees on the express condition that if the debt with interest is not repaid on the due date, he, Shylock, will have the right to extract a "pound of flesh" from the merchant of Venice, anywhere on the merchant's body. Antonio's ships do not arrive on time, and the problem of the unpaid debt takes hold.

This pound of flesh cannot be related to the phallus, to the male sex, to Antonio's *plus phi*. This is not a story about castration. This pound of flesh can be extracted *ad libitum* by Shylock, from *anywhere*; as explicitly stated in the contract, the place from which the pound of flesh will be taken is arbitrary, *without meaning*; simply, it a question of taking it from somewhere in the body, in a way *without meaning*. The opposition between a part of the body *with meaning* and a *meaningless* part of the body, resonates with the debt itself. *Schuld* in German meaning both "fault" and "debt", can be a precise fault (*with meaning*) or an unspecified fault, a fundamental guilt (*without meaning* and without any possible explanation), while debt itself means dowry (for the love of the beautiful Portia) or has no meaning at all: money has neither smell nor colour for Shylock. No coincidence that Shylock is a Jew, because what he demands is not the phallus *plus phi*, but the removal of a meaningless part of the body such as the foreskin *minus phi*, likening the removal of the pound of flesh more to a circumcision than to castration.

By the very fact of its function, the zone of the body is a sacred zone, and what is removed, is an insolvent residue. In the first schema of the division of the subject, this residue appears as what is not divisible in the operation of division of the big Other by the question of the subject (and this remainder *a* is inscribed in the third line of the formula). In the second schema of division, this residue is not just waste, it is a residue that remains, that continues, that persists unconditionally in the unconscious. It is the unconditionality of the unconscious, which persists like a stump without a signified, without meaning, but from which something new can and must emerge, a new trunk. The function of an irreducible remainder survives any reduction, any interpretation of a signifier that would give an imaginary interpretation, an interpretation that would give the meaning of such and such a formation of the unconscious. It is an irreducible function because S_1 and S_2 are more fundamental than the signifying chain itself. With the pound of flesh in "The Merchant of Venice", Lacan presents the Jewish solution to the division of the subject, which brings us to $\bar{A}$ and object *a* (foreskin, minus phi), to the second level of the second schema of the division of the subject, the level of anxiety.

The Christian solution to this division is an attenuation of the crucial question posed throughout the Merchant of Venice. For the Christian, the A is not really barred. The Christian makes himself the object of the *jouissance* of the unbarred Other, of the imaginarised big Other, and what's more, he identifies with the one who made himself the object *a* of God in his anxiety, creating God's anxiety by making himself object *a*. He identifies with Christ for redemption, to save the world, but this is to save things without the possibility of a new trunk springing from the stump, a new invention. In the Christian or the neurotic solution, the subject's desire is modelled on and conforms to the demand of the Other, and he assumes that the demand of the Other will conform to his desire. How do we respond to this false Christian and neurotic solution, to this Western vision, centred on desire, demand, the phallus and castration? Lacan had returned from Japan, where he had encountered Buddhism. Buddhism states straightaway that *desire is an illusion*. This, then, is the way out of the Christian and neurotic solution, a false solution that consists in revolving around desire, in the imaginarisations of the subject and the Other, and the positivity of the object *a* (*plus phi*).

4   Buddhism's challenge to desire: the scopic object

If desire is only an illusion, what can still be or not be? With the question of being the question of the function of truth is also raised. What is the truth of Buddhism?

That desire is only an illusion also means that it has no support, that it has no out-let, that it has no aim. Here we find a strange similarity with Kant's higher faculty of desire, or the unconditional moral law, which is not supported by phenomenal sensibility, which has no outlet prescribed by pleasure, which has no externally determined goal. With these characteristics, Kantian ethics diverges radically from all previous ethics, which were conditioned by the principles of pleasure and reality. It introduces what we might call the "principle of *jouissance*", something essential to the specific functioning of the unconscious: unconditional and impera-tive. In *Beyond the Pleasure Principle* (1920), Freud had already cited the Buddhist *Nirvana*, raised by Barbara Low as a fundamental principle of psychic function-ing, not unrelated to the death drive.[4] Examination of the Buddhist thesis on desire could thus return us to the upper level of the schema of division: to the level of *jouissance*.

What is the truth of Buddhism? To say that desire is an illusion is not so much to reduce it to a pure nothing. It implies the use of negation, as we find in Zen and in the *wou* of *wou wei*, "to not act". Instead of thinking in terms of dualism, of subject and object for example, Buddhism moves in the direction of non-dualism, of *not* assuming the prior substances of subject and object, nor does it promote monism. Firstly, negation simply highlights the fact that we are distancing ourselves from any substance of subject and object: if there appears to be an "object" of your desire, it can be nothing other than something that comes from "yourself". From the "subject", we might think? But that is nothing personal, and the "subject" is just as inadequate as the "object". Far from any substance of a so-called object and subject, we must retain the impersonal it or id: "*Tat tvam asi*" in Hinduism, taken up by Buddhism, means "you are that", "you are somewhere this absolute move-ment prior to you"; this prior movement is the causality of the subject, the object and of everything. But everything remains in this movement: "you are that", and causality is nothing other than a reciprocal action within the subject, the object and the whole of the universe.

"You are that", in this structure of generalised reciprocal action, implies the field of the eye, i.e. the reciprocity of the world (of the vision of the world) and of the gaze on the world. The eye serves as the mirror of the world, and the world is only what is reflected in the mirror. This structure of the world and the eye is prior to anything that might later seem to be inscribed in it as an illusion. The scopic field is there before anything, like the surface of a mirror that reflects nothing, that captures no object, a mirror without any trace.

Solomon may be astonished at the trace of the eagle in the sky, the trace of the snake on the earth, the trace of the boat in the sea. But there is no trace of the man with the young adolescent woman: no phallic trace on the girl will make her become a woman, and the Freudian hypothesis of *Penisneid* and castration leads nowhere. The erasure of the trace is precisely the very definition of the signifier, of S_2: meaning is erased.

If the mirror, which reflects nothing, has value first and foremost because it is "without trace", this is not an ordinary object that we might have before us. It is the eye itself that is a mirror of the world, where the world organises itself in space, not in a given space, but as a questioning of space itself in the reciprocal action between the eye and the world, in reflections, inter-reflections, infinite references between the world and the eye. The eye is a mirror and it is the world: it is the system of reciprocal action that makes it eye and makes it world and mirror. It is to see it as the organisation of all, on which all knowledge depends.

It is what is at stake in the question of knowledge – itself always dependent on how the eye, the mirror and the world are organised. What can I know? Nothing that is not first played out in space and time, says Kant (transcendental aesthetics). Nothing that is not first played out in topology, according to Lacan's questioning of space and time.[5] Like the mirror that reflects nothing, topology is also without trace, purely empty, possibly waiting to be inscribed secondarily. Space-time, the condition of all seeing and all knowledge, is empty in itself. This is the third form of nothing, according to Kant, but it is not a nothing at all, it is the *ens imaginarium*, the absolute empty place, absolute not only in its emptiness, but also in everything that can be inscribed and imagined within it.[6] The topology of the cross-cap (dependent on the signifying process) is empty. It fundamentally presupposes the operation of emptying out the entire imaginary and yet it is something absolute, without which there is no image that can be inscribed. It is the eye-mirror-world that alone allows knowledge. It is the fundamental empty phantasy, which declines the questions posed by the original phantasies which attempt to replace it, such as intra-uterine life for the beginning of everything that happens, the primal scene for the conception of the subject, seduction for the birth of sexuality, castration for the *plus phi* or the *minus phi*.

In resonance with the scopic field, Lacan describes a temple and speaks of the Buddha of Kamakura, then of the Buddha of Nara. Manifestly neither the Kamakura nor the Nara temple Lacan is referring to a temple in Kyoto, the *Sanjusangendo – san ju san* = three ten three = 33 –a long temple with 33 intervals occupied by 1,000 Buddhas in the making, human-sized, which the visitor passes through before finally arriving at the main statue, which is three metres high. "You are that" is addressed as much to the visitor as to the 1,000 Buddhas, who are nothing other than what is at play in the main statue, the very principle of the 1,000 other human statues. This principle is not to be understood as desire, which is merely an illusion, but as that which precedes all substantiality and personification, inscribed as *jouissance* at the upper level of the schema of division. The principal statue, moreover, does not represent an completed Buddha, but a Buddha *in the making*, a bodhisattva, a figure who has not yet succeeded in achieving complete disinterest in the salvation of humanity (the Buddhist school of the mahāyāna, the great medium dedicated to the salvation of all humanity, while the small medium hināyāna is confined strictly to individual salvation and is disinterested in the desire to save humanity). The compassion of the bodhisattva is still caught up in desire (the illusory desire to save), but it still depends on the pure *enjoyment* represented by the completed Buddha, who is disinterested in the salvation of humanity – the bodhisattva's compassion a perfect illustration of Lacan's aphorism: "only love allows jouissance to condescend to desire".

More than a specific bodhisattva, the principle statue represents Kannon, the Japanese translation of Avalokiteshvara, the bodhisattva who embodies the compassion of all Buddhas. All the etymologies given for Avalokiteshvara make reference to the scopic field: "the lord who *sees* in every direction", "the lord of what we *see, of the eye* and of the world", "the one who has a *gaze* of compassion" or "the one who *gazes with his eyes*". Avalokiteshvara clearly identifies the scopic field, which serves as a principle for all those who wish to advance to the state of Buddha. But was Buddha a man or a woman?

In India, Avalokiteshvara was a man. In his passage to China, in Kumarajiva's translation of Buddhism into Chinese, Avalokiteshvara became Kwan Yin, an obviously feminine divinity (a woman raised to the dignity of a true divinity). And in Japan: was Kannon (Kwan Non) male or female? The question resonates between the level of *jouissance*, a domain which is clearly more feminine than masculine, and the level of desire, which is more masculine than feminine. Doesn't the main statue of *Sanjusan-gendo* represent the feminine principle of *jouissance*, while the 1,000 statues we pass on the way before reaching it, represent men (still caught up in the illusion of desire)? But isn't the principal statue not still caught up in the compassion, anxiety and love that lie *between* jouissance and desire, between woman and man? So woman or man? Lacan's guide had never asked himself this question. For Avalokiteshvara, Kwan Yin or Kannon, for all Buddhas, the principle of compassion transcends the bipartition of the sexes. The eye is neither closed nor half-closed: just a thread of the white of the eye and the edge of the pupil indicate the empty structure of *se-paration* (from the Latin *se parere*, to engender) in which every object is generated. It corresponds to the *ens imaginarium*, the space-time of Kantian aesthetics and Lacan's topology.

The eye of the Bodhisattva Kannon is neither object nor subject, it is not any substance. It is the reciprocal action of the eye and the world in the mirror, the *se-paration* from which the thousand statues derive their existence. And all the other forms of object *a* (oral, anal, phallic, vocal) will be illuminated by the separation brought into play with the eye, the blind mirror of the world.

LESSON 18[7]: THE DIALECTIC OF OBJECT *a* IN THE SHADOW OF THE SCOPIC OBJECT

Anxiety – as experienced and as studied in this seminar – has as its function to set us on the path of "reviving the whole dialectic of desire", the path that involves the signifying division and its three levels of *jouissance*, anxiety and desire. It is this division that sheds light on the function of object *a* in relation to desire (object *a* *cause of* desire).

Common parlance speaks of the oral object, the anal object, the phallic object, the scopic object, the vocal object: there are, it seems, five objects. Yet, we have only one question, that of objectality, which is inscribed in the schema of signifying division, more precisely at the level of anxiety. When we are talking about these so-called different objects, we are, in fact, talking only about different ways to approach the question of object *a*: the oral, anal, phallic, scopic or vocal way.

In the previous lesson, desire was denounced as an illusion by Buddhism from the scopic perspective of Buddha's eye. Reviving the dialectic of desire means continuing to question it from every angle. This lesson will focus on the oral and phallic aspects of object *a*.

1   The oral object as amboceptor?

However, psychoanalysts in general regularly fall back on the oral aspect of object *a* to explain what makes an object an object, to explain objectality. The paradigm of the oral object is the amboceptor, and it can be used to understand other aspects of object *a* and reduce them to the properly oral model. The point here is not to set out given facts that could be applied secondarily in the reality of the clinic and in the reduction of the other facets of the object *a*. The point is to distinguish, from the oral model of the amboceptor, the structure of the division that allows the dialectic of desire as a function of *jouissance* and anxiety to be renewed.

In Ehrlich's theory of immunity, the amboceptor is an intermediary capable of reuniting two biochemical elements by means of two specific receptors. In the oral context, the two elements to be brought together are the mother and the child, the amboceptor being the breast, with two receptors, one on the child's side and the other on the mother's side. This amboception can be represented by two overlapping circles (Figure 8.2).

The child and the mother overlap, with the breast cross-referenced between the child and the mother. The breast belongs to the mother and the child. It is a receptor on both sides, an amboceptor. A similar amboception takes place at birth between the child and the mother. But here the amboceptor is the whole of the cord, the envelopes and the placenta. It is a receptor on both the child's and the mother's side.

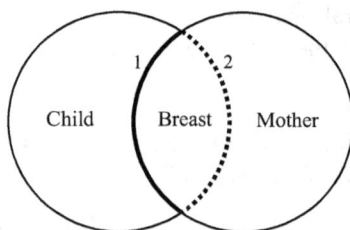

Figure 8.2 The breast as the intersection between child and mother.

It is remarkable that each time (for the breast and the placenta), the cut between the child and the mother is twofold: the non-mother (cut 1) is the child without the breast, and the non-child (cut 2) is the mother without the breast. Note that in both cuts, the breast (vs. the placenta) is negativised: without the breast (as *minus phi*?).

With these two cuts, we can distinguish a point of anxiety and a point of desire. For the oral object, desire is situated between the breast and the child, the child desires the breast, whereas anxiety is situated between the mother and the breast, where anxiety is that the breast might dry up. Desire (desire for the breast) is on the side of the subject (S or the child), while anxiety is on the side of the Other (A or the mother).The cut at birth is twofold in the same fashion: the cut between the child and the cord is the possibility for the child to desire, while the cut between the mother and the placenta, i.e. the delivery, locates the point of anxiety where the fallen object (the placenta) is the continuation of a big Other no longer able to respond to all needs (A̶). But Lacan is drawing on biological considerations to show that the child's relationship to the mother is more primitive than the appearance of the placenta, which is why we will retain the term oral object (rather than "placental object"). In the child's vampiric relationship with the mother, the cut made by the vampire's teeth between the breast and the mother is the point of anxiety. The child vampirises its mother, in other words, deprives her of her substance.

Freud's phrase that "anatomy is destiny" now takes on a whole new meaning. Anatomy is dissection, but it must also be understood as dissection, in other words as *two* different cuts. Why this duality? From where do they come? With the ambo of amboceptor, we initially assumed two quite separate entities, the mother and the child, represented by the two Euler circles. And with their intersection, it was only secondarily that the object *a* appeared. We can measure the abyss separating this conception of object *a* as amboceptor from the conception of the scopic object introduced with Buddhism, as the principle of the primordial *in-between* (before the two): far from being an advance on the previous lesson, the amboceptor remains in the shadow of the scopic object. Instead of having a reciprocal causality that makes the two sides of the in-between spurt out, the conception of the object *a* equal to an amboceptor first posits the subject (S, the child) and the Other (A, the mother) in a face-to-face relationship that is not unrelated to the double torus characteristic of neurosis. In a conception such as this, object *a* does not relate to the question of the fabrication of the object starting from the signifying process. Fundamentally, the problematic of object *a* (objectality) is not even posed, and what we call "object *a*" is easily reduced to an ordinary object, comprehensible in a formalist logic, as testified to by the use of Euler circles.

2   The phallic object

During his exposition of the oral structure of object *a*, Lacan alluded several times to the phallic side of object *a*. For example, the mammary gland of the platypus needs to be stimulated in order to take on consistency; otherwise it remains hollow and empty. The following Aesop's fable is another example of this sliding from the oral object *a* towards the phallic object. Aesop's master had asked him to prepare a meal of the finest dishes; all the courses, from starter to dessert, were recipes for tongue. The guests were disgusted. So, the master asked Aesop to prepare a meal of the worst dishes. More recipes for tongue. The guests were similarly disgusted. Aesop earned a reprieve from his master and acclaim from the guests with the following explanation of his unchanged choice of dish. Because, he explained, *la langue* – the tongue – in its effect, is the best and the worst of things and all will be well, as long as you understand it as the tongue of language, as the object that transcends good and evil, but also see in it a phallic symbol.

The phallic object can also be represented by two Euler circles, within the framework of object *a* as amboceptor. The two presupposed persons here are man and woman, and depending on them, the phallic object *a* is their intersection. This intersection is inscribed from the outset as *minus phi*: man and woman share what they don't have (not the phallus as male sexual organ, but as *minus phi* in its detumescence) (Figure 8.3).

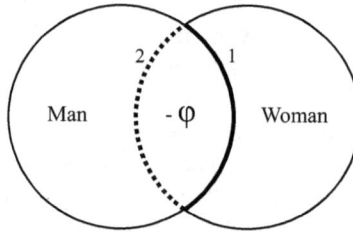

Figure 8.3 Minus phi as the intersection between man and woman.

The first cut (1), specified as non-man, characterises the woman insofar as she escapes all logic on the man's side and the phallic question (she corresponds to what Lacan would later call the *not all* = not the logic that functions according to the formalist model of universals, particulars, affirmatives and negatives). The second cut (2), which is specified as non-woman, characterises man under the impact or the threat of castration, but a castration that concerns the *minus phi*, a castration that would result in man being incapable of loving, more precisely, of giving what he does not have; this is the real point of anxiety. The first cut, the one that systematically cuts itself off from everything that is man, is the opening of desire, insofar as desire must be situated from jouissance (on the woman's side), in a logic other than formal logic, the logic of the engendering of the question of the subject and the question of the object.

For the oral object and the phallic object, we must distinguish between the cut of anxiety and the cut of desire. This distinction is crucial, since the purpose of the seminar is to start from anxiety in order to revivify the dialectic of desire. If we compare the two diagrams for the oral object and for the phallic object and substitute the man (in the second diagram) for the child (in the first diagram) and the woman (in the second diagram) for the mother (in the first diagram), then we can see an inversion of the two cuts: the cut of desire giving way to the cut of anxiety and vice versa (in the two diagrams, the cut of desire is noted as "1" and the cut of anxiety as "2").

The non-coincidence of the point of anxiety and the point of desire indicates the difference between anxiety and desire, but also the two possible and opposing ways of understanding object *a*: on the one hand, the object of desire (the object that is desired) appears as primary (a perspective initiated by the oral object); on the other hand, the object of anxiety (the second level of division) is the *cause of* desire (a perspective advanced with the *minus phi*). The first way that led to the first schema of division (on the side of knowledge and Hegel) is now radically challenged in the previous lesson by the Buddhist doctrine of desire as illusion. This second way leads to the true position of the object *a* as cause of desire and as *minus phi*. At the same time, this second way, at the same time, requires us to free ourselves from any attempt to define the object *a* within a formalist logic... including the spherical perspective of the Euler circles!

This brings us back to the concept of the phallus: *plus phi* or *minus phi*. How should we conceive of the organ that unites man and woman? It is not a hook, in other words it is not an amboceptive organ, and the schema of the intersection of man and woman as *minus phi* remains approximate and insufficient. Certainly, *minus phi* serves as the first lack, the first detumescence, the first detumescence already sketching out the cut. But the fact remains that the schema first presupposes the two primary substances of man and woman, in other words someone, man or woman, who should submit to castration.

Is castration to be understood as the castration that threatens the man who comes in the place of the little child, in the place of the subject? Or is it castration that affects the woman who comes in the place of the mother, in the place of the big Other? In any case, this question of castration remains posed from the two substantified sides of the S and the A: castration of the little boy or castration of the big Other. Everything is played out starting from the supposition of two personifications. The interest in the big Other *insofar as it is secondarily barred* is to insist on the fact that the big Other will never respond, S(Ⱥ). But the question of where to start from remains: from *plus phi* or from *minus phi*?

Starting from *minus phi*, we have to say that castration anxiety concerns detumescence of the organ, not its erection. Now, orgasm refers to detumescence, and it arises in the very line of anxiety, not the anxiety of losing the organ, but the anxiety of letting this *minus phi* slip away. Lacan can therefore say that, of all anxieties, orgasm is the only one that really comes to an end, that comes to an end with the *minus phi* that is really there. It is also from this *minus phi* that we can understand the subject's anxiety at finding himself amputated, castrated, etc.: *minus phi* is already there and the subject is in anxiety about losing its trace.

In contrast to this departure into a primordial *minus phi*, we can now imagine a schema revolving around *plus phi* and corresponding to the schema of the Freudian conception of analysis and the end of analysis (a schema not found in Lacan's seminar). The analysand replaces the child of the oral schema and the analyst is the big Other replacing the mother: (Figure 8.4)

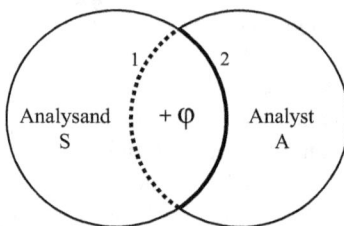

Figure 8.4 Plus phi as the intersection between the subject and the Other.

The patient, whether male or female, reclaims the phallus that we owe him. The phallus is positivised; it is not *minus phi*. We have returned to a properly oral schema – where *plus phi* has the very structure of the oral object, which can be treated spherically, that is, placed inside or outside the circle. The male analysand at the end of analysis does not want the phallus to belong to or to return to the analyst; he has no need of interpretation, good advice or the phallus of the analyst; he cuts off the analyst's phallus to keep it for himself. This is cut "2", which corresponds to the position of the child in the oral schema who vampirises his mother. The female analysand, by contrast, does not have the phallus; it would fall to her to have to desire it indefinitely. It is cut "1" that corresponds to the child's desire in the oral schema. And she does not finish her analysis, waiting indefinitely for her analyst to give her *plus phi*, some good interpretations, good advice, a good ending that would satisfy her completely. These two endings of analysis come up against the rock of castration in two different ways, but each time on the model of the object *a* in its oral form, leaving Freud's conception of the rock of castration in the shadow of its relation to the oral object.

Is it enough to distinguish *plus phi* from *minus phi*? The choice between *plus phi* and *minus phi* is still situated in the binary perspective (typical of the Euler circle and formalist logic). With the aim of calling into question the dialectic of desire, Lesson 17 highlighted what could well serve as another *plus phi*: the scopic object, the eye-mirror, the equivalent of the world. The *ens imaginarium* (topology, space-time) is completely void, and at the same time it can contain the whole universe. This is an absolutely extraordinary power: it is *plus phi*. To maintain such power, man is ready to accept his little castrations, his own little impotences. This is the structure of the neurotic: accepting one's impotence in order to preserve the infinite power of *plus phi* in the big Other.

The scopic object is a valid *plus phi*, the mirror-eye of the world that justifies the jubilation of the mirror stage and narcissism. This is the foundation of transcendental aesthetics, of space; the structure excludes only one thing: the eye, that is, the act that founds it (and this is already the question of doing – what must I do? – specific to the vocal form of object *a*). To sustain this infinite power, the eye is always a *double* organ; as such, it cancels out the mystery of castration – everything that is double refers to what is impossible to castrate.

Buddhism, however, introduces the third eye, starting from desire, a point of ripping away of desire, a zero point, where desire is called into question by anxiety. This zero point, the third eye is no longer an amboceptor; it does not correspond to Euler's schema of two circles. It already indicates the form of object *a* that will be dealt with in the next lesson: the vocal object.

Notes

1 Lesson of 8 May 1963. Chapter XVI in the Seuil edition.
2 Édouard Dhorme (translator of the *Bible* in the Pléiade edition), *L'Emploi métaphorique des noms des parties du corps en hébreux et en akkadien* (1923).
  https://archive.org/details/DhormeEmploiMetaphoriquePartiesCorps/mode/2up
3 We would have to read this analytic carefully before subscribing to Lacan's assertion on this subject. See in particular the remarks made above about the opposition between Kant's formal logic and transcendental logic.
4 Sigmund Freud, "Beyond the Pleasure Principle", in *The Standard Edition of the Complete Psychological Works*, Volume 18, translated and edited by James Strachey,London, Hogarth Press, 1955, p. 3.
5 "Isn't topology what mathematical discourse leads us to, and which requires a revision of Kant's aesthetics" (Jacques Lacan, *L'Étourdit*, in *Écrits*, Paris, Seuil, 1966, p. 472).
6 Immanuel Kant, *Critique of Pure Reason*, London, J.M. Dent, 1993, p. 1011.
7 Lesson of 15 May 1963. Chapter XVII in the Seuil edition.

Part Five

The vocal object

Chapter 9

The central role of the vocal object

The question of desire remains central to psychoanalysis and Seminar X, *Anxiety*, aims at renewing the dialectic of desire. With Freud, it might have seemed that desire was a matter based on persons playing out between individuals prior to desire, or again, between the Subject and the big Other. The dialectic of desire based on the substantiation of the Subject and the Other is fundamentally neurotic and is exposed in the topology of the two entwined toruses. With the *Subversion of the Subject...* (the reversal of a substantial consistency imputed to the subject), Lacan opened up the renewal of the *...Dialectic of Desire*,[1] having already done so by following the path by which the Freudian invention makes its way, the signifying process and the invention of object *a*.

In *Anxiety*, the "dialectic of desire" is made explicit through the signifying process (the second conception of the signifier) with S_1–S_2, where S_1 is a signifier charged with the imaginary and S_2 is the same signifier emptied of all imaginary. This structure of the signifier explains at once the greatest difficulty encountered in the order of knowledge and the greatest restlessness in the order of movement (cf. the nine-box reference table or grid). If the signifier S_1 is emptied of all imaginary, knowledge is reduced to its zero degree, to non-knowledge. The most turbulent movement, the invention of the unconscious, implies death, the death of the imaginary. What unites the zero degree of knowledge and the most turbulent of movements is *anxiety*. It is in this that it does not deceive.

In this dialectic, nothing exists independently of everything else and anxiety appears and is treated only with the help of the neighbouring boxes on the grid, with acting out and *passage à l'acte*. In *passage à l'acte*, not-knowing is at its height, where the most turbulent movement is replaced by a simple reaction, possibly a flight reaction. In acting out, movement remains the most turbulent, but the radical not-knowing is replaced by a questioning that hopes for and seeks an interpretation, particularly on the part of the analyst.

The signifying process, on which *jouissance* depends, is not founded on a consistent and substantial Subject and big Other. These emerge only in the history of the signifier, in the myth invented in the signifying process: how the Subject and the big Other can exist on the basis of the signifier? The position of this first mythical level of the subject's questioning (*subversion of the subject*) is fundamental for the renewal of the *dialectic of desire*, and its crucial point is S_2, the void,

DOI: 10.4324/9781003477822-14

the not-being: it is *jouissance*. It is followed by a second level, that of anxiety, where the non-existent S is replaced by the barred big Other, $\cancel{A}$ (the non-existent Other will not provide the solution, it is non-knowledge at its height) and where the non-existent Other is replaced by object *a* (it is the turbulent movement of invention at its height, inscribed in the signifying process). It is only from the object *a* and its most stirring movement of invention that desire and the completely subverted subject, $\cancel{S}$, can appear: the object is the cause of desire, the third level of the signifying process initiated at the first level of *jouissance*.

The renewal of the dialectic of desire thus passes through object *a*, situated at the level of anxiety and dependent on the level of *jouissance*. Now, in anxiety, object *a* (as the cause of desire) remains outside knowledge in its turbulence and its radicality. It can only be approached from an oral, anal, phallic, scopic or vocal angle. Yet there is always a tendency to reduce it to something, to an object, to an ordinary object. As a phallic object, it is then understood as *plus phi* or as another form of positive object (breast, faeces, eye, voice), each of which can serve as a currency of exchange between a subject and a substantial Other (a return to the neurotic conception of desire). In contrast to this vision of a *plus phi* that would sustain desire between two persons, the entire Seminar insists on the dematerialisation of the phallus, on *minus phi* and on *jouissance*. From the outset, the woman is closer to this *minus phi* and to *jouissance*, whereas the man, encumbered by his *plus phi*, is always already engaged in the problematic of an already constituted desire. The woman as analyst is freer in analytic practice due to her position closer to *jouissance*.

The object *a* is what makes that an object is an object. It then appears as an *ens imaginarium*, the empty place, the space-time where all objects can be inscribed. It is the bilateral correspondence between the eye and the world; the eye that mirrors the world allows us to see and know everything, but at the same time, the most restless movement disappears. With its all-seeing, all-powerful look, the question of the object's constitution in act is dismissed, the signifying process (at the level of *jouissance*) that leads to powerlessness, nothingness, blindness and not-knowing is forgotten. The optical, theoretical perspective (in the etymological sense in which seeing leads to knowledge) results in a disembodying, a sidelining of the body arising in the signifying operation S_1–S_2. This purely optical perspective is an acting out: the "act" side of the signifying process is explained or demands to be explained externally.

Psychoanalysis is not first and foremost a practice of observation, inserted into a scopic field, in a given space and time or topology. It is founded on the ethical unconscious; starting from *jouissance*, the object *a* must be heard in its vocal form, which implies a radical not-knowing.

LESSON 19[2]: THE SHOFAR AND THE PLACE OF THE VOCAL OBJECT

1   The vocal face of object *a* introduced by the shofar

Whatever the multitude and the resonances of the detailed information proposed in Theodor Reik's study of the shofar, his method remains on the side of analogy, which as we have seen remains an insufficient method in approaching anxiety, or again, on the side of a possible cumulative knowledge. This forces us to return again and again to the fundamental key: the S_1–S_2 process at play at the level of *jouissance*.

The shofar is a simple wind instrument (without piston or slide) carved from a ram's horn. Like the bugle, which is used for calling or reminding, it produces only a few tonic harmonics through variations in the tightening of the lips. Four fundamental rhythmic compositions refer to the major differing uses of the instrument. These are the shofars (the "trumpets of Jericho") that trigger the collapse of the walls of the city of Jericho during the conquest of the land of Canaan by the Hebrews.[3]

The shofar is also regularly heard, particularly on the two Jewish festivals of Rosh Hashanah and Yom Kippur, thus giving us an idea of its function and that of the vocal object *a* that it represents. Rosh Hashanah is the New Year feast around November, a new beginning. Yom Kippur, a few days later, is the Day of Atonement, where forgiveness is sought for all offences committed against those close to us. We will return to the new beginning and to guilt with regard to the vocal object *a*.

To speak of the shofar, Lacan draws on two references from Exodus, *before* the handing over the Tablets of the Law or the Ten Commandments (serving as a new beginning), the shofar is heard during Moses' dialogue with Yahweh, amidst a tumult of storm, thunder and lightning and *after* the handover, at the moment when the Hebrew people *see* the smoking mountain and stand far away.[4] It is guilt, on each occasion, that prowls around the edge of Yahweh's voice and in relation to what we can see or know of it (we hear the shofar in the excommunication ceremony, Spinoza's in particular). But what guilt? At this point in the text, Lacan does *not* quote the Ten Commandments: *the shofar is not the voice that articulates the Ten Commandments*. If the shofar is intimately correlated with the moral law and guilt, it is by no means through the intermediary of a given content of the law or of this or that fault (be it incest with the mother or the murder of the father), it is by no means through the biases of the Ten Commandments, still less through other laws or other secondary ordinances and regulations. If object *a* is correlated with the ethics of the unconscious, it is in not through the intermediary of a superego inherited from civilisation's imperatives, social or familial. It depends on the superego that opens onto jouissance ("Jouis!"). In other words, it has its starting point at the level of *jouissance* and not at the level of desire.

The key to understanding what is at stake with the shofar – the key missing from Reik's study – is the new beginning from the perspective of fundamental guilt, the New Year *Rosh Hashanah* from *the* perspective of Atonement *Yom Kippur*. This new beginning is played out in the signifying process, where S_2 the evacuation of all imaginary, the evacuation of all imaginary fault, leaves the void open to invention in *jouissance*. A new beginning originating from the unconscious.

The Jewish festivals were about renewing the covenant with God, a repetition of the covenant. But repetition has two opposing meanings: on the one hand, the indefinite repetition of a past event that occurs x times and continues to occur throughout life, but produces nothing (a sterile repetition, with no new beginning), and, on the other hand the S_1–S_2 repetition, an event that introduces the need to invent a genuine renewal against the background of a guilt or a moral law emptied of all content, a creative repetition, with a new beginning. The repetition at work in analysis should not be the automatic repetition linked to the necessary return of signifiers in the signifying chain that overlap and repeat things already said. True repetition gives meaning to the interrogation carried by the locus of the Other. The meaning of the question (*Che vuoi?*) awakens the memory, the memory of God himself, but of a God who does not respond (in particular, who does not respond with the Tablets of the Law).

2   Two kinds or two faces of the superego

A clear distinction must be made between two types, or rather two ways of understanding the superego. On the one hand, the superego, as it is most often understood, is made up of a multitude of residues of commandments, of more or less strict, stereotyped regulations, which hinder our freedom, awakening the memory of past commandments. On the other hand, the superego is on the side of *issuing* the law: "Jouis!" which sounds like "I hear". It is the superego of the voice of *jouissance* and of the signifying process, freed of all meaning to leave only the hearing *l'ouie*, or even the yes – *oui* – of the movement of invention and creation proper to the unconscious.

Drawing on Conrad Stein's analysis of *Totem and Taboo*, Lacan specifies that it is indeed a question of the signifier, neither solely nor principally a signifier articulated in the signifying chain, but a *vocalised* signifier. This means that the signifier in question is not first inscribed in a system of linguistic oppositions, of possible metaphors and metonymies that open the door to interpretation; it moves forward with a new dimension, the *vocal* dimension. Lacan says: it is the "*emissive*" dimension of emission. Unfortunately, the Seuil edition uses the word "emissible" instead of "emissive", which suggests that a prior subject would already have the meaning of commandments that could possibly be emitted, or vocalised (the first conception of the signifier). This is the opposite of the emphasis on the purely emissive dimension of the S_1–S_2 signifying process or the second conception of the signifier. For the very reason of the primacy of the signifying process compared to any conception of a prior subject which would express a meaning, Lacan has reservations about what Conrad Stein advances in his text as the "act" implied in this primordial signifier. Act presupposes a primordial subject, whereas the vocal object *a* must be understood as *without a subject*, before the subject. The vocal object *a is* just the emission, without intention, without meaning, without a prior subject.

The pure emissivity of the signifier is further illustrated in the sacrifice of Isaac. God commanded Abraham to sacrifice his son Isaac, clearly not a question of sacrificing any old thing but of sacrificing the flesh of his flesh. With Isaac, the entire imaginary world, *without exception,* must be sacrificed. This carries the imperative to abandon everything, including what was richest in imagination, his own son. But it is still too little, still too imaginary, this sacrifice: at the last minute, the angel of God stays Abraham's hand, the one carrying the knife, ready to slit Isaac's throat. And Isaac is replaced by a ram, the ram that cries out in the ram's horn that is the shofar. For the shofar is not simply a bugle intended to transmit orders. It is the pure voice, the superego *without content*, purified of all imaginary, that opens *jouissance*: *Jouis! J'ouïs. Oui.*

Where can we find the voice? It can certainly be found in the voice of conscience or in the hallucinatory voice. But such clinical and phenomenological data on the vocal object are nothing more than waste: the dead leaves of the voice. Such references as those of conscience or psychosis only reveal the waste products of the vocal object *a*, the decay or degraded forms of the voice. The voices in psychosis and the voices of the conscience of the obsessional superego represent the voice only secondarily and will not help us to understand the vocal object proper. Conversely, it is the object *a* in its radical, properly vocal aspect that can illuminate practice and know-how in the encounter with these dead leaves that are the voices of psychosis and consciousness. It is the vocal object *a* that will show the way to setting ourselves in motion in what appears to be all signposted in the scopic field.

3   Space and the eye put in question by the vocal face of object *a*

A whole series of ideas, schemata and ways of thinking and practising in psychoanalysis imply their own given space and the eye that situates them in their space. Thus, we speak of field, place, role, of cases and the case, of theories, topography, topology and so on. Each time, space is implicated at the same time as the eye that situates them in these pieces of space. It is precisely all of this that needs to be called into question by means of the vocal object, precisely what is at stake with the voice.

Space is generally understood as the space of objectivity, as a space given as a framework in which the various objects of the external world and, by extension, all the objects at play in the psychical world are naturally placed. We are in *objectivity*. This approach to space will not enable us to renew the dialectic of desire at play in psychoanalysis. It is not verifiable objectivity advancing into the field of the representable that is at play in the unconscious, but *objectality*, in other words, the object, always in its relation to desire and dependent on the unconscious. The relation of the object to desire does not consist in seeing the object as an ordinary object targeted by a tendency that we would call desire (which would only be a mode of objectivity). The relation itself must reveal "object" and "desire" in their genesis from the relation made explicit by the schema of division: jouissance – anxiety – desire. The space in question in psychoanalysis is therefore not space as commonly understood, but the space from which the object and desire emerge.

Let us specify here that when Lacan says that this space is not the space of "transcendental aesthetics", in reducing Kant's space to ordinary space (in the order of objectivity), he completely underestimates Kant's transcendental aesthetics, where, rather, the questioning of space (the metaphysical exposition of space) and the questioning of the object (the whole *Critique of Pure Reason*) are explicitly presupposed by Kant. It can be shown that Kant's transcendental aesthetic in his metaphysical exposition corresponds strictly to Lacan's schema L.[5] Moreover, the latter exactly situates topology as a revision of Kantian aesthetics.[6]

The questioning of space starts with common, ordinary space. As such, ordinary space is objectively empty: it is "an empty intuition without an object" or "*ens imaginarium*", which serves for Kant as the third form of nothing.[7] With the all-seeing omniscience of the eye mirror of the world, the scopic point of view and a certain way of seeing the "scopic object" (within the framework of common, unquestioned space) systematically avoid object *a* in its vocal aspect, in its objectality. Ordinary space is thus separated not only from the ordinary object in the perspective of objectivity, but the very questioning of space in the perspective of objectality is separated from the real question of object *a*, which remains elided in the scopic perspective. Desire, seeking its support unencumbered by anxiety, takes advantage of this space where object *a* appears in its scopic form, and relies on phantasy insofar as it is primarily visual. What is thus elided by phantasy and its visual forms is what would lead to the vocal object *a* and the anxiety it implies.

Space in principle is, for its part completely homogeneous, nothing is apparently separate from space, everything is in space. However, space is not outside of sensibility. Even if it frames knowledge, absolute knowledge, the subject supposed to know, space is not an idea (not an idea of reason such as the world, the soul, God). Space essentially has to do with the body, not the mind.

What is the relationship of space with the body? Lacan says that the eye as body is attached to space. The Seuil version, however, says that it is space that is attached to the eye. This latter version may have some truth to it, because everything depends on object *a*, which is primary, but it is not object *a* as eye, it is object *a* in its *already vocal* dimension that is primary. So let us return to the "the eye is attached to space" version, which consists in locating the eye in space, as is done for no matter which body.

When physicists talk about a body in space, they represent it as a point. This body is not an individual, this body is impenetrably reduced to an unbreakable point. Starting with the scopic field and the scopic object, Lacan touches on the second antinomy of quality: is the world infinitely indivisible or not? In other words, can one always cut off indefinitely any part of the world, or is it made up of atoms, an atom being indivisible? Lacan seems to answer as follows: yes, there is an unbreakable, indivisible unit, an atom, and it is object *a*.

Yet space itself is only of interest in supposing a sectioning, in supposing that it can always be cut. Despite the appearance of the supposedly undividable point that would be object *a*, space is always homogeneous, and it can always be cut. We see this in discursive practice, which is the only way of approaching object *a* with its different aspects, and in handling topology, where each point can be split in two to reveal two points (as resulting from reciprocal action, from the primordial in-between). Contrary to the purely physical optics, in a manner of speaking, of the object represented by a point, in our practice, every point is and must always be called into question; there is no feasible "point of focus", because the point always diffracts into two. There are no points that are fixed once and for all as realities, either in our clinical practice or in our conceptual practice. The "point" will therefore be schematised by a multiplicity of approaches Real, Symbolic and Imaginary approaches, like a triple spiral or *triskel*. Or again, the "point" that interests us in the topology of surfaces can only be circumscribed by an interior figure of eight, this being the central "point" of the cross-cap.

4   Questioning knowledge in the scopic field

The specular image, noted as i(a) and characteristic of the mirror stage, opens the field and virtual space of the ego and for the ego. This opening of the field and virtual space provokes a feeling of power, even of omnipotence, which is the source of the jubilation characteristic of the mirror stage, as well as the jubilation in front of the opening of knowledge, insofar as it searches for the right shapes in the visual field.

In this space – and I do mean space – constituted by the specular image, let us introduce a stain, a fly, an anomaly, a grain of sand, a beauty spot. We could return to Lacan's account of his excursion on a small boat with a Breton fisherman, where a small sardine can floating on the ocean glistens in the visual space, making a mark. With this object (valid as object *a* in its scopic dimension determined by the initial area), seeing the space itself is called into question. It is no longer Lacan's eye that looks and mirrors the world, it is the glistening sardine can that looks at him and challenges him, via the voice of the fisherman: "you see that little can, it doesn't see you, it's not in the order of vision, but it looks at you", in other words, it completely calls into question the visual field and the field of knowledge (proper to the eye that mirrors the world).

The field of knowledge or of scopic space is found in Jeremy Bentham's *panopticon* where a certain architectural layout lends itself at all times, to monitoring, disciplining and managing the conduct of prisoners. Whether this scopic space (panopticon) is set up in a penitentiary or in any other surveillance system, it makes it possible to see, compare, educate, direct and manipulate people and crowds based on something that is entirely of the order of seeing and knowing (panopticon). Such a scopic space is called into question by the tattoo, by the stain, which itself is blind. Because it lies outside this space of seeing and knowing, "there is nothing more blind than a stain". It is by refusing this panopticon that the scopic object *a* ("gaze") can open onto something that is outside of seeing, outside of knowledge and of understanding.

But the stain, the gaze, the sardine can are *exceptions* in the field of vision, whereas, in desire grasped from the scopic side, that is, from the side of seeing, of knowledge (and of the phantasy), the object *a* is systematically elided. With this elision, anxiety remains masked, as if nothing were missing. If we remain in this field of vision that dominates everything, we will only grasp semblances, appearances, *dummies*, mannequins, puppets, fake objects that satisfy a primary need (which is nothing other than the avoidance of anxiety). Everything is appearance. Everything is a phenomenon; there is no object in itself, Kant would say. Everything is inscribed in pure intuition, in this space without remainder. There is no anxiety

Everything changes from the moment the gaze (object *a* for whoever is under that gaze) of a voyeur appears. The voyeur's eye is not an object *a* for him; it is nothing more than the mirror eye of the world, the supposed panopticon, and the voyeur is not in principle anxious, except when he is surprised by someone else who serves as a gaze (an object *a* for him). Then he is anxious. From being omnipotent as a voyeur, he comes to be seen, really seen: he is impotent. With this voyeur who is now the one seen, desire (voyeur) is opposed to anxiety: the desire of the voyeur who believes he can see and know everything and master everything in his phantasy is opposed to the anxiety of the one who is seen who experiences something that goes completely beyond what he imagined himself to be on the side of phantasy, of seeing and knowing. But in the scopic field, apart from the exceptional irruption of the gaze, the point of anxiety remains covered by the point of desire, and we remain in a field of appearance, phenomenon and knowledge. The relation of desire to anxiety is presented as masked in the phantasy, the ordinary phantasy on which desire is based when it remains caught in the scopic space. Such a phantasy is an illusion as far as the real questioning of the structure of desire is concerned: it gives an appearance (phenomenon) of knowledge.

It is to overcome this lure that the vocal aspect of the object *a* is fundamental. Seen from the point of view of the phantasy that supports it imaginarily, the structure of desire is necessarily missed, and the point of anxiety hides behind the point of desire. This coincidence is unmasked in the voice, where the place of anxiety is primordial. The renewal of the dialectic of desire necessarily passes by way of anxiety, maximal anxiety, as it is represented both in the nine-square grid (ISA) and at the median level of the schema of division (between *jouissance* and desire).

As long we start from desire – presented in its scopic form, supported by phantasy and structured around the mother's desire as primordial desire – we remain in the realm of vaudeville, where the murder of the father would be no more than an avatar of this (scopic) desire, to use an expression of Conrad Stein's referenced by Lacan. We cannot begin from the question of desire, as if it were something we can see and know. The starting point, the origin, is the murder of the father as it underpins the signifying process and the schema of division, where *jouissance* and not desire, is primordial. The question of the father's *jouissance* must be seen starting from the signifying process rather than from the mythical *jouissance* of the father of the primitive horde, even if the latter imagines the former. How can a subject emerge in the signifying process? As is reflected in the myth, how can the sons become subjects? They can only do so by bringing the big Other into play, but by barring it: the murder of the father is the murder of the imaginary in the passage from S_1 to S_2.

Here is the fundamental starting point of the seminar, the key to the seminar. It is also the key that renews psychoanalytic practice by revising the dialectic of desire. From the murder of the father onwards, the shofar is equivalent to the bellowing of the bull or of the ram with its throat cut. Original desire is not desire for the mother as object (object a is not the object targeted by desire). It is the desire made explicit by the murder of the father, the radical bar on the big Other, or the bar on any imaginary interpretation of S_1. This big Other barred ($\bar{A}$) is thus situated at the level of anxiety and must be preceded by the level of jouissance, the first line of the division of the subject and of the principle of *jouissance* already implying the "*nihil negativum*", object a in its vocal form.

LESSON 20[8]: TEACHING AND *MINUS PHI* (MORE ABOUT THE VOCAL OBJECT *a*)

If knowledge is so radically called into question with the vocal object a, is there still a place for teaching in the field of psychoanalysis and of the dialectic of desire?

1   Teaching and pedagogy

Any discipline and any field of enquiry offer different levels of understanding, starting with a common understanding and moving on to more elaborate levels of elucidation. In physics, for example, we moved from a pre-Copernican cosmology to a Copernican elucidation of the world, then on to Einstein's system of relativity. To move from Copernicus's system to Einstein's system requires a certain effort and eventually some teaching. For a mind sufficiently developed and open to mathematics, the transition from one system to the other is relatively easy, provided it is properly explained. Einsteinian equations are certainly more complicated, but anyone who follows the explanation properly will quickly see and understand how Einsteinian equations include Copernican equations as particular cases in their system. In short, there is a teaching of Einsteinian physics.

The same applies to psychoanalysis. A preliminary understanding of all psychical phenomena was first imposed, obeying the pleasure principle. Then psychoanalysis was renewed with Freud's introduction of the death drive and of enjoyment *Beyond the Pleasure Principle*. The elucidation of desire is central every time and is the object of psychoanalysis. With *The Subversion of the Subject and the Dialectic of Desire*, Lacan introduces a new dialectic of desire (in contrast to *Wunsch*, the Freudian wish), in which we can grasp Freudian psychoanalysis as a particular case of this dialectic (where the line of *jouissance* is avoided). The seminar on *Identification* introduces yet another reworking within Lacanian thought itself; it operates the passage from a theory of neurosis, represented by the two intertwined toruses, centred on the signifying chain (the first conception of the signifier) to the signifying process $(S_1–S_2)$ from which a new psychoanalytic practice emerges, according to the structure of the fundamental phantasy represented by the cross-cap.

The topology of the cross-cap is certainly more complicated than the topology of the two toruses, but the two toruses are part of the furniture, a specific part of the theory of the cross-cap. The seminar on *Anxiety* makes the transition from a Freudian theory of desire centred on the phallus *plus phi* to a new theory centred on *minus phi* and dependent on *jouissance*: Freudian desire thus appears to be no more than a particular case of the general schema of the signifying division with its three levels of *jouissance*, anxiety and desire.

To move from one system of physical science to another, to move from one dialectic of desire to another in psychoanalysis, results in resistance and requires an effort each time. To take the step, a teaching is required at the same time as its pedagogical method, not only to teach others, but above all to teach oneself. For a transmission integral to the passage or the way in question, each one has to do and re-do the work themselves over and over again; this is the sense of the matheme: "I can, I want to, I have to do it myself". That is what teaching is and to clarify his own teaching method, Lacan is going to critique two pedagogies, Stern's and Piaget's.

Stern's method[9] consists in letting the child do its own thing, letting him follow his own interests at his own pace, when and how he wants: he will move forward on his own at the right moment. It is a method that genetically follows the child's development in his own becoming; this method appears as an extreme simplification of the matheme: *I do it myself*, where the modalities of desire (*I can, I want to, I have to*) are erased behind what actually happens. Unlike Stern's method, Piaget's method takes account of the fact that this development does not come about without obstacles: there is a fault, a gap, a hole between childish thinking and the scientific path that only the adult can follow. Students and children cannot learn just anything at any age. Such a method is still genetically conceived, but we have to take into account and wait for the right moment, and not short-circuit the student's real possibilities. Whether we follow Stern's or Piaget's conception, the method consists in following the movement, allowing that the fruitfulness of the teaching itself is reduced to almost zero where it is enough to follow the child's general development (possibly taking into account the impossibilities of learning such and such a thing according to his age). Basically, there is no teaching in these two support methods.

Lacan replies: "But, teaching exists". Where is the teaching of psychoanalysis? Where is the teaching of the reading of the psychoanalytic cure? The teaching of psychoanalysis – particularly by Lacan – does not consist in providing references; the new elements introduced by Lacan from his knowledge of Chinese, from mathematics, from Saussure, from logic, from philosophers, etc. doesn't in any way constitute the core of Lacan's teaching. What makes his teaching is the discourse insofar as it introduces and imposes what makes it possible to move forward, to take the step from one position of knowledge to another more powerful position of knowledge (from the Copernican system to the Einsteinian system, from one conception of the signifier to another, etc.). And this step (which implies the modalities of desire: power, duty, will) can each time have real effects of opening, even of unleashing.

But how do we measure the possibility, necessity and willingness to take this step? We can start from the idea that access to certain things, to certain concepts, would not be possible before puberty. Whatever the truth of this assertion, we must recognise that adolescence is the age when everything is called into question, and it is this questioning that makes it possible to take a step that might not have been possible beforehand. But why does this step become possible?

Or again, how can we understand the step of adolescence? Or, how can we understand the function of relaunching inherent in the phallus? It is not at all situated in the positivity of the phallus, but in *minus phi*, which opens access to the dynamic of object *a* – Lacan's only invention – from where the effect of opening and unleashing its advances for psychoanalysis can be situated. Lesson 20 logically continues with the phallic function as *minus phi*, then secondarily with the question of orgasm, which Lacan had linked to anxiety, and finally with anxiety insofar as it always occurs in the place where *minus phi* should be, but might not be, in play.

2   The phallic function as *minus phi*

The phallic function as *minus phi* would be the key to opening up pedagogy a little more, with object *a* as *minus phi* making it possible to situate castration anxiety.

Yet, it is the phallus as *plus phi* that is regularly invoked, particularly in relation to object *a* where we compare the breast to an erect phallus, or note the similarity between faeces and the phallus, and see a phallic omnipotence in the all-seeing eye. Freud's interpretation of the end of the treatment is played out precisely in terms of the positivised phallus, with both sexes stumbling over the rock of castration: the man wanting to keep his positivised phallus, i.e. his power, his ability to manage on his own, without the intervention of the analyst; the woman waiting indefinitely for the same positivised phallus in the form of the gift, the right interpretation from the analyst that would fulfil her.

To grasp *minus phi*, which is fundamental to the conception of object *a,* it is absolutely not enough to start from the positivised phallus and to secondarily deny it by means of subtraction: "there is the phallus, and I don't have it". This so-called castration is completely accepted by the neurotic: "I don't have all the possibilities, and I accept this willingly". This essentially masculine and neurotic position does not pose a problem for him, as long as the Other is not castrated.

An analysand tells me the following dream: "I'm not castrated". Her associations make it immediately clear that this not to infer that she has a positivised phallus; she has a perfectly normal female body, nothing has changed in it. With this dream, one can infer that she does not fit into the Freudian conception of a woman as essentially castrated. The dream states: "I do not subscribe to the conception that assumes the primacy of a positivised phallus". Like the dream of the Butcher's Beautiful Wife (which contradicted Freud's thesis that every dream is the fulfilment of a wish), this dream contradicts Freud's theory of positivised desire as a function of a phallus *plus phi*. The dream of the Beautiful Butcher's Wife contradicts Freud's positivised desire, of positivised desire as the essence of all dreams.

These dreams reflect the passage from a first level of understanding to another level, more complex to be sure, but understanding the first level as a particular case or instance. Starting with *minus phi* we must then see how *plus phi* will interfere and provoke the question of anxiety, the question becoming one of discerning at the very heart of what presents itself as *plus phi*, the more fundamental and hidden thing that is *minus phi*. Starting with the visual field, the eye mirror of the world sees, knows and masters the whole universe. It presents itself as *plus phi*, where phantasy (in its visual dimension) structures our whole relationship with the world, phantasy therefore going hand in hand with the phallus. In the phantasy of the primal scene, it is the visual that is at stake, the *question* of the phallus is everywhere, but everywhere it is retracted, not seen, disappearing, assumed. This is also what is at play in the phallic phase: the little boy does have a little thingamy, but in the end, it doesn't measure up to the big brother's or the father's and everything else we might expect from them. And the little girl may have something too, but it's so small, it's not much in any case.

In the Wolfman's dream, the window opens: the window of the phantasy, as we have already seen, serves to frame anxiety. The window opens and the phallus is there everywhere: in the catatonia of the tree, in the alert wolves, in the fur of their tails, and so on. But it is only there in a retracted form: not *plus phi*, but *minus phi* which is played out in the place of *jouissance*, to be understood as the place where it is shouted out (that is, from where the voice comes from) that the universe (the universe, the eye, mirror of the world) is a flaw in the purity of non-being (in the purity of the void, of S_2).[10] The positive phallic being is supposed to articulate the universe (the eye, mirror of the world), but it is a defect, it is a particular case in the purity of non-being, in the *minus phi*.

Jouissance is the basis on which the anxiety provoked in the dream of the Wolf Man can be understood. In the analysis of the Rat Man, Freud himself noted the patient's *jouissance* as he recounted the rat torture in his analysis. In any case, we would need to understand *jouissance* not in terms of *plus phi*, but in terms of *minus phi*, even if *jouissance* can pass rapidly to another level, as in the case of the Wolfman, as Freud infers: at the moment of the primal scene (of *jouissance* and anxiety), the little Wolfman would have immediately defaecated; a hypothesis supported by his anal symptomatology following the dream. The symptom is necessary and replaces anxiety. Referring to the grid of anxiety, the anxiety that was there with the maximal difficulty of knowing (not-knowing) at the very place of the essential setting of things in motion (birth and death, conception, emergence of a new life) is replaced by the positivised symbolic: a possible knowledge, where anxiety is reduced to the acting out of defaecation, a movement of reaction to an external event where the anal resonates with scopic. The Wolfman, plunged into maximal anxiety dependent on *jouissance* and the *minus phi* inherent in the primal scene, moves on to the symptom that combines acting out and *passage à l'acte*. *Passage à l'acte*, as seen from the side of the phenomenon of the symptom, appears at the junction of emotion and embarrassment, where, in the instance of an anal *passage à l'acte*, cf. the Wolfman's obsessional neurosis, the moralising assumption specific to the anal stage can be built. But at the same time, an acting out persists as seen from the fundamental side of the symptom where the question of birth and death is maintained and movement in its radicality and maximum creative vigour remains underlying. Acting out persists, even if reduced to the level of obsessional knowledge and morality where the ferocious face of the superego hides its inventive, "enjoy" ["*jouis*"] face. Instead of having the pure handling of the moral law that implicates pure vocal emission, the vocal object *a* represented by the shofar, it is a "moralising assumption" that is required, a law distributed in different rites, in different commandments that require observance.

3 Approaches to *jouissance* and the drive

By presenting the orgasm in the sexual act as the equivalent of anxiety, Lacan was at the same time assuming that the sexual act was the only relation "that does not deceive", that it "is not without object", and so on. At the same time, the formulation of this equivalence raised three types of question: (1) in the orgasm, is it the same *jouissance* that is at stake as in the sense explained above? (2) rather than being the equivalent of anxiety, shouldn't we say that the orgasm covers anxiety and makes it disappear and (3) what about orgasm and *jouissance* in women?

(1) The satisfaction of orgasm is not played out at the level of *jouissance*, as defined in the seminar on Anxiety; it is not at play at the properly mythical level of *jouissance as a principle*, something never properly materialised in itself. (2) In order to deal with the question of the possible covering over of anxiety by the orgasm, we have to take note of the fact that the orgasm is not very satisfying anyway; it does not bring absolute satisfaction. If the orgasm masks anxiety, it can only do so very partially. (3) The question of the orgasm is not played out at the same level in men and women. In the schema of division, for women, the question is played out at the level of *jouissance*, starting from *minus phi*, whereas for men it is played out at the level of desire, starting from *plus phi*. At all costs, consideration of the phallic function changes completely.

At the oral level, the drive can still be explained by need and demand: it is demanded that the need be satisfied, and with satisfaction, there is no longer any need. At the phallic level (Lacan says "genital") – the most primitive level of the drive – the drive must be understood as the relationship between desire and demand. And above all, desire must not be lowered to the level of need (which does not come into play in the schema of division). Desire can be understood in terms of the phantasy (with emphasis on the scopic that characterises it), as this is inscribed in the graph of desire on the intermediate line between the upper line of *jouissance* and the barred big Other and the lower line of the signifier and the response to the message. This is the neurotic position of desire. But this is not enough. We can – and must – also understand it in the renewal of the dialectic of desire starting from *jouissance* and in the formula of the drive inscribed on the upper line as an articulation of the subject $\mathcal{S}$ and the demand D arising from the side of the big Other: $\mathcal{S} \lozenge D$.

What is the demand involved in the drive, $S \lozenge D$? The most primitive drive is sexual and is played out at the phallic level, again as understood from *minus phi*. But who is asking? What is being asked? Who is being asked? To answer these three questions, we can *first of all* set aside an almost inevitable presupposition (which will shed light on the first and third questions) and *secondly,* highlight a biological correlation (which will shed light on the second question). *Firstly,* we need to set aside the presupposition of *individuals* preceding the phallic function and the sexual question. The sexual relation fundamentally transcends individuals. We don't firstly have two individuals who then have sexual relations. What first arises is a sexual relation, which is eventually played out between two individuals. We could say: "there is no sexual relation" between two given individuals. The two questions "who is asking?" and "of whom?" remain unanswered by the drive itself. *Secondly,* "What is being asked?" is clarified by the clear biological correlation between bisexuality and the death of the individual. Of the question of the individual? Sexuality proper only appears with the death of the individual, of individuality. Again, in no case can we assume that the individual or individuality are primary.

It is not only the presupposition of individuality that is discarded, it is also death that is advanced. What is being demanded is death, the "little death", including, as Lacan says, to die laughing, to laugh at all the explanatory expectations that collapse and fall away. That is what is called making love: starting from the collapse of all attempts at explaining, to die laughing – it is a sense of comedy.

4   Anxiety: object *a* and the barred big Other

Who demands? We could say: the big Other. But only insofar as it is barred ($\cancel{A}$), insofar as it implies the development of the question of *jouissance* with anxiety. From then on, desire changes meaning: it can no longer be the desire of the subject, but the desire of the barred subject S, in its dependence on anxiety.

Anxiety asserts itself in all its vigour where the structure of *jouissance* – anxiety – desire is interrupted, as in coitus interruptus where the sexual act is short-circuited. Here, the question of the drive and the demand of the Other implied in the drive (the precedence of the drive over the actors and the demand for death) are reduced to a purely physiological and mechanical problem. In the first Freudian theory, anxiety is nothing other than the automatic conversion of accumulated libido with no way out, arising par excellence following the practice of coitus interruptus. Anxiety would thus be the automatic transformation of a libidinal biochemical substance. Yet anxiety is not correlated with the absence of ejaculation. But the first Freudian theory of anxiety duplicates and covers up the short-circuit that consists in erasing the sexual relation and the question of *jouissance* and drive, reducing it to a biochemical mechanism. Might we say that this first theory of anxiety is itself the cause of anxiety?

As we have just seen, anxiety appears as a structural insistence in response to the forgetting or setting aside of this same structure that depends on the level of jouissance and with it the drive. It insists by displaying both object *a* and the big Other barred Ⱥ, which is why it does not deceive, insisting as it does at the very place where something comes to block the inventive power of object *a* and of the fundamental non-knowledge of Ⱥ. Anxiety is thus anxiety of death, little death, fear of dying, etc., in the field of the death drive, understood as the possible renewal of life. It arises in response to the closing over of this field.

In Freud's second theory, anxiety was conceived of as the signal of a threat to the "status of the defended *I*" where the "I", the "subject" defended itself with the five classic objects that protect it: the breast, the relationship with the other and his demand, the phallus, recognition of the other (how one is seen), the social demands of the superego. These are the five possible losses that threaten the subject in the chronological succession of the child's development: loss of the oral object, loss of the anal object, loss of the phallic object, loss of the scopic object and loss of the vocal object. In this Freudian schema, we find traces of Lacan's five forms of the object *a*. But each time, the possible loss is played out only through a *positivisation of* the object *a*, through *plus phi*. Anxiety, then, always relates to the "underneath" of this "well-defended I" by means of one or other of these positivised objects. It affirms a and A and depends on the *jouissance* that goes beyond our limits and implies the real of *jouissance*, non-being and the Nirvana principle.

The positivised object, the organ, *plus phi* does not take us very far in the field of the call of *jouissance*. It gives up prematurely. Genital consummation is generally not very brilliant and the positivised phallus is quickly reduced to a small rag, a token of tenderness perhaps? But if we let go of the ideal of genital fulfilment with the positivation of the phallus, with *minus phi* we then touch on something essential, hidden behind the castration complex, namely desire on the part of the woman.

In this connection, Lacan quotes the poet T. S. Eliot, a naturalised Englishman born in America and winner of the 1948 Nobel Prize. The extract is from *The Waste Land,* where it is a question of the void. Eliot wrote this collection of poems following a tumultuous divorce that left both himself and his ex-wife deeply distressed.

When lovely woman stoops to folly and
Paces about her room again, alone,
she smooths her hair with automatic hand,
and puts a record on the gramophone.

"When a charming woman stoops to madness", the madness of sexual intercourse,

"and walks around her room alone again", when the intercourse is over.

"she straightens her hair with an automatic hand": this is the introduction of a desire that is not modulated by *plus phi*, but by *minus phi*, this is the desire of woman.

In other words, there is sexual intercourse and it is a madness when it is over quickly. Then supervenes the changing of the record: starting from jouissance.

This is because at the level of the phallus something has been realised and yet not realised, *something else* that can appear immediately afterwards on the basis, not of *plus phi*, but of *minus phi*, something of the phallus that is not realised. It is in this non-fulfilment of the phallus that the encounter of the desires of man and woman can be played out, and not in the madness of sexual intercourse based on *plus phi*.

Again and again, it is this *minus phi* that is missing in Freudian theory and practice, particularly in relation to the end of analysis for a woman. She would ask the analyst for the penis. Without a sufficient response, the analysis continues indefinitely. In contrast to the lack of the penis (*Penisneid*), but still within the perspective of *plus phi*, a woman can claim actual possession of it. This is a feminine masquerade: she has the penis, she has *plus phi* better than the man does; she makes a claim for the non-detumescent phallic object, which is displayed in all her feminine attributes, all *plus phi*, all signs of omnipotence.

To understand analysis based on *plus phi* is to do a real disservice not only to the desire of woman, but more originally, to *jouissance*, because the woman's desire is first played out, based on *jouissance*. If we push her along a path comparable to man's desire, centred on *plus phi* and not starting from *jouissance* and *minus phi,* we halt the very efficacy of the phallic function, which opens up the renewal of the dialectic of desire starting only from *minus phi*. It is the relaunch of the phallus that is blocked, the positivised phallus then serving only as an object of appeasement, an object aimed at acquiring the clemency of a God or a man already caught up in a dialectic of desire centred on *plus phi*. All of this is not without provoking anxiety that insists on object *a* and the barred big Other, that have been blocked by the positivised phallus.

Notes

1 Jacques Lacan, "The Subversion of the Subject and the Dialectic of Desire" in *Écrits, The First Complet Edition in English,* translated by B. Fink in collaboration with H. Fink and R. Grigg. New York, W.W. Norton & Company, 2006, pp. 672–700.
2 Lesson of 22 May 1963. Chapter XVIII of the Seuil version.
3 *La Bible*, New York, W.W. Norton & Company, 2006, pp. 413–415 (Joshua, 6, 1–21).
4 *La Bible*, New York, W.W. Norton & Company, 2006, pp. 151–153 (Exodus, 19, 16–19 and Exodus, 20–18).
5 See Christian Fierens, *Lecture de l'identification de Lacan. De l'utopie d'identité au moteur de l'invention,* Louvain-la-Neuve, EME, 2020.
6 Jacques Lacan, "L'Étourdit", in *Autres écrits,* Paris, Seuil, 2001, pp. 472.
7 Immanuel Kant, *Critique of Pure Reason*, London, J.M. Dent, 1993, pp. 1011.
8 Lesson of 29 May 1963. Chapter XIX in the Seuil edition.
9 Not to be confused with the Steiner method or Steiner-Waldorf pedagogy (as the Seuil edition does), whatever the possible resonances.
10 Jacques Lacan, *Écrits, The First Complet Edition in English,* translated by B. Fink in collaboration with H. Fink and R. Grigg, New York, W.W. Norton & Company, 2006, pp. 819.

Chapter 10

The vocal object *a* in the structure and in the clinic

LESSON 21[1]: THE VOCAL OBJECT IN THE PHALLIC STRUCTURE

Object *a* is regularly understood to be a positive object, *plus phi*, whereas it should firstly be understood as a lack. At the same time, there is the question of the dependence of desire on *jouissance*: notwithstanding this dependence, desire is represented and sustained by something of the order of *plus phi*, whereas in its dependence on *jouissance*, it firstly presupposes a fundamental lack, the void, the radical nothing inherent in *jouissance*. The renewal of the dialectic of desire consists in understanding object *a* as the *minus phi* inherent in the schema of division: *jouissance* – anxiety – desire.

1 The phallus and the phallic function

The phallus eminently poses the following dilemma: something or nothing? *Plus phi* or *minus phi*? How is this question answered when posited at the intersection of man (M) and woman (W)? This intersection can be imagined as positive, *plus phi* which is the Freud's conception of the phallus that resonates, as we have seen, positively with the scopic perspective of the eye mirror of the world, with the possibility of being all-seeing and all-knowing (Figure 10.1).

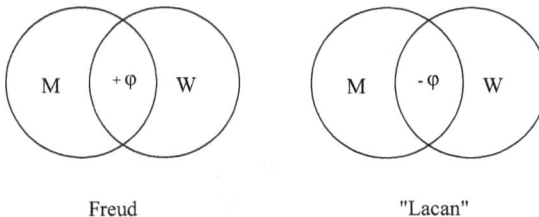

Freud   "Lacan"

Figure 10.1 The dialectic of desire between man (M) and woman (W) according to Freud and Lacan.

To expose Lacan's displacement in relation to Freud in the dialectic of desire between man and woman, we can first replace the positivity of the phallus *plus phi*,

DOI: 10.4324/9781003477822-15

with *minus phi*: *minus phi* now taken to be the intersection between man (M) and woman (W). This is only the first stage in the displacement, explaining why "Lacan" is placed in inverted commas in the diagram. This is because Lacan's introduction of *minus phi* as a function of the signifying process itself S_1-S_2 (the second conception of the signifier) engages in a complete subversion of the conception of the phallus and of desire. From the perspective of formal logic and spherical topology, the two schemas (Freud and "Lacan") still presuppose positive elements, objects inscribable in sets M and W. But, prior to the phallic function, "Man" and "Woman" cannot be persons, but positions arising – secondarily – in the course of the development of said phallic function, which remains the primordial question. The phallic is thus inscribed in the signifying process represented by an interior eight, where *plus phi*, full of the imaginary (S_1), is represented by the big loop, while *minus phi*, emptied of all imaginary (S_2), is represented by the small loop (Figure 10.2).

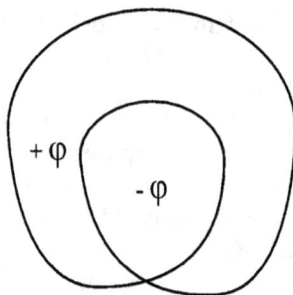

Figure 10.2 Interior eight representing the phallic signifier.

With this schema of the phallic signifier $(S_1-S_2,$ *plus phi–minus phi*), it is no longer possible to inscribe man and woman in separate boxes; they inscribe each other in continuity in the same interior eight. And since "woman" (W) and "man" (M) retain a whole series of imaginary meanings, they are necessarily inscribed in the big loop: (Figure 10.3).

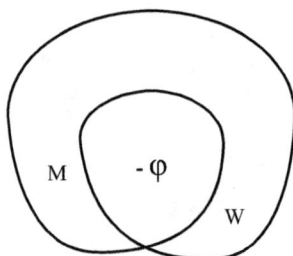

Figure 10.3 Man (M) and woman (W) represented with the phallic signifier.

We can read the signifying process inherent in the phallic function $(S_1-S_2,$ *plus phi–minus phi*) in the story of the Wolfman, particularly in his dream, where the phallus is always present and at the same time always lacking: it is lacking where it is awaited and at the very moment when it appears positively in the dream, anxiety arises. This positive appearance of the phallus (*plus phi*) goes hand in hand with the withdrawal of the signifying flow (*minus phi*) proper to the full development of the phallic and sexual function. This is what is at stake in coitus interruptus, as we have seen: when the flow of sexuality retreats, "it shows the sand" says Lacan. When the flow of the signifying process withdraws, it shows the pure instrumental object, pure organic functioning. The sexual organ as such then provokes anxiety, that is, a reminder of the fundamental structure (object *a* and the barred big Other): this is castration anxiety.

It is insofar as it is fundamentally inserted into the signifying process that the phallus is called upon to function as an instrument of power. The phallic function, the phallic signifier, is thus essentially something of the order of the signifier and of relaunch. Any signifying process can be understood as this development of phallic relaunch, as long as we understand that the phallus is essentially *minus phi*. The power of phallic relaunch is thus always in the process of vacillating, always in the process of eventually disappearing and showing the sand, and then provoking castration anxiety. We don't expect power and revival to be everywhere and always.

But the necessary, inevitable and intermittent appearance of *plus phi* provokes castration anxiety just as necessarily, inevitably and intermittently. To counter it, we can imagine omnipotence (this is not the only solution). The omnipotence of the phallus is no more than an escape from this point where all potency – the real of phallic power – vacillates and, fundamentally, is no more than a simple relaunch. This imagined omnipotence resonates in the scopic field, where the eye supposed to be omnipotent, the eye of God, sees all and knows all. It is an illusion of omnipotence engendered as a response to castration: not "I am indestructible", but "the indestructible is guaranteed by the big Other". So, the neurotic accepts all the little castrations, all the little personal frustrations, as long as he can count on the all-seeing eye of God, on the omnipotence of the big Other who can answer everything.

We can follow how imaginary omnipotence insinuates itself into the very heart of narcissism. In the development of the ego, the question at the time presents itself as *what am I?*, then, turns to the past to find support in the ideal ego and transfers this support to the future in the form of an ego ideal that would be able to direct action. As a function of this question and its unmistakable hole, the ideal ego and the ego ideal remain essentially perforated. The necessary appearance of *plus phi*, however, gives a semblance of omnipotence to this narcissism where the ideal ego is no longer centred on a hole, on object *a* as lack, but on an object that has no lack (a positivised object *a*). And the ego ideal is no longer centred on *minus phi*, on opening up at the heart of the ego ideal, the power of creation inherent in the unconscious; instead, the ego ideal is filled by the big Other or by the object *a* of the big Other, which provides the imaginary and illusory consistency of power and omnipotence. In general, this is what is at play in the formation of crowds. Crowds have an unshakeable confidence in their leader, who is supposed to have all the answers, and who stands as the complete and plugged ego ideal. By the continual reference to this *plus phi* where the ego Ideal is fully consistent, as signalled by the Hitler salute, by the sign of the cross, the imaginary omnipotence of *plus phi* is given to the crowd, to the church, to the army, and possibly to the schools of psychoanalysis.

The omnipotence inherent in a certain form of narcissism, inherent in a narcissism that has already been filled up and diverted, is what is at stake in the professional ideal in general. The professional ideal corresponds to the ego ideal constitutive of a group; one registers in a given profession as if in the crowd of practitioners of that profession. Psychoanalysts can fit into such a professional ideal. From this formation of a professional ideal, a professional dignity is established, not without a certain taste for omnipotence, which however plugs the central lack, the impotence, the fundamental *minus phi* inherent in the intermittent, limited power of the phallic function and its relaunch.

Normal male homosexuality parallels the same structure as professional dignity where everything revolves around this positivised ego ideal. We come and go in a milieu of good social ties and friendships; this applies to male homosexuality, to professional dignity and to all groups in general. Lacan insists that female homosexuality is not of this type: no social function is at stake and the omnipotence of desire is not played out around a *plus phi*, but is played out at the level of love, of homosexual love, which depends primordially on *minus phi*, at the level of *jouissance* and anxiety.

The support of desire – as *minus phi* – is not made for sexual union: the support of desire insofar as it originates in *jouissance* and anxiety, that is to say, from the phallic function as the signifying process and the interior eight does not presuppose man and woman to be united, nor does it create them in order to unite them. The support of desire takes them both at the same time in its own movement, which follows the "round" (in the form of the interior eight) of the formulae of sexuation (Figure 10.4).

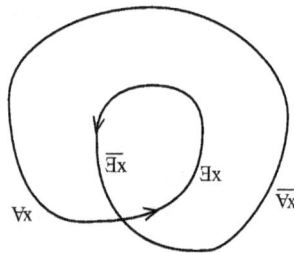

Figure 10.4 The formulae of sexuation represented on the movement of the phallic signifier.

In the signifying process of the phallic function, we always begin by imagining, thereby, plunging us inevitably into formal logic and spherical topology (see the diagrams of the intersection of man and woman). And phallic power imposes itself on everything, on every x, on every man, on every mortal, on every Greek, and so on. These are universals. The universal dominates in Aristotelian logic, and particulars are inscribed within the framework of the universal: this is the meaning of the first phallic formula: for any x phi of x, any x is inscribed within the logic of universality and the particulars that depend on it. Aristotelian logic raises the question of who imagined it: on whom or on what does it depend, that might be reducible neither to the universal nor to the particular. Singularity – the singularity of the S_1–S_2 signifying process (the second conception of the signifier) – empties the imagined universal; there is something outside the universal (and particulars), there is a singularity: there exists an x non-phi of x (the second phallic formula). This singularity must still be denied, it cannot take on an imaginary consistency that would bring it back into the field of the universal by taking it to be a simple particularity: there is no such thing as an x non-phi of x (third phallic formula). Existence, which goes hand in hand with particularity in classical logic, is denied in order to reveal anything else that has no place in formal logic (as in the first formula). From this void of non-existence of a particular, it is the very ex-sistence or process of invention and creation proper to the unconscious that is summoned insofar as it is irreducible to formal logic, to the logic of the Universal. This brings us to the right-hand side of the diagram and the fourth phallic formula: not all x phi of x. This is by no means a particular formula; the signifying process in its movement of creation in singularity, liberated from all imaginary constraints, is, in its creative way, all-powerful, giving the "all" of the first formula a new vigour.

These phallic formulae will not be proposed until later in Lacan's teaching, but they are already implicit in the treatment of the phallic (*plus phi/minus phi*) in the line of the S_1–S_2 signifying process. There is no sexual union because there are no preliminary objects posited as man and woman. It is the movement of the phallic structure that precedes this, with the contradiction of *plus phi/ minus phi* and the implication of *minus phi*, of the hole that rightly allows for the invention at the heart of this question of the sexual relation. "There is no sexual relation", far from being a negative formula, opens the moment of phallic relaunch.

2   The movement of the structure

Let us return, however, to the schema of sexual union, represented by *minus phi* as the intersection of man and woman. On the man's side, *minus phi* is always worth placing under the threat of castration; on the woman's side, it stands for *Penisneid*. Between the two sexes, a choice must be made, and with whichever choice is made, the phallus is automatically positivised. This positivisation is part of the structure and goes hand in hand with what needs to be known, with the question of seeing and of knowing. It is the very reason for the introduction of the eye, and especially, the third eye. A first way of looking at the third eye is to situate it between the two eyes, as in the schema where the phallus serves as the intersection (*plus ph*i or *minus phi*) between man and woman. (Figure 10.5)

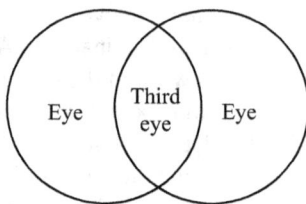

Figure 10.5 The third eye as the intersection of two eyes.

However, with the development of the phallic function and following the interior eight of the signifying process, we pass continuously from the "masculine" to the "feminine" and vice versa. It is in this passage that we can situate Lacan's marked interest in the sex of Avalokiteshvara and his guide's puzzled non-response. The bodhisattva passes from a masculine figure to a feminine one, in an interior figure eight, with the third eye more correctly registered at the heart of this movement (Figure 10.6).

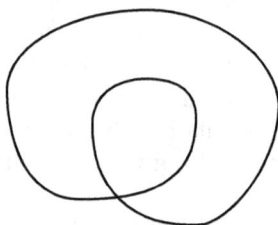

Avalokiteshvara from male to female

Figure 10.6 Avalokiteshvara from male to female.

We are confronted not with an alternative between *plus phi* and *minus phi*, between the *plus phi* of desire and the *minus phi* of *jouissance*, but with an experience that engages these two antinomic ways of seeing the phallic, the eye and everything that concerns object *a* in general. It is not a question of synthesising these two ways but of resolving it differently, that is, by situating the question *upstream of* the distinction between the two ways, the question having been already posed in anxiety ever before it was made explicit in the phallic function. It was posed in anxiety insofar as it separates and gives rise to *jouissance* and desire.

This impasse, which is at the root of the false alternative between *plus phi* and *minus phi*, is the radical distinction between the level of *jouissance* and the level of desire, not only in our theory, but especially in our practice and in our listening. Even if our interior eight diagram of the formulae of sexuation seems to indicate a direct continuity between the feminine and the masculine, we need to make a radical distinction between S$_1$ and S$_2$ (the big loop and the little loop). Even if psychoanalytic practice centred on the signifying process (the second conception of the signifier) never avoids the interpretative practice of the signifying chain (the first conception of the signifier), it does not follow that there is a continuity between the two: we need to very clearly distinguish between a type of psychoanalysis centred on *minus phi* and jouissance, and another type centred on *plus phi* and desire that is caught up in the imaginary capture of the scopic field and phantasy.

The distinction can be made with the scopic field and even within it. Starting with the difference between apes and humans, the monkey is almost perfectly situated in the scopic field, where with its ability, it can do almost anything as long as it can see, as long as it is in the operative field of vision. But the monkey does not have the mirror stage. In other words, there is no narcissism in the sense of the development of the ego; and if there is no narcissism, there is no impasse as just mentioned, between *jouissance* and desire, between the feminine and the masculine, and so on. There is no S_1–S_2 signifying process.

It is therefore essential to avoid the "ubiquitous libido" of the ape and the scopic field, where the eye is simply the mirror of the world. In contrast to this ubiquitous libido, which seems to master the world through the scopic field, narcissism has always been at an impasse, because of its question (who am I?) and in its answers (the object *a* as lacking in the ideal ego and the *minus phi* at the heart of the ego ideal). This something of the order of a not-seeing, a primordial not-knowing generates from a void, not from reflections and images, but the reflexion proper to narcissism. Narcissism is essentially non-specular; it cannot be reduced to seeing, to seeing oneself, or to seeing a part of the world. Something new – outside seeing and outside knowing – is injected, but injected as a void (*minus phi*) – into the scopic field: not the eye, but the gaze, the stain, the beauty spot, the scopic object *a*, and we will find this void at the heart of the ideal ego in the form of the object *a* as lack and at the heart of the ego ideal in the form of *minus phi*.

In the scopic field *without this void* (like the monkey), what is sought is the right form, the field of insight, of all-powerful seeing and knowing. It is here that of the field of universality is found, the field of scopic seeing and the knowledge of Aristotelian logic (universality and particularity). But beneath the visible, there is the eye that actively sees and *questions itself.* Beneath the desirable, there is a desiring. The experience of narcissism is that there is a desirer, a *question of* desire and of reflection prior to the image which justifies the image. When this eye or this desirer appears in the very place of the all-powerful seeing and knowing of the right form, then the uncanny, the *Unheimlich,* is produced: something of the desire dependent on anxiety comes to life at the interior of the scopic field.

The third eye of Buddhism (and Hinduism), the "eye" of knowledge, but also of wisdom, is not just the all-seeing eye. Even as it appears restful and neutralised in and by the scopic field, it already implies in itself the questioning movement of the eye and of the whole scopic field. If it were to come to life explicitly in the statue of the Bodhisattva, it would appear completely strange or uncanny (*Unheimlich*). It is animation, latent in the third eye that introduces strangeness and anxiety. The scopic object, the third eye, the stain, any of which may appear simply as a point of not-knowing, are much more than points, points simply being what represent any object in the classical scopic field. Here, the point cannot be reduced to a point inscribed in space; it exists only for the movement of turning around, in an interior figure eight, with the signifier. This is the real beginning at play, starting from the mirror stage or from narcissism.

Our praxis consists in returning to this primordial structure already present in narcissism, this structure introduced by narcissism that goes far beyond the practice of seeing and knowing in the scopic field. Narcissism already poses the question *of the subject*: how can the subject emerge in the field of the Other? It is the question of the division of the big Other articulated with its three levels: *jouissance*, anxiety, desire. We can and we must understand this question in terms of narcissism. Such a practice, from the outset, goes beyond language as communication, including the communication of desire in a so-called interpretation.

Both narcissism and the schema of the division of the big Other by the subject, who does not yet exist, begin with this question: who am I? The answer necessarily takes shape in the locus of the Other in the form of: "you are…" even if there is no Other to answer. "You are…" remains without an attribute, "you are…", an ellipsis: we don't know. "You are…" is an ideal ego with an empty object *a* inside, and the ego ideal is also used as a "you are…" or "you are what you are going to be able to become", but with a void, with minus phi inside.

Roman Jakobson suggested that psychologists place a recorder in nurseries to record the monologue of very young children as they begin to speak, on the verge of sleep, and listen in to what is said when there is no one else in the room (this is before the mirror stage, where the Other is personified). This is very different from Piaget's so-called "egocentric" language, which is nothing more than the monologue a child engages in when he is engaged in a joint task with his classmates. Jakobson's experiment reveals the precociousness of the primordial tensions of the unconscious, the precociousness of the signifying movement that is already complete, with the question "What am I?" and the answer "You are…", but with a void in the middle of this "You are", "What am I?" along with the development of narcissism and the development of the ego.

Beyond the dream as the "fulfilment of a wish" according to Freud, we must understand, according to Lacan, the function of the dream from the structure of the signifying process (S_1–S_2 with the void and *minus phi* inherent in the process). In other words, we must understand the dream as the implementation of the question of the subject, understood both in terms of the development of the ego and narcissism and in terms of the division of the big Other by the question of the subject. There is a true invention of the self in the dream where the dreamer is most often represented by different people in different places as long as we preserve the holes, the voids, in these different places and people: the object *a* as void, the primordial *minus phi* on the side of the relaunch of the phallus. For everything is played out in the perspective of a becoming, of something that is invented. This is a serious displacement compared to the Freudian thesis of the dream as the fulfilment of a wish or a desire, where the dream appeared to be the royal road to knowing the unconscious, to knowing how to analyse and to desire.[2]

3   The royal road to the unconscious: the voice

Throughout the seminar, through *jouissance*, the dialectic of desire is transferred or displaced from the wish towards something other than the wish. This displacement (*Entstellung* distortion) was already present in filigree in Freud's work, when, after stating his thesis that "every dream is a fulfilment of wish" in chapter 3 of the *Traumdeutung*, he comes in chapter 4 *Distortion in Dreams* to the question of anxiety, the anxiety notably present in a certain number of dreams that don't appear to be fulfilments of desire: these being the ones that bring into play a "distortion" (*Entstellung*) that masks the fulfilment of a wish, this distortion introducing something other than the supposedly primary desire that functions under the primacy of the pleasure principle. Distortion implies movement, ongoing work, which is not unrelated to invention. Jakobson's experiment in recording the monologues of toddlers in nurseries shows that this ongoing work is present from the very beginning of the first word. It appears on the side of the voice, not at first the voice that can be recorded, but the pure voice without the plug of signification, the pure voice opening up invention and creation from the outset.

The voice, intimately linked to the question of emptiness, is absolutely central to our practice. It is present from the very beginning of speech. The vocal face of object *a* is not a question of sonority, still less of signification, but it is it that allows sonority, it is the condition of sonority (and then of meaning). To emphasise this vocal object that precedes all sonority (and all meaning), Lacan engages in a number of considerations about the anatomy of the snail's ear, which is made up of a certain number of resonances; because the apparatus of the ear precedes sound and is its condition; here, the ear in its anatomy is an exhibition of the vocal object. The inner ear, composed of these multiple resonances, can be compared to an organ, with its multiple (empty) pipes. Each pipe resonates at its own frequency with its own harmonics (the shofar being a rudimentary organ consisting of a single pipe). The ear's apparatus, which is an exhibition of object *a* in its vocal form, is played out, not around sound, but around hollows and emptiness. Now, the ear or the organ are not given from the outset: the void must be created, the vocal face of object *a* must be let happen. The void must be created, as the potter who, in shaping his pot, creates the void. The void of object *a* is not passive or negative; from the outset, in its composition, it presumes the movement of invention and creation, which will then resonate in a new invention (like the shofar, creator of a new alliance).

How and where to invent or create the vocal object? The voice is not an object situated like a point in a given space. It can be grasped in the phatic function of speech, namely, from the very first moment of contact, in a remark emptied of all meaning: "how are you?", "the weather's fine today", "hello", "good morning". By dint of repetition, the word has lost its imaginary meaning. It is a signifier devoid of message, where the imaginary is erased. From the perspective of language as communication (the first conception of the signifier), it is of no importance and could disappear. But from the perspective of the signifying process (the second conception of the signifier), it serves as the already completed outline of the process, it has value as S_2 and as the first appearance of the voice. We can take this into account very concretely in practice. Contrary to the tension of a certain type of consti-pated psychoanalyst who allows only "signifying" interpretations to come out of his mouth (first conception of the signifier) supposed to always only take account of the poetic power of the signifier (even if it means remaining completely silent), we should, on the contrary, give these words that have already lost their meanings all their possible value as S_2 (second conception of the signifier). This is where the voice can already be at work in its phatic function. The void of the Other, Å, can resonate there.

The voice, as vocal object a, is not the sonority of speech or the melody of song or music. It is the emptiness of the potter's vessel; it is there in the void created by the phatic function of these signifiers without meaning ("hello", "how are you", etc.). This emptiness is rich with all the power of the Other, but of the Other insofar as it does not respond Å,. This is why our own voice (deprived of the significations it carries) appears foreign to us: it is the voice of the Other, the empty voice of the Other, which does not respond in my place.

The signifying process involves incorporating the voice. This incorporation (*Einverleibung*) can be understood in two different and complementary ways. Firstly: making mine what is of the Other. Secondly: giving the voice a body.

First: the voice in identification. With the signifying process, I can emerge as a subject if I am represented by a signifier (S_1, "good morning", which literally means "good morning") for another signifier (S_2, "good morning", a voice that no longer means anything) that invites invention. The process of analysis consists of this identification, starting with the division of the big Other by the subject and leading to desire (*jouissance* – anxiety – desire schema). The end of analysis – its aim as well as its end – should then be understood as the analysand's identification with the vocal object a. It is an end of analysis that remains within the signifying process (starting from *jouissance*, passing through anxiety and sustaining desire). Note that this is not the end of analysis as proposed as the "end of the neurotic torus" in "*L'Étourdit*", an end where the analysand, in order to be fully the subject of desire ($) , lets the object a fall at the same time as his analyst (who is holding the place of semblance of this object a).[3] In line with the very renewal of the dialectic of desire, it seems more judicious to retain the very principle of *jouissance* at work beyond the end of the analysis, and thus to conceive of the end of the analysis with the radical assumption of the function of the vocal object a. The analysand truly incorporates the object a at the end of the analysis: it gives him body, incorporation being the setting of the body, the living body which is nothing other than the living force of the S_1–S_2 signifier.

Secondly: to give body to the voice. To explain this, Lacan refers to a physi-ological characteristic of the daphnia, commonly known as the "water flea". Its organ of equilibrium contains a few particles of sand. The incorporation of these grains, which remain unassimilated, enables it to situate itself in the verticality of water (the particles fall and point downwards, like a compass pointing down-wards). Similarly, the voice is not assimilated, but it is incorporated, thus acting as a foreign body that serves as a compass for locating the signifying process and for situating oneself in relation to it. It is in its own functioning that it takes shape at the same time as it opens the signifying process with its emptiness. The fundamentally empty object *a* takes on a body, and this taking on of a body – incorporation – is understood in two ways. On the one hand, the modelling of the void in incorporation is played out in its product, in what is created or invented. On the other hand, preventing any invention and blocking it, object *a* is provoked (which means *for the voice*), by a positivised object that short-circuits its emptiness. Returning to the daphnia to better understand this provocation, experimenters introduced iron filings instead of grains of sand into the daphnia's organ of balance (the ear). Subjected to a magnetic field, the daphnia found itself completely disoriented or, more accurately, reoriented by the experimenter's magnet, which acted as the big Other. The same applies to the incorporation of the vocal object. In function of its very emptiness, which only demands to be filled, the vocal object is always reoriented by the incorporation of the desire of the Other, which is supposed to take shape in its demands and commands. In other words, the void of object *a* (which justified the purity of the superego "jouis") takes shape, incorporating the various imperatives and prohibitions which are composed in the ferocious superego.

This incorporation of the voice through the demands and commands of the big Other is what is at play in the neurotic, toric structure. It implies the degradation of a purified superego that impels creation and invention, into a ferocious superego, where commandments predominate with their forbidden face. These two sides of the superego correspond to two forms of guilt: the guilt of *not having done something* ("of having given way on one's desire") and the guilt *of having made* mistakes in relation to the command of the Other. In most cases, these faults fail to explain the often disproportionate extent of the guilt, which should lead us back to questioning the first form of superego and of guilt. For these commandments, in relation to which the said guilt is situated, are not the empty voice, are not the object *a* in its vocal form. Quite the contrary, they block the void of the voice… they block the way. Let us recall that the shofar, the ram's horn, is fundamentally empty, and that the Ten Commandments of the Tables of the Law do nothing more than fill this void.

Freud understood anxiety as a signal of the danger of losing the object of desire (which can be combined with the five positive forms of object *a*). But what is the real danger? Is it not the danger of losing the void, of losing object *a* in its vocal form, rather than the danger of seeing the void filled by iron filings subjected to the magnetism of the big Other? Guilt will be understood and treated in consequence. Sometimes the guilt concerns not having obeyed this or that demand of the big Other, and it will be a matter of waiting for forgiveness from the Other and the erasure of this fault. Sometimes the guilt concerns not having given the vocal object its full place of emptiness, and it is a question of supporting a commitment starting from the barred big Other and the erasure of the imaginarisation of the fault; forgiveness here becomes *par-don* [literally *by-gift*], the height of giving, which consists in giving "what one doesn't have", in committing oneself to inventive and creative love: reopening the primordial emptiness that promises invention.

Outside of the path of the vocal object, we are necessarily caught in the network of desire revolving around *plus phi* and in the confrontation with an unbarred big Other. Caught in this network, the problem consists in capturing this big Other and his good graces. Sacrifices to the gods consist not in giving them something to eat (they don't need to eat), but in making them desire *directly*, that is, independently of the level of *jouissance* and of anxiety. The sacrifice must avoid distressing the Other at all costs; to do this, the victims must be without blemish. Mindful of the stain, the victim is indeed situated in the scopic field, but "without stain", remaining outside any question of the *Unheimlich*, of the gaze, of the scopic object *a*. The sacrifice aims to make the gods desire the field of seeing and knowing, but without provoking the anxiety of the gods. The sacrifice of Christ is quite different: Christ is God made victim, he has a stain, he has taken upon himself the sins of the world to provoke the anxiety of God... the Son. This is a masochistic position that calls everything into question as a function of anxiety and the question that precedes anxiety, the possible emergence of the subject in the question of the signifier, in the "Word", and this is the place of *jouissance*.

LESSON 22[4]: THE VOCAL OBJECT *a* HIDDEN IN THE OBSESSIONAL SYMPTOM

1   The obsessional symptom and its cause

The aim of analysis is always to discover and set a desire in motion. The seminar *Anxiety* makes desire heard in the structure of the division of the Other through the question of the subject: desire depends on the question of *jouissance* through the intermediary of anxiety. The question of *jouissance* is the question of the subject in the locus of the Other: the subject receiving its own message in an inverted form. The message-question "who am I?", a narcissistic question, is followed by the message-response of the big Other "you are...". This "you are..." given by the big Other is part of the signifying process. But a "you are..." emptied of all imaginary, it is "holed" at the interior of the ideal ego and the ego ideal. Starting from this hole, this nothing inherent in the question of *jouissance*, we must commit ourselves – but not without anxiety and even before becoming a subject, before object *a* as lack and before the big Other who does not respond. And it is only at the third level (after *jouissance* and after anxiety) that the subject of desire can emerge, a subject immediately barred by all that precedes it. We can now better understand what is meant by "the desire of man is the desire of the Other".[5] The Other is not any person, it is the Other as signifying process, implicated in the question of the subject (at the level of *jouissance*), the Other who does not respond, the big Other barred (at the level of anxiety). The "desire of the Other" is the question of desire at stake in the question of *jouissance* and anxiety, not the desire of an Other subject. The desire of man is appended to the "desire of the Other" and this can only be played out in pre-subjective love, the love that allows *jouissance* to condescend to desire.

It can only be played out "through the antecedent constitution of object *a*"; in other words, object *a* has to be made (*fabriquer*) and it has to be constituted *before* any question of desire. The Seminar has already insisted on this *made before-hand*, notably with the thesis of object *a* as the cause of desire. Our task is now to construct this cause of desire based on the clinic, which is where the obsessional symptom will verify the question of object *a*, cause of desire. The obsessional symptom reprises OCD *Obsessive Compulsive Disorder* in general, the compulsion to repeatedly check that a door is closed, that a gas tap is turned off, that there is no monster under the bed, etc. This is where we need to identify the object *a* as the cause.

One explanation of the obsessional symptom is that it is directly related to anxiety. It would be presented as a conduit of defence and the avoidance of anxiety: if the obsessional does not check everything that needs to be checked, he becomes anxious. Anxiety is there from the start, and to avoid it, the obsessive checks the tap, the door, etc. Maybe, but anxiety is not locatable there. Anxiety is not correlated with the symptom as such, and it is absolutely pointless to explain to the obsessional that there's no reason to be anxious, that the door is locked and there's no need to go check it.

Instead of this easy explanation, which sees the symptom as a defence against anxiety, we must follow the symptom itself and its structure. With what the obsessional tells us, we can follow the sequence. *Firstly*, the demonstration of OCD: how it works (including the appearance of anxiety if we try to do violence to the symptom). *Secondly*, the question of the cause of the OCD: "after all there has to be a cause". For the obsessional, the symptom will only be truly constituted as a symptom when the question about its cause is asked. As long as this question is not asked, the OCD in question remains no more than a peculiarity of conduct or behaviour that the outside observer may or may not notice. To constitute the symptom is to constitute it with the question of cause (not unrelated to object *a* cause of desire). With the question of cause, it is a matter of "grabbing the symptom by the ears". These ears are not the ones that have already heard everything and could interpret the symptom, they are rather the ears attentive to the voice, to the empty object *a*, to the S_2 without imaginary, without meaning and without interpretation. This remains unassimilated by the subject, and once we think we've found the cause or the ears that would explain the symptom, we become disenchanted. The cause of the symptom remains in default, at fault (Lacan's Seminar XXIII bases the symptom on fault or on *sin*, in order to bring the cause into play, a problematic cause however, never assimilated and always to be reinvented).

In the interpretative approach (the first conception of the signifier), the aim would be to find the cause of the symptom. However, the cause found does not remove the symptom; the problem is not solved, and the question of the cause persists. The symptom (constituted with the cause) persists as a persistent enigma. The cause is then only a cause that is implicated, invoked with the constituted symptom.

How do we understand the cause? This can be done in two ways. *Firstly*, the cause is supposed to be deterministic, and, with it, we could explain to the analysand why the symptom appeared and possibly how it could disappear by removing the cause; this supposed cause generally explains nothing, and the symptom remains unchanged. *Secondly,* the cause is a cause by freedom on the side of the invention of the unconscious beyond knowledge and explanation, but mobilising creation and engagement. The first type of causality is inscribed in the dialectic of desire insofar as it could be explained (first conception of the signifier), while the second type mobilises the level of *jouissance* where the question of the subject arises from the signifying process (second conception of the signifier). The cause of the symptom lies in the in-between of these two types of cause: between the deterministic, supposedly objective cause and the cause of freedom of invention. It is in the same in-between position that the object *a* is situated as the cause of desire: a cause rooted in *jouissance*, a cause of freedom to invent the unconscious, a cause that produces desire, including its determinations.

2   The transference from one cause to another

Object *a* as the cause of desire, in the ambiguity of the cause, is also what allows transference to unfold. Transference first of all summons the subject supposed to know, the subject supposed to know the causes of the illness, the symptom, etc. Here, causality is deterministic, and the oral, anal and scopic faces of object *a* are presented as the cause or causes of a corresponding desire on the side of an oral need, an anal demand, a seeing and a scopic knowing that account for the explanatory, understanding side of knowledge in psychoanalysis. But transference is also the fall of the subject supposed to know, where the big Other no longer responds and a fundamental void appears. So within the transference there is room for self-invention and for causality becoming causality through liberty (to be understood as the liberty inherent in the unconscious).

To carry out an analysis of transference neurosis is to construct transference neurosis around this explanation of the cause of desire: *firstly,* cause on the side of needs, demands, and in an explanatory framework, etc., is deterministic and *secondly,* cause by freedom on the side of a causality that goes beyond all-seeing and all-knowing in a perspective of invention.

If analysis merely produces a transference neurosis and nothing more, the result can only be perplexing. In transference neurosis, where is the desire of the analyst? What does the analyst want? Is there a renewal of the dialectic of desire that the analyst wants, and how? Is there a "transference" as a displacement from one way of seeing the dialectic of desire to another? The truth of transference and at the same time the truth of the desire of the analyst lies in this "transference". And in this seminar, Lacan intends to effect a transfer from one type of cause to another, he intends to *transfer* – that's the word, it's a question of transferring, it's the truth of the transference – the cause at play in Kant's *transcendental aesthetics* to the cause of *transcendental ethics*.

Starting with the *transcendental aesthetic* in Kant's *Critique of Pure Reason*, causality is inscribed in the order of *knowledge* (what can I know?) as the second dimension of the category of relation: cause is deterministic, determining the object in general; in psychoanalysis, the search for the cause of the symptom is inscribed in the perspective of the first figure of the transference: the subject supposed to know. For Kant, cause in *transcendental ethics* corresponds to the *Critique of Practical Reason* where causality is played out at the level of action (what must I do?). The imperative is imposed from the unconditional unconscious and is played out in the dimension of movement; the cause of the symptom is inscribed in the perspective of the second figure of the transference with the barred big Other and the object *a* as empty, which opens up the freedom of the unconscious to invent, to invent the self, to invent everything it can invent.

The transfer of the cause within Kant's philosophy of the transcendental aesthetic to the cause of the transcendental ethic of Lacan's psychoanalysis, the transfer of the subject supposed to know to the barred big Other, is not a diachronic operation. It has always already taken place. To make this transfer, we don't have to leave one cause for another, but to interrogate the very structure of the transcendental aesthetics and of the space-time that constitutes it.

Space – and the space of the transference – is not the locus of a correlation between the object and the subject (the ego of L-schema) because the object only exists with the conditions of the object (the space of the subject) and the ego only exists with the conditions of the ego (the big Other or infinite space). This is how Kant's metaphysical exposition of space is at the same time Lacan's topological exposition in schema L.[6] Kant's philosophy and Lacan's psychoanalysis are therefore not reducible to a correlation between object and subject or to a matter of transference-countertransference between analysand and analyst. We must always start from the axis of conditions, namely the symbolic axis of desire (Figure 10.7).

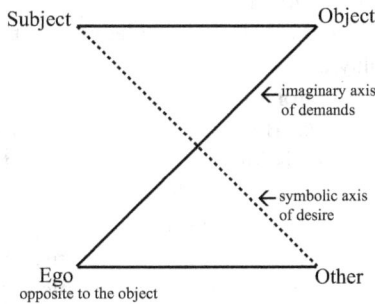

Figure 10.7 Schema L with its imaginary axis of demands and its symbolic axis of desire.

The renewal of the dialectic of desire (as aimed at in this Seminar on Anxiety) consists in requestioning the symbolic axis of the big Other and the subject. Undoubtedly, the engendering of the subject from the big Other is always played out through the imaginary filter of demands between the ego and the object. And it is always possible to present the subject and the big Other as an intertwined couple as in the neurotic perspective of the two intertwined toruses that can be interpreted in the dialectic of demand in the signifying chain (first conception of the signifier). But the real questioning of the emergence of the subject in the locus of the Other is none other than what is inscribed as the signifying process (S_1–S_2, second conception of the signifier) in the schema of the division of the big Other by the question of the subject.

Removing the cause from transcendental aesthetics does not consist in rejecting the question of space, but of finding in it the question that goes beyond its reduction to the imaginary axis of demand. It was therefore necessary to plunge the axis of desire back into its true question, finding its true origin and point of departure in the signifying process at the level of *jouissance* (at the upper level of the graph as well as at the upper level of the schema of division). Space is not a given, it must be constituted in the very movement of the signifier. This is how space is part of the real. It is a matter of allowing it to arrive in the ambiguity of the signifier: sometimes as a signifying chain involving the demands and desires of the subject and the Other, sometimes – and above all, not to be forgotten – as S_1–S_2 in the interior eight, the Moebius strip and cross-cap, in a renewal of topology and psychoanalytic practice.

It is the clinician who must do this work of interrogation of his space, and who must see how the scopic, seeing, knowing and understanding – as we shall see in relation to Piaget – must always involve the interrogation of space based on these multiple torsions implied in the division of the big Other by the subject. Desire can be grasped through the perspective and support of phantasy, but with the signifier S_1–S_2, it must be plunged back into its descent from and dependence on *jouissance*, which serves as its principle. This immersion entails an inevitable loss of knowledge (S_2 being equivalent to the zero degree of knowledge). This loss can be read in the gap of the cause: it is in the hole in deterministic causality that causality through freedom can play out, it is in the hole in knowledge that the freedom of invention of the unconscious can play out.

The cause concerns the motor of what happens, it is *propter hoc*, the "why" of which something happens. But since it always implies a gap, a hole, a hollow (where the unconscious is inscribed), it is easy, in the order of knowledge, to replace the motor with temporal antecedents: the motor comes before the movement it produces. To grasp the cause, we replace "*propter hoc*" with "*post hoc*" where the effect comes after the cause or the cause comes before the effect. This is, moreover, how the category of cause is made noticeable in the Kantian schematisation where "because of that" is replaced by "after that". Now, this schematisation of cause is confusing, if it is the means of inferring that by considering the temporal succession of two phenomena, we have reached the cause. Thus, to state that the Oedipus complex always comes *before* the neurotic symptom, is not to infer that what happened at the time of the Oedipus complex is the true cause of the symptom (as a psychoanalysis, which remains within the ambit of subject supposed to know, the signifying chain, the topology of the torus, etc., too easily assume). The question of the primordial cause is *prior to* any temporal phenomenology but importantly, it is not part of the perspective of knowing and seeing. Object *a* as the

cause of desire is therefore not reducible to its oral side or its anal and scopic resonances. It is of the order of invention, creation and ethics. Questioning space and
questioning time, the object *a* in its vocal side as the true cause of desire completely
subverts transcendental aesthetics (and the whole phenomenological approach) in
favour of transcendental ethics, the ethics of the unconscious.

The symptom is entirely implicated in the cause, insofar as it involves the schema
of the division of the subject. The symptom is at the centre of the nine-square reference table (inhibition-symptom-anxiety) and, in this, all the levels of the *jouissance-*
anxiety-desire schema must be understood. It cannot therefore be reduced to a
structural element. Notably, the symptom is not the effect of a supposed cause; on
the contrary, it bears witness to the irreducible gap between cause and effect, the
gap in which the question of the dynamic unconscious is inscribed. The symptom
appears as something very concrete, we would say a precipitate of the structure:
it can be observed. The strategy of analysis does not consist first of all in making
the symptom disappear (it persists), but, on the contrary, in bringing it to the fore
to open up the questioning of structure, to locate in it the question of cause (and
thus to constitute the symptom as symptom) and set in motion the causality of the
unconscious based on the fundamental defect in knowledge, based on the *sin*, in
other words, to make it a *sinthome*.

The proper effect of the cause in its ambiguity (deterministic cause/cause by
freedom) is not the symptom, it is desire. Object *a* is the *cause of* desire, on condition that the mysterious side of the cause is preserved. Desire will then remain
an effect indefinitely, but an effect that is not carried out. It is in the gap between
the object and desire, in the gap between the cause and an unfulfilled effect, that
Lacan's "transcendental ethics", the ethics of the unconscious, the ethics that is the
very working of the principle of *jouissance*, is introduced.

3   Piaget and transmission

The question of the gap in the cause is completely elided in Piaget's experimental
study of the cause. This is why his study can be likened to an obsessional symptom
where the aim is to *understand* the cause and to dismiss any gap in its understanding, in other words to avoid the fundamental and primordial position of *not understanding*. Piaget's initial error was to believe that speech essentially has the effect
of communicating what we understand. In his experimental study, Piaget set up a
kind of wireless telephone: he transmits a message to a first child, who transmits
it to a second child, and so on. The idea is to follow how the understanding of the
cause – in concrete terms, how the understanding of the tap as the cause of the flow
or stagnation of water – is passed from one child to another.

Piaget notes that the first child, who has to pass on what Piaget has explained
to him, systematically omits in his own explanations what he has already understood so well. Conflating understanding and explanation directly calls Piaget's system into question: if he presents himself at the beginning of the chain as having
understood everything, he shouldn't have to explain anything and the experiment

would not take place. More concretely, explanation conceals a fundamental non-understanding, suggesting that the explanations we proffer all too easily are a sign of the profound nastiness of any pedagogical position.

Transmission is not just played out in relation to a deterministic causality (a tap that determines the passage of water through it or not), but also in the transmission of stories (where another causality is undoubtedly at play)? From the outset, we can see once again what Piaget is avoiding. If, for example, the intention is to pass on the myth of Niobe, this undoubtedly comes to grief, as the myth is reduced to a banal, unremarkable little story that has lost all the original force and reason for the myth. As happened with his understanding of the tap's causality, Piaget is instead studying the entropy of understanding in the transmission of a story.

If there is a wastage of understanding, it is because such stories are not real stories; they're just little stories without the force and interest of myth. The cause of the myth, however, is to be found in anxiety and in the question of the subject. From the outset, the real cause of the story has been short-circuited by the reduction of the myth to a little story without anxiety or interest. In the case of understanding the tap, the cause was not truly touched upon either. For Piaget, the cause would consist of an open tap, the effect of which is that water flows through it, and a closed tap, the effect of which is that it doesn't. But the tap as cause is not whether it is open or closed, it is whether it is closed, the effect of which is to prevent flooding or to fill the bowl without it overflowing. Regarding both taps and stories, causality is not just deterministic, it always involves action, the action, for example, of turning off the tap to avoid flooding or turning off the tap so that the bowl doesn't overflow, the action inherent in the context of myth. This is an action in physical space-time, no doubt, but, above all, it is what is at stake in desire, in desire dependent on *jouissance* and anxiety.

The action inherent in the question of cause is absolutely obvious in the story of little Hans, who compares the widdler to a small tap that can be unscrewed. Faced with a tap, a child doesn't so much want to explain or understand (as Piaget would have us do), he wants to take it apart, he wants to act and act on the cause. He wants to produce an acting out. In other words, yes, he wants to know, he wants to explain how the cause can be symbolically manipulated by dismantling the tap, but at the *same time*, what is already at stake is the question of the essential movement of birth and death that he is already putting to the test in this dismantling. Beyond the deterministic cause that occupied Piaget, we must return to the cause of desire emerging, in *statu nascendi*, for the tap as well as for the story of Niobe. In any case, we must situate object *a, the* cause of desire, in the schema of division starting from *jouissance*.

4   The forgotten face of object *a*

We can now inscribe the first four forms of object *a* in diagrams that broadly take up the *terms* at play in the division of the subject starting from *jouissance*. Potentially, all the forms of object *a* refer to the vocal form, central, as we have seen, to the question of *jouissance*. Yet, they appear in a logic in which the terms they imply are already supposedly given.

1 The first form of object *a* (oral face) revolves around need in the Other (Figure 10.8).

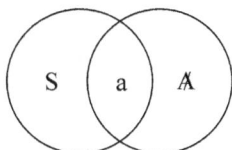

Figure 10.8 Object *a* as the intersection between the subject and the barred big Other.

Within our terms, it corresponds exactly to the upper and middle levels in the schema of division: *jouissance*, A and S; anxiety, a and A̶. The child's enjoyment *jouissance* of the breast corresponds to the cut between S and a. The mother's anxiety of a dried-up breast corresponds to the cut between a and A̶.

2 The second form of object *a* (anal face) revolves around the demand in the Other (Figure 10.9).

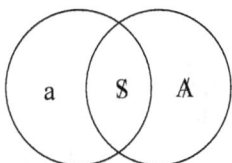

Figure 10.9 The barred subject (S̶) as the intersection of anal object *a* and barred A (A̶).

Within our terms, it corresponds to the middle and lower levels in the schema: anxiety, a and A̶; desire, S, the anxiety of losing a and the person demanding, A̶. And then the barred subject of desire that occurs at the intersection of the two: S̶.

3 The third form of object *a* (the phallic object) turns around *jouissance* in the Other (Figure 10.10).

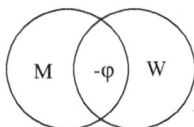

Figure 10.10 Minus phi as the intersection of man (M) and woman (W).

Jouissance in the Other brings *minus phi* into play, which is the only valid intersection between man (M) and woman (W); in other words, that takes account of the feminine way of perceiving the phallic question from the side of *jouissance* and of the void.

4   The fourth form of the object *a* (the scopic object) revolves around power in the Other (Figure 10.11).

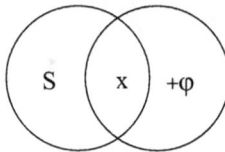

Figure 10.11 Any object (x) as the intersection of the subject and *plus phi*.

This we have made sufficiently clear: the unbarred subject in the scopic field in front of the eye mirror of the world, in contemplative possession, serving as the absolute positive phallic instrument for approaching any object x. This is a positivisation of the phallus that extends to the omnipotence of knowledge, of God or of the big Other (including the alleged omnipotence of Freudian psycho-analytic explanations).

The fifth form of object *a* (the vocal object) revolves around desire in the Other. Here, there is no figure, no schema. The vocal object *a* is unrepresentable, outside any possibility of phenomenalising it, and above all, irreducible to the two circles schema and their intersection.

Object *a* in its vocal form is, however, signalled by anxiety and guilt in the obsessional (which is not to say that the obsessional symptom has the aim and function of avoiding anxiety). In the obsessional's anxiety, we must understand desire in the Other and desire in the Other starting from the level of *jouissance*. This desire in the Other starting from *jouissance* is repressed in the obsessional, and, in its place, all attention is focused on the demands of the Other, that is, the commands of the Other, which make up the whole varied content of the fero-cious superego. This placing of the demands of the Other in place of the desire of the Other is an avoidance of the question of object *a* in its vocal form. The fifth form of the object (vocal) is repressed in the obsessional; it is replaced by the demand of the Other, that is, by the anal question. Anal anxiety character-ises the obsessional (as we see, for example, in the Rat Man) because it conceals the side-lining of the function of the vocal object *a*. To do this, the anal face of the object goes hand in hand with its scopic face and the phantasy that comes to plug the hole.

Notes

1 Lesson of 5 June 1963. Chapter XX of the Seuil edition.
2 "The interpretation of dreams is the royal road to a knowledge of the unconscious activities of the mind" (Sigmund Freud, "The Interpretation of Dreams" in *The Standard Edition of the Complete Psychological Works*, Volume 4 and 5, translated and edited by James Strachey, London, Hogarth Press, 1953, p. 608).
3 Jacques Lacan, *L'Étourdit*, in *Autres écrits*, Paris, Seuil, 2001, p. 487. See also Christian Fierens, "Topologie de la fin - Lacan 1972" in *En finir avec la psychanalyse?* Actes du colloque organisé par la revue PSYCHANALYSE YETU et l'association *Le Pari de Lacan*, les 11 et 12 juin 2022, Paris, Les éditions de l'insu, 2023, p. 39ff.
4 Lesson of 12 June 1963. Chapter XXI in the Seuil version.
5 Jacques Lacan, *Subversion of the Subject and the Dialectic of Desire*, in *Écrits: The First Complete Edition in English*, translated by Bruce Fink, New York, W. W. Norton & Company, 2006 (*Écrits*, Paris, Seuil, p. 814).
6 Emmanuel Kant, *Critique of Pure Reason*, London, J.M. Dent, 1993, p. 785; Jacques Lacan, On a Question Preliminary to any Possible Treatment of Psychosis, in *Écrits: The First Complete Edition in English*, translated by Bruce Fink, New York, W. W. Norton & Company, 2006 (*Écrits*, Paris, Seuil, p. 548–549); Christian Fierens, La parole neutre, in *La parole et la topologie*, Louvain-la-Neuve, EME, 2012, p. 10ff.

Part Six

The truth of anxiety

Chapter 11

Obsessional neurosis in the structure

LESSON 23[1]: THE FIVE FACES OF OBJECT *a*

Lesson 22 was centred on the obsessional symptom insofar as it helps to demonstrate the structure of object *a*. Lesson 23 continues the discussion, starting with object *a* as cause, then interrogating the anal phenomenology present in the obsessional symptom, and finally arriving at what is essential, namely the structure of object *a* in its scopic face, the only means by which the anal problematic of the obsessional can be understood. It is the movement of the structure of object *a* in these five faces that is heard. And the obsessional symptom serves as a support for putting it in play.

1 Synoptic presentation of object *a* as cause

(Figure 11.1) The ordered presentation (1, 2, 3, 4, 5) of the five faces of object *a in the* form of this bell diagram shows the oral (1) resonating with the vocal (5), the

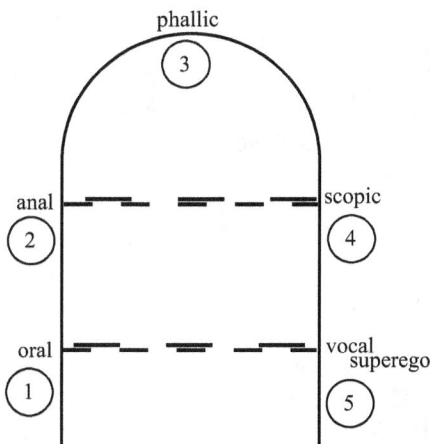

Figure 11.1 The five faces of object *a*.

DOI: 10.4324/9781003477822-17

anal (2) resonating with the scopic (4) and the phallic (3) dominating the whole picture. The resonances of the bell diagram (the oral and the vocal on the one hand, the anal and the scopic on the other) suggest a to-ing and fro-ing where all regression is at the same time progression, and not all progression is without regression. In the practice of analysis, there can be no progression without the mobilisation of the primitive forces of childhood, without the most infantile sexuality, the motor of progression. At the same time, everything that appears as regression is rich in possibilities for progression. And every mechanism of defence plays on the opposition between progression and regression.

Any face of object *a* thus summons up the global structure of object *a* involving its function in the constitution of the subject in the locus of the Other, that is, in the division of the big Other by the question of the subject, with its general function more precisely situated at the intermediate level of anxiety, between the level of *jouissance* and the level of desire (Figure 11.2).

$$\text{A} \mid \text{S} \qquad \text{jouissance}$$

$$\text{a} \mid \text{\AA} \qquad \text{anxiety}$$

$$\text{\$} \mid \qquad \text{desire}$$

Figure 11.2 Second schema of the division of the Other (A) by the question of the subject (S).

Located at the middle level of anxiety, object *a* is the cause of desire. In the previous lesson, we saw how the symptom, to be truly constituted, must claim to be dependent on its cause. A phobic person who systematically avoids public transport and gets by without realising it and without any trouble in his life is not suffering from any symptom. For a symptom to be present, one has to say to oneself something like "that's strange, I can't get on a bus, *there must be a cause*". This doesn't mean that the cause is reached, and even less that the symptom automatically disappears as a result. On the contrary, when we talk about the cause, we encounter a double hollow: *I don't* really *know* what the cause is, and the cause doesn't actually have *the expected result*. This is anxiety, locatable as the maximum in the difficulty of knowing and the maximum in the difficulty of movement.

On the side of knowledge and not-knowing, the cause goes beyond a purely logical process. The demonstration of a theorem is not the cause of the truth of that theorem. And cause announces much more than the antecedence of cause over effect, where "because of this" is not reduced to "after this"; the fact that one event comes after another does not imply that the first is the cause of the second. And yet confusion easily sets in, while giving itself the illusion of filling the causal gap in the order of knowledge. For example, someone suffering from an embolism a fortnight after a vaccination: "now we know, the vaccine must be the cause of the embolism". On the contrary, it is a not-knowing.

On the side of effect: the cause is *also* always the cause of something that has not yet taken place. In other words, there is no direct, immediate link between cause and effect. There is a gap; there is a hole between cause and effect. This is fundamental to understanding object *a* as the cause of desire: with object *a* rightly mobilised, desire is not automatically acquired, it remains unfulfilled, fundamentally unrealised. The effect of object *a* remains a suspended effect. It is in this suspension, in this "condescension" that desire depends on *jouissance*, on this mythical line of *jouissance* (the big Other and the question of the subject). All this forces us to distance ourselves from the facile question: how does psychoanalysis work? How does it achieve results? Such a question places psychoanalysis in the field of knowledge, where effect is not discernible. The question therefore needs to be shifted towards engagement, towards a doing, a doing that is not programmed, that is in suspense.

From the point of view of knowledge, we cannot confine ourselves to *insight* and a reduction of the scopic object to the scopic field, where we could see everything, know everything and understand everything (as can the monkey!). The scopic object *a*, insofar as it is inserted into the structure of five forms of the object, is the stain, the blind spot arising in the scopic field and destroying all its operative pretensions. Or again, the scopic field of seeing and understanding with the first conception of the signifier (the signifying chain being able to cast a net of knowledge over the world and the subject) is defeated by the second conception of the signifier, by the S_1–S_2 signifying process.

From this point onwards, a new *Critique of Reason* establishes itself. This critique of reason is twofold: a critique of knowledge (corresponding to Kant's *Critique of Pure Reason*) and a critique of the effect of the cause (corresponding to Kant's *Critique of Practical Reason*). *Firstly*, we cannot know, and it is starting from the scopic field that the radical subversion introduced by the scopic object is played out, as out-of-field, as gaze and not as eye. *Secondly*, from this first form of gap, it becomes impossible to practically keep to a deterministic cause. What can we do? We do not know, and we find ourselves plunged into the question of the dynamic unconscious. Practical reason is summoned into our practice of the cause. Deterministic cause gives way to faith in the causality of freedom characteristic of the ethical unconscious: it has to happen, or more precisely, it has to be allowed to happen.

This is true transcendence, where, instead of the idea of the *Umwelt*, our world, the world we inhabit and to which we are accustomed, instead of the world we think we can master through the knowledge and collaboration of a big, unbarred Other, we are invited to put our faith in the causality of the free, inventive, dynamic unconscious. Such a causality completely transcends the *Umwelt*, even if it is played out within and from it: transcendence of the unconscious in the immanence of our world. This transcendence provokes anxiety. A similar transcendence (transcendence within immanence) explains the anxiety aroused in animals during an earthquake, an eclipse, etc., because their *Umwelt*, which they inhabited and to which they were accustomed, is fundamentally disrupted and upended. The earthquake for man – which provokes the animal's anxiety – is not first and foremost an earth tremor, it is the tremor of the signifier, of the signifying process, namely that he cannot respond in a suitable way in his world, in his world of language, on the side of the signifying chain.

Opposite the scopic face of object *a* in our bell-shaped diagram, transcending the scopic field, is the anal face.

2   The anal object in question

Can the anal object enlighten us in terms of knowledge? By dealing with the excremental or anal, we might think we're getting closer to the matter, to the concrete nature of what we need to know in analysis. Would analysts be right in flattering themselves at being able to deal with such unpalatable, unpleasant and scatological things? They could be dealing with the substance of substance, the final matter of what we need to know. With the bell diagram, it is easy to bring the anal problem and the (scopic) knowledge problem closer together, as in the notable case of the great obsessionals (see the Rat Man) where the two come together. Correlatively, it is easy to see a properly obsessional mechanism in possible scatological interest (knowledge of the anal) in psychoanalyses.

Lacan proceeds quite differently. His starting point was a long article by Ernest Jones, *The Madonna's Conception through the Ear*, which sought to demonstrate that the conception of Jesus in the Virgin could be explained by an anal wind coming from the Holy Spirit and entering the ear of the Madonna. Jones' article teems with references from multiple domains, all converging to prove the thesis of the crucial importance of the anal wind. There are multiple competing analogies that highlight the anal wind in the creative process. Thus, according to the *Upanishads,* Brahma would engender humanity through the anal wind, explaining why the anal wind is more important than a normal phenomenon such as breathing. Lacan points out, however, that breathing is rightly involved *in anxiety*, in the suffocation of anxiety and in the panting of sexual intercourse.

But the displacement operated by Lacan is far more radical. Instead of delving into Jones's thousand and one references and analogies (analogical method), he replaces the anal with the synoptic and unique structure of object *a*, in which its five faces are articulated. Lacan equally questions the embryonic origin of the anal function. Is this not an introduction to a supplementary reference? Far from fitting in with the analogical method, this leads to *the key* that will allow us to rightly situate the anal object.

Embryologically, the excremental function is present as a blastopore long before the differentiation between oral and anal, between mouth and anus. In the evolution of the embryo, the blastopore is both the gateway to and exit from the gastrula (Figure 11.3).

Blastula   Gastrula

Blastopore

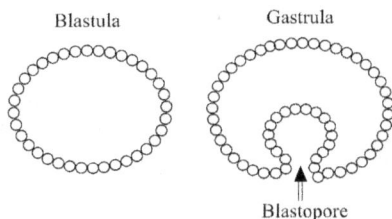

Figure 11.3 Formation of the blastophore.

The peripheral cells of the blastula surround a void. An invagination in the blastula transforms it into a gastrula, which like a sack, has only one way in and out. The blastopore serves as both mouth and anus. This brief embryological consideration serves to emphasise a function that predates any differentiation between the two extremities of the digestive tract. This allows us understand the central functioning of object *a* before grasping its different expressions. Moreover, excrement can be recuperated (and swallowed) making a certain wealth from it, and Lacan goes so far as to evoke the Shoah and the recovery of waste from the bodies of the Chosen People to make bars of soap out of it bringing it into the economic circuit. All these considerations, including the equation of excrement with money, would only lead to infinite analogical possibilities.

The question of the anal form of object *a* must again be considered with the appropriate key. For the analyst, this key is none other than the division of the big Other by the question of the subject. In other words, the object in its anal face appears in the process of subjectivation with the emergence of the question of the subject in the locus of the big Other (at the level of *jouissance*), the emergence of the object *a* and the non-response of the big Other (at the level of anxiety) and the appearance of the barred subject (at the level of desire) (Figure 11.4).

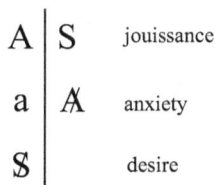

$$A \mid S \qquad \text{jouissance}$$

$$a \mid \cancel{A} \qquad \text{anxiety}$$

$$\cancel{S} \mid \qquad \text{desire}$$

Figure 11.4 Second schema of the division of the Other (A) by the question of the subject (S).

The key here is again the signifying process S_1–S_2 the key that applies to all the other forms of object *a*: the anal form of object *a* arising only in connection with the other forms through this key.

3   Subjectivisation or the anal face in the synoptic structure of object *a*

In its anal form, the signifier first presents itself as the demand of the big Other, asking the child to hold back or sometimes let go of the excrement. Each time, this is the demand of the Other. Doubtless this demand is accompanied by the satisfaction of caring, the erogenous effects of touch, smell and so on. We can process these multiple references and construct a whole series of analogies from which the anal object *a* would be reduced to a general object *a*, an agalma to which we would secondarily add an unpleasant, nauseating side, which would ultimately be no more than an effect of the discipline that is practically imposed in the gestation of the object *a*.

But we must go back to the key, to subjectivisation, to subjective constitution, to the division of the big Other by the question of the subject, because it is from there that we can understand the connection of all the forms of object *a* and the particular place of the anal face in the structure of its five forms. Without connecting all the forms of object *a*, we can understand nothing about the obsessional.

Let us take up the sequence of forms of object *a*, starting with the most regressive, the oral form, which also resonates with the most progressive, the vocal object; this shows that we cannot isolate any one form from the whole. Following the progression: 1, 2, 3, 4, 5, each of the five forms corresponds to the key of signifying division and the three levels of *jouissance*, anxiety and desire.

This allows us establish the following table, with the five forms of object *a* on the ordinate axis (1: oral, 2: anal, 3: phallic, 4: scopic and 5: vocal) and the three levels of the schema of the signifying division (desire, anxiety and jouissance) on the abscissa. The five rows of the table correspond to the five forms of object *a* (starting at the bottom with the first) and the three columns correspond to the three levels of the key to the signifying division (Figure 11.5).

5	X	*a*	Desire of A
4	Image	Power of A	
3	Desire	Anxiety *minus phi*	*Jouissance* of A
2	Trace	Demand of A	
1	~~Anxiety~~	*a*	Desire x of A

Figure 11.5 The five forms of object *a* in relation with the division of the big Other by the subject's question.

The now familiar desire-anxiety-*jouissance* sequence at the third line is written explicitly at the level of the phallic object insofar as the phallic form of the object *a* is understood as *minus phi*. This best reveals the structure of the key and it is also why the Seminar on *Anxiety* adds this additional form to the four classic forms of object *a*. Note also that in this diagram of three columns, the last two columns, those of anxiety and *jouissance*, are merged in the second and fourth rows; in other words, in their anal and scopic expression (which refer to each other and characterise obsessional neurosis) the distinction between anxiety and *jouissance* is effaced.

Detailed presentation of the five lines of the table

The rest of Lesson 23 systematically displays each line of the table. The forms of object a will follow one another, starting with the bottom line (1, 2, 3, 4, …) and the time taken to display them increases logarithmically as you move up the rows of the table: 3 minutes for the oral line (1), $2 \times 3 = 6$ minutes for the anal line (2), $2 \times 6 = 12$ minutes for the phallic line (3), $2 \times 12 = 24$ minutes for the scopic line (4). And with the lesson over, the vocal line (5) will not be exposed.

The oral form

The exposition of the oral form essentially presupposes the resonance of the voice as in the bell diagram, and therefore, from the outset, the level of *jouissance* (desire of A) and the level of anxiety (object a insofar as it might be lacking in the mother and Ⱥ). Desire is not articulated as anything other than the mother's anxiety: not constituted as such, and in its place, anxiety, that is barred is written. The subject is not constituted, it is reduced to what is stuck onto the mother's chest; there only as a mythical subject that does not yet exist as such, and anxiety is simply the cry represented by "a". To represent the oral object by means of the Euler circles, we have the elements at play at the levels of *jouissance* and anxiety, to the exclusion of the level of desire (represented only by "anxiety" that is barred) (Figure 11.6).

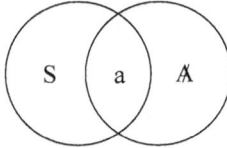

S (a) Ⱥ

Figure 11.6 The oral object.

The anal form

The signifier is presented here in the form of the demand of the Other, which covers the two merged levels of *jouissance* and anxiety. Here, the radical question of the signifying process is already confused with anxiety. With the Euler circles, the specific place of *jouissance* merges into that of anxiety, and we are left with only the elements at play at the levels of anxiety and desire, at the two lower levels of the division of the big Other by the question of the subject: a, $ and Ⱥ.

The demand of the Other (or where *jouissance* and anxiety merge) is always double-edged, turning around "keeping or giving it". With these two phases of demand, the recognition of the subject – whatever he does – will always be ambiguous and double-edged. From the outset, ambivalence is inherent in the anal form of the anal object a, where, there is already an Other who wants and doesn't want this something that is good and bad. It is the very definition of the *nihil privativum*, one gives something and one takes it back; light is given and light is withdrawn, heat is given and is replaced by cold: nothing budges. This mechanism where one tension is annulled by an opposite tension, is the very mechanism of original repression (which controls all repression): a counter-investment opposes the investment to be repressed. When we see such a counter-investment in our practice, it is not difficult to suspect an equally significant investment that has remained hidden and invisible. Signs of absolutely exaggerated love and attention are sure to conceal a fundamental hatred that has had to be repressed. In other words, primary repression is regularly and clearly visible through its counter-investment side.

The big Other, who here wants to take and not take, reject and not reject, is no longer directly in touch with the signifying process (at the level of *jouissance*); fundamentally, it does not answer (Ⱥ) for what it really wants, and this is the anxiety in front of the contradictory object *a*, the anal object (taken and not taken, rejected and not rejected). And the barred subject $ (at the level of desire) appears in Euler's circles as the consequence and intersection of what is played out at the level of anxiety (Ⱥ and a) (Figure 11.7).

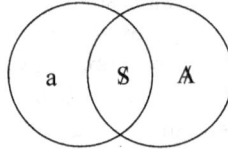

Figure 11.7 The barred subject ($) as the intersection of anal object *a* and barred A (Ⱥ).

This is the first ownership by the subject of what is clean, in both senses of the word. *Firstly*, serving as the trace of the demand of the Other, he is clean (without stain!) like the rest of what the big Other demands, the remainder of the anal object (with its two faces, good and bad, clean and dirty): *secondly*, this same trace, which it is, serves at the same time as a limit, a wall for what he is in and of himself. The subject (already barred by the demand of the Other) is delimited in his property (what he is in his own right) and the same trace (which serves as a limit) serves him to build the walls of defence (of repression, including foreclosure, denial and negation) within his own property.

The phallic form

We could undoubtedly understand the phallic object as the common interest of the two partners already constituted (at the anal stage?). But these two "partners" in their sexual desire only meet and exist through the effect of the sexual ("object *a* is the cause of desire"). We have already seen that the phallic object must first be understood not as *plus phi*, but as *minus phi*, detumescence, emptiness, as what they do not have. This is the only way that love can emerge as "giving what one does not have" (Figure 11.8).

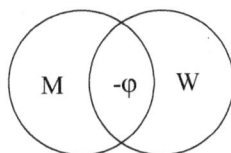

Figure 11.8 Minus phi as the intersection of man (M) and woman (W).

In contrast to the anal form and the demand of the Other, we are here fully in the signifying process (S_1–S_2, the second conception of the signifier) insofar as the phallic is operating as lack in which something charged with the imaginary (S_1) is emptied of all imaginary to produce a void (S_2 valid as *minus phi*). This is the *jouissance* of the Other.

Only love enables *jouissance* to condescend to desire. And love, which consists in "giving what we do not have" finds "*what we do not have*" in the signifying process (at the level of *jouissance*) in S_2, in the void, in *minus phi*. To love is not to give *plus phi*. Giving what we do not have can only be a *metaphor*: one can only give nothing by inventing something else that might emerge as a metaphor for love. It is easy to see that to give away what you have, to give away wealth, runs counter to love. The rich person insofar as he or she is rich may not have access to the realm of love, because the place of "what you do not have" is encumbered by the overflow of what you do have.

The second term in the definition of love, "*to give*", is borrowed from the anal sphere, from the demand of the Other. To give scybala, to give shit, to give the gift *par excellence*, shows here the very clear connection between the phallic form and the anal form of object *a* at the level of *giving*. The object to be given is positivised in the anal form (*plus phi* is in fact a structurally *anal* object). The object to be given can only retain its power as *minus phi* through the signifying process (at the level of *jouissance*). *Minus phi* must be made in the signifying process, in other words, the imaginary *plus phi* must be erased; this has to be understood as what happens in metaphor, where one signifier (S_1) is effaced, is voided to make way for the metaphorical signifier (metaphorical S), in the void (S_2) of the first. The symbol of the gift is essential to love, provided it is played out in metaphor. The metaphor of love is present from the outset in narcissism, which serves as the reservoir of the libido, the reservoir from which all love springs: to love oneself. In the development of narcissism, the one who loves is not the same as the loved one. There is a hollow, a void at the heart of the one who loves: what he does not have. It is with "what he doesn't have" that he can love the beloved, which is equal to the ideal ego. But to sustain the reciprocal love between the two, the beloved must also have a hollow, a void at its centre: the egativised object *a*. And yet another hollow will be found in what is sought at the heart of the ego ideal: this is what Lacan notes very explicitly as *minus phi*.

With these first three forms of object *a* (oral, anal, scopic), we have *nothing of* what makes the specificity of the obsessional's relations to his desire. In other words, the anal phenomenology of the obsessional symptom says nothing about its relation to desire. The apparent importance of anality is in fact only a consequence of the resonance between the scopic object and the anal object (as we saw in the presentation of the five forms of object *a* in the bell diagram).

The scopic form

In the scopic field, with the schema of the eye as mirror of the world, the eye itself is elided to allow the illusion of omnipotence to reign over the whole world. The eventual appearance of the eye as gaze gives rise to the feeling of the *Unheimlich*, the uncanny or disquieting strangeness. With omnipotence (the power of the Other), the question of the constitution of the subject in the division of the big Other (that is, the question at the level of *jouissance*) is elided once again. As at the anal level, in the table of the five forms of object *a* and the three levels of signifying division (desire, anxiety and *jouissance*), the columns of anxiety and *jouissance* merge into a single one, in which the power of the Other is inscribed. The scopic object *a* remains hidden in the power of the Other.

This power of the Other makes it possible to symbolise desire (which was unresolved in the previous stages). Desire is symbolised by the image and in phantasies. The obsessional's phantasies remain just that, phantasies; they are not executed, they remain on the side of the image. They present themselves as something to be seen, to be known, to be understood from a theoretical point of view and to be explained in interpretations. Even if we find a series of forms of perversion in certain obsessional families, they are not realised for the obsessional himself, but remaining the stuff of phantasy.

The symbolisation of desire was brought into play at the beginning of psychoanalysis. Freud's thesis in *The Interpretation of Dreams* – that the dream is a fulfilment of a wish – brings desire into play as a result of the power of the Other, the power of Freud's interpretation of the dream. Freud's thesis is itself played out at the level of phantasies in a properly scopic, obsessive mode. And the phantasmatic realisation of desire in the dream has no direct repercussions on reality. Interpretation as an explanation of the dream runs the risk, in this scheme, of remaining purely phantasmatic, and the will to then concretely realise the dream or the phantasy remains frozen in the same scopic point of view controlled by the power of the Other.

Enormous power, omnipotence, is the only mode in which the obsessional can constitute this desire. But this is always impossible, and desire presents itself as impossible. The phantasmatic omnipotence of the image at the scopic level is associated with the impossibility of realising desire in reality as desire remains in the image.

One image in particular serves to highlight the association between the power of the Other and the image at the same time as the obsessional structure. It is the image of the fish in Christian iconography, revelatory of the obsessional structure of Christianity. The importance of the image of the fish does not come from the miraculous catch, but from the pictorial letter. Fish is written in Greek ιχθύς [icthus] or in capital letters ΙΧΘΥΣ. These letters I – X – Θ – Y – Σ form the acronym for "Jesus Khristos Theou Huios Sôtêr", ΙΗΣΟΥΣ (*Jesous*) "Jesus", ΧΡΙΣΤΟΣ (*Khristos*) "Christ", ΘΕΟΥ (*Theou*) "of God", ΥΙΟΣ (*Huios*) "son", ΣΩΤΗΡ (Sôtêr)

"*Saviour*". "Jesus Christ son of God saviour": represents the power of the Other put into image. Jones mentions no fish, no trace of this IXΘΥΣ in *The Conception of the Madonna by the Ear*. It is, however, the key to understanding the obsessional at the same time as Christianity from a certain level of understanding subjective division. The power of the Other thus imaged in Christ enables us to understand why obsessionals regularly construct their phantasies with certain images of Jesus Christ. Such phantasies, which support their sexual practice, depict Jesus Christ with a whole range of obscene, anal and scatological imagery, because Jesus Christ is both God and son: the son of God the saviour, the power of the Other made into an image.

Omnipotence is the power of the Other, where the Other is not just the God of Christianity, but of the gods. The gods are always real, and their reality consists in their effectiveness, in a power that is fulfilled. They realise the Freud's thesis of the dream, the fulfilment of desires, with maximum efficiency: the transformation of desire into satisfaction is immediate. The god himself (as the desirer) is immediately transformed into the object of his desire. It is cinematic, it is the dream according to chapter 3 of *The Interpretation of Dreams*, omnipotence made image. In Greek mythology, the god Apollo desires Daphne, who, terrified, is turned into a laurel tree. But the laurel is none other than Apollo. In other words, Apollo finds satisfaction by transforming himself into the object of his desire. This is the pattern of infinite power attributed to the gods in general. It applies to Yahweh as well as to Plato's god, the Supreme Good. Likewise, The Agathon, that is omnipotent and all-seeing, can explain all ideas, how they work and how they are achieved.

This power of the Other that generates the image can be applied to the process of the development of the ego in narcissism, but omnipotence thus fills all the holes, the hole of the question, the hole of the object *a* in the ideal ego and the hole of *minus phi* in the ego ideal. The ego ideal then takes the form of the Almighty, and the obsessional is founded precisely on a ubiquitous phantasy: he can be everywhere and can have infinite power. Why and how? By being the son who is dependent on the omnipotence of the Other. Jesus Khristos Theou Huios Sôtêr, Jesus Christ Son of God Saviour, is the obsessional himself who is saved by the fact that he imagines himself to be the son of an all-powerful God. The obsessional always believes in God; he always imagines he can be saved by the big Other, the God of science eventually – he will be a scientist – saved by a universal eye cast over all our actions to reassure him and save him on every occasion.

Who would then be the true atheist? He would have to have succeeded in eliminating the phantasy of omnipotence proper to the obsessional, including the imaginary omnipotence that may be attributed to psychoanalysis. Genuine atheism is a genuine asceticism inscribed in the movement of the five forms of object *a*, obliging us to go beyond the fourth optical form towards the fifth vocal form. This asceticism must be called psychoanalytic insofar as psychoanalysis must be rightly understood from the principle of *jouissance*, and with the vocal form of object *a*, it opens onto the invention of the unconscious.

Here, the vocal form of object *a* remains on hold.

LESSON 24[2]: DESIRE AND ANXIETY

Obsessional neurosis is characterised by the effacement of the level of *jouissance* (of *minus phi*) in favour of the foregrounding of *anxiety* and of *desire* in the phantasy. But once again, the point of this lesson is not to explain the obsessional's structure, but the general structure of desire and anxiety in a clinic that lends itself particularly well to this. This structure remains controlled by the question of *jouissance*, and it implies the object *a* (which object a appears cedable (*cessible*) phenomenologically in obsessional neurosis).

1   Object *a* as what can be ceded

The cedable[3] object (*objet cessible*) is an object that can be ceded. It is through being ceded that the object is constituted as such. Here Lacan takes up the question of the origin of the object: for Freud, "…the external world, objects, and what is hated are identical".[4]

The object is thus nothing other than the result of the projection of the hated onto the exterior of the ego. The "subject", in inverted commas, the hypothetical subject, the "I" cedes, abandons, projects something of "itself" (still in inverted commas), outside of itself, to the outside.

To cede is to bring about a separation that results in the constitution of a subject and of an object. Let us recall se-paration (from the Latin *se parere*, to beget) as a begetting of the subject as well as the object. This separation is a radical movement, it involves the birth of the subject and the object (maximal movement) and it takes place independently of all knowledge (the difficulty of knowing is minimal).

The object able-to-be-ceded is thus locatable in the nine-box reference table in the place of *émoi*. The object able-to-be-ceded is *émoi*, and *émoi* is the object able-to-be-ceded or the birth of the object in general, what makes an object an object and this is object *a*. Object *a*, as an object able-to-be-ceded, is thus *é-moi*, *outside* of "I", abandoned outside of "I"; this is the strongest moment of movement (Figure 11.9).

Inhibition	Impediment	Embarrassment
Emotion	**Symptom**	*Passage à l'acte*
Émoi	Acting out	**Anxiety**

Figure 11.9 The nine-box reference table (with inhibition, symptom, anxiety).

In this *émoi* as "outside of I" [é-moi], outside the ego, the subject is at first nothing more than a mythical subject, at the beginning of the division of the big Other. The "subject" yields to the situation, but this does not mean that an already constituted subject vacillates or bends, but rather that, before any constituted subject, something emerges, a separation produces the *émoi*, the object *a* and correlatively, the subject. In other words, before any object *a* and any barred subject, the question of separation is played out at the level of *jouissance*, and the ceding (separation) successively produces object *a* at the level of anxiety and the barred subject at the level of desire.

Such separation can be traced back to the primal scene encountered by the Wolfman when he was one and a half years old. At first, the primal scene of parental coitus upsets, fascinates and petrifies, and the underlying question is that of the subject – what am I? How can the subject constitute himself in the place of the Other? This is the question of *jouissance* in the scheme of the division of the subject. In a second moment occurring immediately afterwards, the anal *émoi* and the production of a stool, an anal object, a transferable object, emerge; this is the moment of anxiety when the anal object is confronted with the non-response of the parents, Å. It is only much later that the subject barred by all the hazards of the adventure can finally be constituted as an obsessional: this is the result of the process in the obsessional neurosis of the Wolfman, which erupts after his dream at the age of four.

With the Wolfman, we have indeed found the anal object again and the obsessional problematic. But both must be inserted into the general structure of the division of the big Other dependent on *jouissance*. The object able-to-be-ceded is therefore not the object of obsessional neurosis or of any diagnosis. It is a question of renewing the dialectic of desire by placing it in the perspective of the key that fits it, in the perspective of the signifying process, or, in other words, of the question of *jouissance* as principle. On this basis, the able-to-be-ceded object can no longer be confined to the anal object but combined in all its forms (oral, anal, phallic, scopic and vocal).

The oral object, the breast, is able-to-be-ceded insofar as the breast is part of the "child". The child abandons, gives up a part of itself and it is this lack that gives rise to desire (at the oral level). Similarly, the new-born baby gives up a part of itself (the cord, the envelopes, the placenta, which have the same genetic heritage as the child). The pure ceding, the definitive abandonment of the breast would put the "subject" (as yet unconstituted) in a position of dereliction, of *Hilflosigkeit*, of extreme helplessness if there were no substitutes, no baby bottles to replace the breast. Because the object is fundamentally able-to-be-ceded, we can find a thousand substitutes for it.

Similarly, organ transplants are substitutions for organs, the transplanted organ itself an object able-to-be-ceded. It is tissue that has been kept alive in its "donor", who is already brain dead. The donor, no longer a subject, no longer considered to be a subject, is supposed to be able to cede a liver, a kidney or something else; clearly the ceding as a separation will not lead to any new constitution of the "donor subject", but will possibly serve as a prosthesis for the other subject, the recipient for whom there is no question of a process of se-paration or ceding. Here, the possibility of transplants introduces a fundamental ethical question that depends on the division at the level of *jouissance*.

The vocal object can also be presented as an able-to-be-ceded object, the recording of the voice from which one can always be separated. But in this ceding, the voice is nothing more than the phenomenal, recordable voice; it cannot be the true form of the vocal object *a*, as we have seen. The same is true of *the scopic object,* which can always be represented as an image, a photograph, a painting, a drawing or a computer file. But the scopic object cannot be reduced to what we can see and master. Rather, it is the gaze and not the eye, it is the questioning of the empty space outside seeing and outside knowing.

That leaves the *phallic object*, and, remarkably, Lacan does not mention the phallus here. Yet it is not uncommon to hear analysands dream of having the phallus in their pocket or of being able to give it away, so the phallic object really does appear to be able-to-be-ceded, but this object able-to-be-ceded appears as a *plus phi*, a form of positivised object *a* (as with the vocal object and the scopic object presented as able-to-be-ceded). If he had cited the phallic object as an able-to-be-ceded object, Lacan would have returned to *plus phi* (which runs counter to the teaching in this Seminar) which would not be without importance for measuring the function of the able-to-be-ceded object as such.

Whatever its form, object *a* insofar as it can be ceded, is not a positive object that would be aimed at by desire as its goal or end. Insofar as it is able-to-be-ceded, it appears in the constitution of the object as object at the level of anxiety and it is the cause of an effect that remains unfulfilled, on hold at the level of desire. The subject is only constituted in this unfulfilled effect that is desire, desire which must be repeated metonymically, repeated par excellence because it is never constituted; desire is therefore this metonymy. Returning to the schema of the neurotic torus: desire subsists in the metonymy of repeated demands that are summed up in desire (the turning of desire on the torus).

We are still in the neurotic (obsessional) structure, an integral part of the structure of *jouissance*, anxiety and desire. The *neurotic* focus on desire makes it apparently dependent on the anal level. But the *general* focus on desire, the symbolisation of desire, makes it dependent on phantasy and the image at the *scopic level*. Nothing about obsessional neurosis can be understood without putting the anal object in resonance with the scopic object.

2   One desire opposed to another or inhibition

At the anal level, desire consists in ceding, in letting go, *and at the same time* in not letting go, in holding back. These two sides of desire determine a wall that separates the clean from the dirty and, at the same time, a wall that se-parates, that engenders the subject properly himself as opposed to the object able-to-be-ceded, improperly called subjective. It is education in cleanliness *propreté* as well as in property *proprieté* that corresponds to the demand of the Other. The two sides of desire, evident in obsessive ambivalence, play a dual role: in the opposition of clean and dirty and of subject and object. An integral part of the fundamental structure of desire in general (much broader than the desire of the obsessional), these two sides are further expressed in the opposition of desire and the law: the law being nothing other than repressed desire. "Desire" and "The Law" or non-repressed desire leaning against a repressed desire, is the very structure of repression in its principle, the mechanism of original repression opposing a counter-investment to an investment, a law to a desire.

Desire – in this dual structure – is thus characterised on the one hand by a halt in movement provoked by the annulment of a movement of desire by the other (not to be able), and on the other hand by repression, where the question of knowing is set aside (not to know). Let us remember in parentheses that repression is not the unconscious: repression dismisses the knowledge of something that can be known (and this is an easy way of resolving the difficult question of knowledge), whereas the unconscious is an irreducible non-knowledge. The difficulty then lies in managing to deal with knowledge from this zero degree of knowledge that opens up the dimension of invention and creation. In its very structure, desire corresponds to the first degree of movement (not being able to) and to the first degree of the difficulty of knowing (not-knowing) in the ISA reference table, it is in the place of inhibition (Figure 11.10).

Desire	Not to be able	...
Not to know	(Symptom)	...
...	...	...

Figure 11.10 The structure of desire in the place of inhibition.

Desire thus appears in a composition of two desires: hating and loving (inhibition of hatred), ceding and not ceding (inhibition of ceding), writing and not writing (writers' block). Inhibition provides the very structure of desire, corresponding to the structure of *Urverdrängung*, of original repression.

This exposition of desire isolates the four upper left-hand squares of the nine-square reference table. At the opposite end of the spectrum from desire (in the same ISA grid), we find anxiety, and later, in this same lesson, we will be able to reveal anxiety in a similar way with the lower four right-hand squares of the same ISA grid. Desire and anxiety are thus presented as two polar correlatives in the same structure, which depends fundamentally on *jouissance* in the schema of division in the question of subjectivisation based on the signifying process (*jouissance*, anxiety, desire) (Figure 11.11).

Desire	Impediment	Embarrassment
Emotion	Symptom	Passage à l'acte
Émoi	Acting out	Anxiety

Figure 11.11 Desire and anxiety as two polar correlatives in the same structure, in the reference table (and the question of subjectivisation based on the signifying process).

This structure of desire as inhibition concern, not only desire as unfulfilled but also the structure of the *act*, which Lacan presents as the only polar correlative to the locus of anxiety. The act is not the doing; as the *result of doing,* it is opposed to doing. At the very point of inhibition and desire, the act fixes the two components of desire or inhibition. The act cannot be defined by motor activity alone, but by motor activity that comes to a standstill (movement is reduced to zero), but at the same time, with the act, there is no longer any question of knowing (the difficulty of knowing is reduced to zero). The definition of the act thus takes the place of desire and inhibition. In the process of division and subjectivation based on *jouissance*, the act is at the same time the appearance of the subject, the subject barred by the whole process that produced it. This conception of the act as inscribed in the structure based on the signifying process contradicts the personalist conception of the act as the production of the person. The subject (as the person) is not primary. The act is part of the *jouissance*-anxiety-act-desire sequence, and therefore depends on object *a*, which precedes subjectivisation proper. Far from being a production of the subject, the act is the fixation of the subject.

The two dimensions of the act (a halt in movement and a halt in knowledge) manifest a *state of* desire, a halt of the metonymic shift of desire. It is in the sense of this halt that we speak of the sexual act, or the testamentary act, where the metonymic shift has been frozen. Desire and the sexual act are made explicit through and in anal desire, with the desire to retain, which only takes on its sense in relation to a primary object supposed to have all its value. The anal object is thus necessarily positivised. And any desire as desire, any act as act, will necessarily be played out in a resonance with anality – including the sexual act. We make love and we are born, *inter urinas et faeces*, between urine and faeces. The focus on desire (where *jouissance* and anxiety are bracketed) necessarily leads to (anal) positivisation of the object *a* and of the phallus: *plus phi*.

But this positivisation of desire presupposes the two dimensions of inhibition: inhibition of knowledge, or not-knowing, and inhibition of movement, or not being able to. Not-knowing poses no problem insofar as we take desire to be a realistic thing: "I have such and such a desire" (in realism, there is nothing to know: things are what they are). To not be able does not pose a problem either, insofar as the impediment justifies stopping, suspending and then metonymising the desire ("impediment" comes from the Latin *impedicare*, to ensnare, to get caught in the trap). In these multiple compulsions (*Zwang*), the obsessional (the sufferer of "compulsive neurosis" *Zwangneurosis*) is caught in the trap of his own desire, where he gets tangled up in the brushes of law and desire, in the two sides of desire. He is continually prevented from adhering to his desire to hold back as well as to his desire not to hold back: he is continually in a state of "not being able to". When confronted with tasks (the movement of reaction at the second level of movement), he doesn't know where or how to respond: this "not knowing" comes to the place of emotion.

He is plunged into the question of desire independently of the question of *jouissance* and, if possible, of anxiety. And it all comes down to the four top left-hand squares of the ISA grid: impediment, not being able (not being able to hold back or not holding back and above all not being able to create) and emotion, not-knowing (not knowing the real signifying process) and his symptom. In this narrowed structure focused on desire alone, object *a* is taken in its anal aspect with the positivisation that depends on it and that is transmitted to the other forms of object *a*.

All these compulsive movements (to not be able) and erratic questionings (not-knowing) encumbering desire, demand an explanation: what is the cause? The authentic cause lies in object *a* insofar as it is necessary for movement in its maximum creative force; it is object *a* in its vocal form, which remains effaced behind desire, behind the subject, behind the act and behind the mechanism of original repression. Therefore, the obsessional's *acting out* mobilises the maximum power of the movement of *object a* (on the side of émoi and the birth of the object) and the obsessional's continual *doubt* opens up the question of the maximum difficulty of knowing, embarrassment about the *cause* (which would otherwise get him going on the side of the causality of freedom of the unconscious). From doubt, the question of the cause is awakened, and from *acting out*, object *a* is mobilised to construct the symptom *in function of object a as the cause of desire* (and no longer as a conjunction of a *not being able to* and a *not-knowing*) (Figure 11.12).

Desire	Not being able to	Cause
Not knowing	(Symptom)	(doubt?)
Object *a*	Acting out	Anxiety

Figure 11.12 The object *a* and the cause in the reference table.

This is the path to putting the narrow dialectic of (obsessive) desire back into the perspective of *jouissance*. Not without anxiety.

3   The reason for one desire opposed to another. Anxiety

How does desire appear? What is the reason for the two-sided, ambivalent structure of desire, desire-law, desire versus desire? The polar correlation between desire and anxiety leads us to the answer. The obsessional is confronted with anxiety not from the anal or scopic side of object *a*, but from the phallic side, castration and *minus phi*. As we have seen, it is at this level that the *jouissance*-anxiety-desire triad is most clearly presented (third line of the five-line, three-column diagram on page 168). Anxiety is necessarily evoked by the phallus (*plus phi*), it's the anxiety of losing the trace of *minus phi*. It's not just a fear in relation to an event (castration) that threatens a positive object. It's above all the question of *minus phi*. This anxiety linked to *minus phi*, can by no means be reduced to the point of view of the possible loss of a positivised organ. What is at stake at the level of the phallic face of object *a* (desire, anxiety, *minus phi, jouissance*)? This is the crucial question, the pivotal question where the drift of obsessional neurosis towards a focus on desire alone (and inhibition) is played out. It is from here that the way out and the unfolding of the complete structure can be played out.

Anxiety is the cause of repression, as Freud said in *Inhibitions, Symptoms and Anxiety*. Freud understood anxiety from castration, as the fear of losing *plus phi*. For Lacan, anxiety, "castration anxiety" is understood as *minus phi*, as the *cause* of original repression, of obsessional desire, of the positivisation of object *a* in its anal and scopic forms, etc. And it is the dialectic of desire centred on *plus phi* that must be revisited by the dialectic of desire dependent on *jouissance* and *minus phi*.

Anxiety occurs at the very place of the lack of the object, and it occurs when this lack is filled. Anxiety is provoked by the prospect of the loss of lack, of lacking the lack, of losing the structure of this radical lack of object. It is clear, then, that the obsessional symptom cannot be reduced to a mechanism for conjuring away anxiety (which is inevitable). On the contrary, the real reason for obsessional desire, caught up in the anal ambivalence of giving and not giving, of letting go and holding back, lies in the way it treats *minus phi* as a simple subtraction of *plus phi*, in other words, by means of a cork or plug. The reason for obsessional desire must be understood from the perspective of *jouissance* and its avoidance. It is the question of giving what we have, oblativity, that needs to be placed in the context of "giving what we do not have", which is inseparable from reopening the question of subjective division. For example, the question of the tap in Piaget's experiment that signals oblativity: the desire to close, to master and control, just as one should master and control one's sphincters, must be put in the context of the void.

With the recurrence of acting out and the doubt that arises in the midst of obsessional neurosis, object *a* as the cause of desire begins to appear and the symptom, along with anxiety, is now constituted (Figure 11.13).

...	...	...
...	Symptom	Doubt
...	Acting out	**Anxiety**

Figure 11.13 The square of anxiety in the reference table.

In the square of desire (the four upper left-hand squares of the nine-square grid) and the square of anxiety (the four lower right-hand squares), the symptom is present in both, the first time bracketed, hidden and latent, the second time well constituted by the embarrassing question of the cause (doubt) and by the evocation of object *a*.

Passage à l'acte is located in the third column, on the side of the cause and its questioning which lies outside seeing, outside knowledge. Doubt about the cause would imply highlighting the cause that escapes, the cause of the unconscious (freedom), the cause that sets invention in motion. But the obsessional reduces it to any kind of movement, such as turning on the tap at some external whim.

Acting out is the spurt of water itself, the movement of bringing life out of death, the maximal and most radical movement, and it requires an explanation, an interpretation of the spurt of water. In other words, a real (the jet of water itself) is or must be symbolised in the explanation. The *acting out* of Ernst Kris' patient[5] may illustrate the point. The analysand, we recall, produces articles in a field close to the analyst's heart and wonders whether everything he writes is plagiarism. Ernst Kris, his analyst, checks if this is really the case and concludes by telling his patient: "No, it's not plagiarism, no, you're not a plagiarist". The analyst's message completely misses the point of the analysand's acting out, which was centred on the question of original writing. The analyst's message doesn't answer the question of original writing at all, which was not at all about evaluating some externally commanded movement, but a movement of life and death, concerning the analysand's wish was to bring something absolutely new to light in his writing. It is at this level, at the level of *émoi* and object *a*, that the analyst should have responded. The analysand continues his interpellation at the third level of movement (the creative movement of writing) while the analyst, as the subject supposed to know, was at the second level of the difficulty of knowing. In other words, the analysand produced an *acting out*, which consisted of checking out the menus of restaurants offering fresh brains. He is not going to eat them, he is simply going to look at fresh brains at the level of seeing and knowing (second level of the difficulty of knowing). This is a question posed by him to the analyst about his mental anorexia, anorexia as far as the mind is concerned, because in suspending his writing, he summons up the nothing, but, already, this is the nothing that is the starting point of true creation, of true writing.

The *acting out* responds to the analyst's wrong position, opening up an *elsewhere* already the patient's, the void of the movement of birth and death around which all his desire to invent already revolves.

A gap is present in the *acting out*, but the obsessional bypasses it in the positivisation of the object – with or without the help of the analyst, whom he summons as the subject supposed to know. The gap, *minus phi*, at the phallic level, is circumvented by the (positive) power of the Other at the scopic level, where *minus phi* is read as *plus phi*. With this *plus phi*, love itself undergoes a metamorphosis; it is no longer a question of giving what one does not have, but of "giving what one has": love is idealised in the sense that the ego ideal (which supports the process of love in general) is no longer centred on *minus phi*, but on filling the hole of *minus phi* with *plus phi*. With this idealised love and *plus phi*, the obsessional imagines that the power of the Other can easily condescend to desire and that's all there is to it, no need to worry about the question of *jouissance*, the starting point of subjectivation: it is taken for granted. For the obsessional man, the woman is the exalted, idealised, full, *plus phi*, which surreptitiously erases the dependence of desire on the signifying process (*jouissance*). Idealised love at the scopic level, fundamental for the obsessional, also explains the reduction of one's love life to the anal, scatological level in return for its elevation to the level of giving, oblativity, altruism in order to save the Other. What is lost is the question of *minus phi*. Just as he loves an idealised image in the woman, so he wants us to love an image in him, of himself. Is this polarisation towards an idealised image a reason for treatment? To distance oneself, for example from ideals and the scopic field? But the real distance is already there at the start of obsessional neurosis, the one that wards off these idealised images (of the woman and of himself) from the question of *minus phi* and *jouissance*. It is the latter, this last distance that is most difficult to reduce in analysis. Rediscovering the real question, placing desire in its dependence on *jouissance*, supporting the vocal face of object *a* and *minus phi* – all these ways of expressing what is at stake in psychoanalysis centred on the S_1–S_2 signifying process are radically out of step with a psychoanalysis (cf. Bouvet) of the obsessional structure that claims to manage transference by establishing the "right distance" between analysand and analyst. This so-called "right distance" merely repeats and reinforces a deplorable distancing from *minus phi* and the vocal object *a* by means of the obsessional structure.

The desire of the obsessional settles in the scopic register with the illusion of the power and omnipotence of the Other, allowing him to do the rounds of all the possibilities, *plus phi*, the idealised woman, the substitute for the positivised phallus. All these possibilities merely encircle, circumvent and avoid radical impossibility, *minus phi*. At the level of phallic desire, the obsessional sustains his desire as impossible: on the one hand bringing into play all the anal and scopic possibilities, but on the other hand all this is played out around what he avoids, around *minus phi* seen as the impossible at the phallic level. In neurotic topology, the figure of the torus offers all the possibilities of demand and the possibility of the desire that brings them together and to which correspond the demands of another torus, the torus of the Other. But what is systematically avoided is the void inherent in the signifier, in the signifier S_2, and thus in the whole topology of the cross-cap. What is avoided nonetheless continues to insist in the doubts and *acting out of the* obsessional. The general structure of the *parlêtre*, the speaking being (starting from *jouissance*, through anxiety and into desire) continues to function.

Lacan's point is indeed this general structure of the speaking being, and the obsessional neurosis is merely an opportunity and an incentive to develop it. Contrary to what is proposed in the Seuil version (which modifies Lacan's statement somewhat), the final lesson will not be devoted to another supposedly specific structure, the so-called hysterical structure, counterbalancing that of obsession. In the final session, Lacan would continue with structure in general, to clear the way for the *Noms-du-Père* the Names-of-the-Father, the intended title of the following year's seminar.

Notes

1 Lesson of 19 June 1963. Chapter XXII in the Seuil edition.
2 Lesson of 26 June 1963. Chapter XXIII of the Seuil edition.
3 Cedable? While negotiable comes close in meaning, cedable includes reference to the transferability of intangible rights.
4 Sigmund Freud, "Instincts and their Vicissitudes" in *The Standard Edition of the Complete Psychological Works*, Volume 14, translated and edited by James Strachey,, London, Hogarth Press, 1957. p. 136.
5 Jacques Lacan, "The Direction of the Treatment and the Principles of its Power" in *Écrits: The First Complete Edition in English*, translated by Bruce Fink, New York, W. W. Norton & Company, 2006, p. 599.

Chapter 12

From anxiety to the Names-of-the-Father

Two tables recur regularly in the seminar helping to articulate Lacan's advances in relation to *Anxiety*.

1 *The ISA (inhibition, symptom, anxiety) reference table (or grid)* with its nine boxes structured by the table's two axes. *Firstly, the vertical axis* differentiates three approaches to *movement*, which can be understood sometimes on the imaginary side as an absence of movement or starting from an absence of movement, sometimes on the symbolic side as a reaction to a stimulus or an event that occurs externally, and sometimes on the side of the real as a movement that involves birth and death, the life drive and the death drive, a truly radical movement. From the point of view of movement, ISA (inhibition, symptom, anxiety) is inscribed as ISR (imaginary, symbolic, real). *Secondly, the horizontal axis* differentiates three degrees of *knowledge* and *difficulty of knowing*; knowledge is sometimes taken on the imaginary side as a simple superfluous duplication of a primary reality (realism), sometimes on the symbolic side as a treatment and modification of this reality by language, sometimes on the side of the real as an impossibility of knowing, a radical not-knowing. From the point of view of knowledge, ISA (inhibition, symptom, anxiety) is inscribed as ISR (imaginary, symbolic, real). The ISA table now corresponds to a doubly ISR table: inhibition is on the side of the imaginary in its movement and its knowledge, the symptom is on the side of the symbolic in its movement and its knowledge, anxiety is on the side of the real in its movement and its knowledge.

How to approach this dual SRI differentiation?

2 *The table of division of the Other by the question of the subject* gives the key to this double differentiation. The key is the signifying process where the second conception of the signifier introduces the real and anxiety, while the first remains a treatment of the symbolic and the symptom. In the signifying process S_1–S_2, S_2 is emptied of all imaginary, opening up the question of the real, of the nothing, at the level of *jouissance*. It is from here that *anxiety* can be situated in the real. To say that "anxiety is not without an object" is not to think that object a is the cause of anxiety (object a is the cause of desire, and desire is not the same thing as anxiety). Anxiety is *not without making the object a appear at the* same time

DOI: 10.4324/9781003477822-18

as the barred big Other A̶. Anxiety introduces castration, a castration that must be understood as that of the big Other, S(A̶). Finally, it is object *a,* appearing with anxiety, that causes *desire.* This differentiation between *jouissance*, anxiety and desire can be found in the suite of Seminars from VI to X. The seminar on *Desire* (VI) must be placed in the context of *jouissance* (*The Ethics of Psychoanalysis*, VII). It is transference love that allows *jouissance* to descend to desire (*The Transference*, VIII, with the introduction of object *a*). The starting point is the signifying process S_1–S_2 (*Identification*, IX, making object *a* explicit) followed by *Anxiety* (Seminar X) and the highlighting of object *a* as *minus phi.*

The "minus phi" introduced in the seminar on *Anxiety* is on the side of the real, and cannot in any way be understood as a subtraction from a pre-existing *plus phi* (as the boy imagines it in the form of a castration that threatens him). "*Minus phi*" is immediately present on the woman's side. Therefore, to still talk about castration, is to talk about castration on the basis of this *minus phi* and no longer on the basis of *plus phi*. The emphasis on *minus phi* marks a radical change of direction in psychoanalysis in relation to Freud, a change that is perceptible in the generally freer way in which women analysts (Barbara Lowe, Lucie Tower, etc.) situate themselves in analysis and in the transference.

The introduction of *minus phi* serves as a turntable in the bell-shaped schema of the five forms of object *a*. It is in function of *minus phi* that each form of object *a* must be thought and rethought about from the *primary* perspective of the void, of the nothing. And it is from this void that the oral form resonates with the vocal form and the anal form resonates with the scopic form of object *a* as indicated in the bell-shaped schema. The introduction of the scopic form and the scopic field by means of Buddhism is played out by going beyond with the introduction of the vocal form as signalled by the shofar.

The final three lessons of the Seminar show how the object in its complex structure and articulated with anxiety, is played out in the clinic, particularly in the clinic of the obsessional. The obsessional symptom is played out through repression and the systematic avoidance of the phallic form and the vocal form of object *a*, these being the two forms that highlight the void, the nothing that completely escapes us. In these lessons, Lacan's aim is not to expose a particular structure (that of the obsessional) that is subordinate to the general structure. On the contrary, the aim is to singularly show how the structure works, with all the cogs continually working in concert, where, by means of his acting out and his awkward doubting, the obsessional will yet get out of the jam in which object *a* is presented as positivised. For the psychoanalyst, the point is to practise with the complete structure in mind, the complete structure encompassing the two reference tables, the primacy of *minus phi* and the articulation of the five forms of object *a*.

The great difficulty – both practical and theoretical – is to move from the scopic level (where seeing and knowing dominate, along with the illusion of omnipotence they imply) to the functioning of object *a*, centred on the void and the real of anxiety. This can only be achieved by overcoming the anxiety inherent in the real.

This overcoming consists of conserving, surpassing, suppressing and raising anxiety, all at the same time (cf. the meaning of the German term *Aufhebung*). This is played out in transference and in transference love. It is the characteristic of a father and of the Name-of-the-Father. The seminar on *Anxiety* leads to the only lesson of the following seminar: *The Names-of-the-Father*.

LESSON 25[1]: STRUCTURE AND ANXIETY

1   Anxiety according to Lacan

Beginning with *Inhibitions, Symptoms and Anxiety* (1926), Freud considers anxiety, as the signal of the danger of loss of an object, to be fundamental to the libidinal economy of the ego. In Freud's text, Lacan identified five types of fundamental object that give rise to just as many types of anxiety, each signalling a specific danger: the danger of losing the breast, the danger of losing the anal object, the danger of losing the penis, the danger of losing the loving gaze of the other and the danger of losing the consideration of the other as a function of a ferocious superego at the vocal level. We can easily recognise the five forms of object *a*: oral, anal, phallic, scopic and vocal. Yet, Lacan's conception of anxiety differs radically from Freud's.

For Lacan, the danger signalled in anxiety is linked to the constitutive character of the *ceding* of object *a*. To constitute itself in the locus of the Other (the level of *jouissance*), the "subject" – the mythical subject that does *not yet exist,* that is not yet constituted – cedes, separates itself from a piece *that does not yet exist* and that, in this *ceding*, becomes the "object". In this se-paration, the *constitution of the object* precedes (at the level of anxiety) that of the subject, and the subject only comes to be afterwards (at the level of desire): the object *a* is the cause of desire. To cede, then, does not consist at all in the subject relinquishing an object that it possesses; on the contrary, the usual focus on the subject gives way to the constitution of object *a*. Here, the function of anxiety is no longer to signal the danger of losing an important object; it is to constitute object *a* in the act of ceding, in se-paration.

For Freud, the object is assumed to be given in advance, and it is the danger of losing a primordial object that arouses anxiety. For Lacan, anxiety is played out starting from the pure signifying process at the level of *jouissance*, and it produces and constitutes the object as an object, as an object able-to-be-ceded. If it still appears as a reaction to a possible danger, the danger here is no longer that of losing a positive object fundamental to the ego, but of losing the trace of the constitution of the object starting from the negativised object (as is object *a* in its phallic and vocal forms).

Lacan had, however, given an entirely different definition of anxiety in the seminar on *identification*: *anxiety is the feeling of the desire of the Other*. In the following apologue, the "subject" Lacan is standing in front of the praying mantis, the little "subject" Lacan (1.75 m high) looks the magnified mantis (4 m high) in the eye and wonders with anxiety: what am I to the desire of this mantis that could devour me to fulfil its desire? In this scopic face-off between Lacan and the praying mantis, the subject Lacan has every reason to be anxious, not only in relation to the praying mantis, which is reputed to devour the heads of its partners after mating, but also in relation to his own image, not only reflected by a single mirror, but by the multiple facets of the eye of the mantis; in its attempt to constitute itself, the ideal Ego finds only a multitude of fragmented facets in place of its unity.

Lacan's apologue not only illustrates *that* anxiety is the sensation of the desire of the Other. It also illustrates *how* the sensation of the desire of the Other is placed *in the context of the constitution of the object and the subject*. To do this, the instance of the big Other is presented as having nothing in common with the subject (which does not yet exist) and, it is as such, that it is the very place where the subject can constitute itself (*jouissance*). This it can only do by first making itself an object (anxiety): "what object am I for the desire of the praying mantis?"

Not everyone has the experience of encountering the big Other modelled on the mantis, a being who has nothing to do with the question of the subject. Usually, the big Other presents itself as a fellow being and not as a monstrous insect. Usually, I see that the big Other resembles me, whatever its dimensions and strength. In other words, it is well suited to fit into the scopic field of seeing, of the eye-mirror of the world and of the omnipotence not of the monster, but of the all-seeing eye. It is a miscognition [*méconnaissance*] based on the semblance, whereby the true nature of the object and of the constitution of the object (the constitution that is at stake in the object *a*) is short-circuited. The *how of* anxiety as a feeling of the desire of the Other is exactly the movement of the constitution of the object (in anxiety) and of the subject (in desire).

2   Starting from the begetting of object *a*

Object *a* is constituted by a ceding, a se-paration from which the object *a* is engendered, which will secondarily permit subjectivisation, that is, the begetting of the subject. This movement of engendering is played out for all forms of object *a*.

The cry of the hungry new-born, the first manifestation of anxiety, is not uttered by a constituted subject and the breast is not yet there. It is the cry that summons the question of the breast, and then the breast itself; we imagine that there is already a desiring "subject", but it is a purely mythical subject. The cry is pure anxiety (cf. Munch's *The Scream*), firstly in the absence of any object or any subject. The scream is a ceding, a scream is released, and then come the object and the subject. This is what happens at birth; the organism that was functioning well in the uterus before birth lets go of something of itself, a hole is made in itself, something completely different intervenes that it has never known before, the big Other rushes into the intimacy of the body and the new-born is suffocated by the air entering its lungs. In this surrender, it begins to breathe.

The breast should not be seen as the primary positive object that the child loses secondarily when weaning. In contrast to this positivisation of the breast (particularly by doting mothers), there are new-borns who, from birth and permanently, wean themselves and cede the breast, which is nevertheless an integral part of the living unit that is the "infant". Meconium – the first faecal matter of the new-born – is given up from the outset, even before birth, even before any subjectivisation. Each time, the ceding is prior to the constitution of the object, and *a fortiori* to the constitution of the subject. The object *a* is constituted in anxiety and the subject in desire. In an anal model, it may appear that *the subject* cedes something (the anal object) in order to constitute himself as a subject in his relation to the Other. The ceding of the object is prior to subjectivisation; in the first oral ceding, the object is first produced (in anxiety) before any subjectivisation. Admittedly, the ceding of the object is not played out according to the developmental order of the stages (oral, anal, phallic, etc.); it always has to be made and remade, this is where we have to maintain ourselves in an analysis. But the structural order of the forms of the object *a* requires us to begin (and always to begin again) with the oral form in resonance with the vocal form, with the nothing that opens the process of constitution of the object (and then of the subject).

However, the obsessional almost systematically dismisses the question of the constitution of the object and the anxiety that accompanies it. He cannot help but hold back (not release) an object that the Other asks of him (the anal object at the anal level). The anal object demanded is fundamentally ambivalent: good and bad. In the opposition of these two faces, the doubt of the obsessional sets in and *secondarily* produces the zero point; he does not know, he is in a non-knowledge, which eventually leaves him at the mercy of any little other. This zero point produced by the reciprocal annulment of opposites (good/bad, investment/counter-investment), this zero point that serves as the anal form of object *a*, is what is at stake in the retroactive annulment typical of the obsessional problematic. But this zero point is evanescent in the obsessional, and he is content to oscillate between one and the other, both well positivised.

From this fading of the zero point in the obsessional, we can better understand the radical difference that Lacan posited at the beginning of the seminar between, on the one hand, Hegel's dialectic of desire centred on the opposition of two desires already constituted, and on the other, the dialectic of desire introduced in *Anxiety*, focused essentially on the zero point as the starting point for the constitution of object *a* (which will be followed by that of the subject).

In Hegel's formula – d(a): d(A) < a – desire of a is equivalent to the desire of the big Other, or again: "the desire of man is the desire of the Other". With two desires in two given people, from this we can arrive at the conclusion that man is the little a. This formula could be likened to the topology of the torus or the neurotic: where two toruses or two subjects are presupposed and then the desire of one matches up with the demands of the other. Kierkegaard replied to Hegel that this equation solved nothing, because we were left with a pure unknown: we still don't know what this desire of a, this desire of man, is, and we don't know what man himself is: d(x): d(A) < x.

In Lacan's formula – d(a) < i(a): d(A) – we don't have two given persons; we only have the movement of the desire of a, the supposed desire at stake in the constitution of object a, which is what determines the fact that i(a), the ideal Ego, is fundamentally equivalent to the desire of the barred big Other. Note that in the graph of desire, i(a) is at the bottom right and S($\bar{A}$) is at the top left: we cannot read the structure, as developed in the graph, in detached pieces. Starting from the desire of the little a in its movement of constitution, we see that it is the whole structure that is implicated, the ideal ego and the ego ideal implicate the fundamental hole (of object a in the ideal ego and of *minus phi* in the ego ideal) and with this fundamental hole, desire in its dependence on the line of *jouissance*, the desire of a big Other that doesn't exist. It is the movement of the development of the ego that implies the whole structure: the movement of the ideal ego towards the ego ideal, both fundamentally perforated and without response from the big Other.

To be on the path to the truth of the formula of desire or the truth of the renewal of the dialectic of desire in the seminar *Anxiety* by way of anxiety, it is now enough to replace the "a" by "0" [symbol for zero]: d(0) < i(0): d($\bar{A}$). The whole dialectic that began with the ideal Ego now turns out to be starting fundamentally from the hole in i(a), from a strange internal cause, on an object a that is not on the side of knowledge, that is ignored, and this hole in the ideal Ego (the 0 inherent in i(0)) is at the same time the zero of object a itself (the 0 inherent in d(0)). The figure of the big Other itself is only a *provisional* presentation of object a by something positive (A) in order to find in it the hole ($\bar{A}$): d(0) < 0: d(a). Recall how, in presentation and representation, we always begin by taking the big Other from the side of the signifier that can have a meaning (A and the first conception of the signifier) to then mobilise the signifying process ($\bar{A}$ and the second conception of the signifier) and produce the object a.

But in the structure, we must always begin with the object a that commands the whole structure where Lacan's formula in truth turns around: d(a): 0 > d(0). Desire here starts from no subject, neither a subject *causa sui* nor a Hegelian subject caused by the intermediary of an Other who would reflect to him what it is in the coexistence of self-consciousnesses. Everything starts from "0", which we already find at the very starting point of the development of the question of the subject, of the development of the Ego, i(a) or the ideal Ego. "Everything is vanity", "everything is wind", insists the *Qohelet*, "everything is zero". *Vanity indicates the zero in the middle of the ideal ego, and the driving wind indicates the zero at the heart of the ideal ego.*

Of course, the zero can be approached by means of the ambivalences of the obsessional. It can be found in the death struggle for pure prestige between the slave and the master, in two senses: in the stakes of death and in the vanity of prestige. But such an approach each time, before the questioning of desire through *jouissance*, presupposes the positivity of the elements or characters. The ideal ego, i(a), is assumed first, followed by the vanity of vanities inscribed within it. Object a then appears as disappointment or even waste, in the actuality of a big Other that does not respond in a contingent way.

Lacan's formula says something quite different: object a is a fundamental nothing, it is able to be ceded, that is, it *arises* from the ceding, from the separation that produces firstly the object (anxiety) and secondly the subject (desire). In this movement, the big Other as a question (*jouissance*) is necessary, and it is necessarily the big Other barred. This is played out most prominently at the phallic level, in the gap between desire and *jouissance* with *minus phi* inscribed at the level of anxiety (Figure 12.1).

5	X	*a*	Desire of A
4	Image	Power of A	
3	Desire	Anxiety *minus phi*	*Jouissance* of A
2	Trace	Demand of A	
1	~~Anxiety~~	*a*	Desire x of A

Figure 12.1 The five forms of object *a* in relation with the division of the big Other by the subject's question.

Minus phi, which is essentially feminine, we recall has nothing to do with the imagined wish for the penis in girls or its loss in boys. *Minus phi* is without a penis. This fundamental *minus phi* (whose question is not covered by the penis) is at the heart of anxiety. This is why Kierkegaard was able to assert that "women are more anguished than men". *Through anxiety, she highlights the desire-anxiety-jouissance structure.*

"Anxiety is made up of the relationship to the desire of the Other", here, the formula of the seminar on Anxiety responds to that of the seminar on Identification, where "anxiety is the sensation of the desire of the Other". In both formulae, it must be understood that the desire of the Other includes *jouissance* within itself, that is, the question of *minus phi*. The first and fifth lines of the five-line, three-column table above resonate with this "desire of the Other", which is inscribed in the jouissance column each time, first as desire x, an unknown and unresolved desire at the oral level, then as a desire for invention at the vocal level. But the structure is only ever given through the veil and intermediary of a positivisation – anal and scopic – in which it should still be possible to read the structure of the void and anxiety that is fundamentally imposed. The greatest difficulty in theory and practice is the passage from the scopic level (positivised) to the level of anxiety taken on at the vocal level (*minus phi*).

3   The structure of the schema of anxiety at the scopic level

Oedipus, the person does not have a castration complex. He is not threatened with castration by a father or a mother. On the contrary, he is the very example of castration taken on and desired, particularly in *Oedipus at Colonus*. He seeks the truth, and this truth that is sought is not the power of *plus phi*, but of *minus phi*. He wants to see and know why misfortune has befallen Thebes. Tiresias reveals the answer to him: incest with his mother Jocasta and the murder of his father Laius have provoked the vengeance of the gods. This is a response of seeing and knowing at the scopic level. Following this revelation, Oedipus gouges out his eyes; he has wanted to see, he does not want to see, but now he sees his eyes gouged out on the ground, he sees the *minus phi*.

Following Oedipus' example, would we have to pass by way of this bloody blinding? Would we have to lead our analysands through the tragedy of Oedipus and of blindness in order to finally have *minus phi* beyond eyes and seeing? No, because the eyes, unlike Oedipus' desire to see and to know, are most often disconnected from their function of seeing. *"They have eyes in order not to see"*[2] Lacan repeats throughout his seminar. Something diverts their eyes from the horrific and tragic things they would have to see. Tragedy and anxiety as such are brought to an end by comedy[3]. Unlike the story of Oedipus at Colonus, we no longer see the hole; anxiety is kept at a distance, ignored and pushed down as by a stopper over the hole. The hole in the ideal ego (object *a*) and the ego ideal (*minus phi*) is no more, and, what presents itself, in its place, is a positivised object *a* and this is *plus phi*.

With the positivation of object *a* and *plus phi*, the nine-square ISA reference table remains unchanged. But each of the boxes, with the exception of anxiety, appears in a different colour, veiling the original phenomenon. All the terms, except "anxiety" are modified to produce the table of the scopic level in the ordinary human comedy. The trick will be to awaken the general structure of the schema of anxiety, hidden behind these phenomena inherent in the scopic field (Figure 12.2).

Desire not to see (inhibition)	Impotence (impediment)	Concept of anxiety (embarrassment)
Miscognition (emotion)	Omnipotence (symptom)	Suicide (*passage à l'acte*)
Ideal (*émoi*)	Mourning (acting out)	Anxiety

Figure 12.2 The reference table in the scopic field.

Instead of inhibition, the desire not to see appears in the ambivalence of seeing and not seeing; everything to do with tragedy is avoided and we remain in comedy. At the same time, we remain in the absence of movement, in distancing from and ignorance of object *a*. We remain in the scopic field (the eye as pure mirror of the world) without it being called into question by the scopic object *a* proper, without which the gaze may not be summoned.

Instead of emotion, which appeared as a reaction to an external event, miscognition [*méconnaissance*] is reduced to a pure "not-knowing" or to the minimum degree of difficulty in knowing, without the question of movement being raised (not even in the form of a reaction).

Instead of impediment where the "not being able to" tries to explain itself at the symbolic level, powerlessness sticks to a literal affirmation of the "not being able to", to the minimal degree of movement: "it's a fact and there's nothing to explain".

Instead of the symptom, where the median degree of knowledge and the median degree of movement merge, the *omnipotence of* the scopic field arises following the erasure of the hole in knowledge (the erasure of $\cancel{A}$), the erasure of the hole that is the source of radical movement (the erasure of the vocal object a), allowing knowledge and the seeing of the eye-mirror of the world to encompass everything with supposed absolute efficacy.

Instead of embarrassment, which took account of radical not-knowing, the concept of anxiety reduces the subject's unease and the associated implications of not-knowing to a conceptual matter. Introduced by Kierkegaard with unprecedented audacity, this concept radically challenges the entire Hegelian perspective centred on absolute knowledge and the subject supposed to know, and calls into question the very concept of cause, but as a concept, it does not in itself imply any movement, nor does it directly challenge the subject.

Instead of émoi, as the unquestioned motor of invention and creation, the ideal arises as a goal already there for invention and creation. The hole of the ego ideal is already plugged (*minus phi* is replaced by any *plus phi*) and the ideal ego on which the ego ideal was based is also already plugged (object a is positivised). The ideal is the very motor of the development of the ego, as can be seen in the tragedy of Hamlet. Before the murder, Hamlet's father equalled Hamlet's ideal ego, and his mother, Gertrude, was the father's ideal and, consequently, Hamlet's ego ideal. Everything was positively in place in an apparently unproblematic scopic field (with Hamlet's father rich in the positivity of object a and his mother rich in the positivity of *plus phi*). With the father's murder, every ideal collapsed (the ideal ego and the ego ideal); *émoi* imposed itself and, with it, the very root of radical movement. But Hamlet remains indecisive and inactive. He has not mourned the loss of an Ideal still imagined in the scopic field as having to support his action and his subjectivisation.

Instead of an acting out, mourning comes as a radical setting in motion (life and death) at the level of a median knowledge. Hamlet's mother had not begun any mourning process: the leftovers from the funeral meal for Hamlet's father were able to be used for the wedding feast with Claudius. How will Hamlet be able to mourn his Ideal, which would be equivalent to his own setting in motion in a certain knowledge? To begin to move, Hamlet will need to encounter a genuine process of mourning in the person of Laërtes mourning his father and, above all, his sister, Ophelia. The problem with mourning is not so much that the loved one has disappeared; it is that the Ideal that he or she represented continues to function positively. Mourning consists precisely in emptying this Ideal and finding the hole in it: the *minus phi* in the ego Ideal and the vocal object a in the ideal ego. Mourning consists in regaining the strength of object a without refusing or destroying the consistency of the narcissistic i(a), developed in particular in the dimension of knowledge (median level of the difficulty of knowing).

Instead of passage à l'acte, suicide causes the subject who drowns in the scopic field (like Ophelia) to disappear. The *positivised* object a, charged with hatred, triumphs over the ego which collapses; this is melancholia. We could call it radical anxiety, but if anxiety abandons movement in its principle of engendering death and life, to fall back on a level of movement in reaction to an external fact, it is *passage à l'acte* in the form of suicide, the suicide of the melancholic.

Mourning, in its structure is first played out at the scopic level. It is a question of getting rid of the ideal from a narcissistic point of view and of assuming it in another way: mourning is completed with the full assumption of object *a*, as a *vocal object a*, with its central hole energising the ideal ego and the ego ideal, this vocal face of object *a* leading to invention and creation.

Beyond the prevailing appearance of the scopic level and all the phenomena that depend on it, it is indeed the fifth level – the most fundamental – that responds and that needs to be awakened, that of the vocal form and the pure superego (jouis!). It is summoned in the "Name-of-the-Father".

4   The Name-of-the-Father and love

The "father" is the one who knows to which object *a* desire refers and this is not a positivised object *a*, nor any *plus phi* whatsoever. This is the one that plays out the whole structure (*jouissance*/anxiety vs. love/desire) and makes it resonate in his own history. The real father incarnates the structure, i.e. the real, the symbolic and the imaginary. He is the subject who has gone far enough in the realisation of his desire to reintegrate it into its cause – on the side of anxiety and the object *a* – whatever that may be. He is the one who doesn't give in on his desire, whatever that may be.

With anxiety, object *a* is caught up in its irreducible, unexplainable force, where the difficulty of knowing is maximal, as is, at the same time, the movement of creation and invention. Object *a,* by definition, unknowable and unrecognisable, necessitates opening the way to it through and in the field of the Other; it is *jouissance* taken as a principle and not as something made into a phenomenon.

Transference is the encounter of object *a* in the field of the Other. However, the "field of the Other" remains ambiguous, because the Other, both unbarred or supposedly so with its omnipotence deployed in the scopic field, is, at the same time, the barred big Other, the vocal, summoning the question of anxiety. Through transference, through transference love, it is possible to "overcome" anxiety, to "overcome" meaning to surpass, suppress, conserve and elevate all at once (as in the German term *Aufhebung*). Anxiety is preserved, but it is gone beyond in the global structure that also implies *jouissance* and desire and which is brought into play by what we call a real father. This is, of course, in radical opposition to melancholia, where i(a) is, on the contrary, abandoned and the question of narcissism collapses under the power of the destructive positivised object.

The global structure starting with the signifier is the key to overcoming anxiety in the love that "alone allows *jouissance* to condescend to desire". And this key plays out in transference love, the *name* being the emergence of a nomination that brings together the one loving and the one loved. Nomination is thus a process of love from which the lover and the beloved can emerge. The love of the father (objective and subjective genitive) is equivalent to the nomination of the father.

Therefore, the Name-of-the-Father is not, in any way, a name, a label stuck onto something called the father. It is the movement of bringing forth the complete structure of the signifying process, insofar as it "overcomes" anxiety and is present in transference love. The foreclosure of the Name-of-the-Father would consist in extracting oneself from the Name-of-the-Father and situating oneself in a place where there would no longer be any access to the structure of movement made explicit in all the diagrams of this Seminar. Later on in Lacan's teaching, the different constituent dimensions of the RSI structure will be presented as different Names-of-the-Father. In our reference table, the three entries for movement (inhibition, emotion and *émoi*) and the three entries for the difficulty of knowing (inhibition, impediment, embarrassment) are already "Names-of-the-Father".

The analyst must be the one who has been able "to make his desire enter sufficiently into this irreducible *a* to offer a real guarantee to the question of the concept of anxiety". This final sentence of the Seminar speaks of the desire of the analyst insofar as it is a question of overcoming the concept of anxiety "by a real guarantee", which is to be found with the irreducible object *a*. The desire of the analyst is to push things beyond the limit of the concept or the facts of anxiety, the desire, so specified "of the analyst" only because it mobilises the Name-of-the-Father, that is, this global structure deployed throughout the seminar. To offer the question of the concept of anxiety "a real guarantee" *is not to erase anxiety with any kind of reality, but on the contrary, to go beyond the maximum difficulty of the concept of anxiety in the order of knowledge (as major embarrassment in the scopic tableau) by offering it the real side* in the order of movement. How can this be achieved? By making his desire return to this irreducible object *a*, which is irreducible to knowledge and representation, irreducible to any phenomenality whatsoever, irreducible to transcendental aesthetics. Why? To let its fundamentally negative vocal form – *minus phi* – work at the invention of the unconscious "transcendental ethics". Overcoming the concept of anxiety (embarrassment of the cause, upper right-hand square of the ISA grid) means engaging it with the object *a* in its vocal form, in *émoi* and in the ideal (lower left-hand square of the ISA grid). The guarantee is not to be sought in any knowledge, but starting from non-knowledge (embarrassment at the concept of anxiety). The guarantee is found in bringing the irreducible vocal object *a* and its invention into play. Analysis is not guaranteed through knowing, not even by the maximum degree of difficulty that is radical non-knowledge. It is guaranteed by the maximal movement (the vocal object *a*) in the dimension of transference love.

LESSON 26: NAMES-OF-THE-FATHER SEMINAR[4]

The single session of the seminar on the *Names-of-the-Father*, held in November 1963, is an integral part of the seminar on *Anxiety* and constitutes its conclusion. Lacan learns the evening before the seminar that he has been struck off the list of didactic analysts of the *Société Française de Psychanalyse*, the price he has to pay for the *Société* to be recognised by the IPA, *The International Psychoanalytical*

Association. Lacan decides that he will never give his seminar, except for this first lesson. In January 1964, he will start his seminar afresh seminar with Freud and *The Four Fundamental Concepts of Psychoanalysis* where his most advanced thought on *Anxiety* was not to the forefront.

The first part of the *Names-of-the-Father* lesson resumes with the question of object *a* and its five forms, corresponding respectively to the need of the Other, the demand of the Other, the *jouissance* of the Other, the power of the Other and the desire of the Other. Beyond the one who speaks in the locus of the Other, what is the voice that speaks when the Other does not respond? This is the question of the *Name-of-the-Father* which should return to the whole problematic of *anxiety*, but which remains in abeyance with the interruption of the seminar.

1   The *jouissance* of the father for Freud/the sacrifice of Isaac for Lacan

To grasp what is at stake in the *Names-of-the-Father*, we will begin with the myth of the father in Freud's *Totem and Taboo*. The all-powerful father of the primal horde has the enjoyment, the jouissance, of all the women; his sons decide to murder him, not without anxiety; this murder leads to the guilt that is the foundation of the law and desire. The myth apparently takes up the three levels of subjectivation or the division of the field of the big Other by the question of the subject: (1) *jouissance* in the father of the primal horde, (2) anxiety at the moment of the father's murder (barred big Other), (3) the joint emergence of desire and guilt (desire and the law). There is no doubt about it. It should be noted, however, that the schema of division presupposes the characters even before the signifying process, still locating us in the Hegelian perspective of the struggle of self-consciousness.

With Lacan, however, let us return to the question of *jouissance*. It is approached through the *jouissance* of the father of the primal horde, who has the status of a god. For the *jouissance* of the gods, the victims had to be flawless. Lacan insists that the mysticism of all traditions, *except* the Judeo-Christian tradition, is centred on the flawless *jouissance* of the gods or of God, where, the victims to be sacrificed must be spotless, immaculate for the perfect enjoyment of the gods. This conception of *jouissance* corresponds to the Freudian conception of psychoanalysis. As we saw, however in the seminar *Anxiety*, the renewal of the dialectic of desire depends on a *different* conception of *jouissance*, one that is independent of the pleasure principle. According to Lacan, if psychoanalytic theory and practice broke down after Freud, it was because nobody dared to go further than Freud. The key to going further is precisely the question of *jouissance*, which first drives anxiety and then desire.

The overtaking of the Freudian conception of *jouissance* is illuminated by an episode from the Judeo-Christian tradition, the scandal of the sacrifice of Isaac (on which Kierkegaard, once again, pondered at length). God asks Abraham to sacrifice his son Isaac, then changes his mind and dispatches an angel to stop the knife at the very moment of sacrifice. Where is the cut? The real cut is not the one that would cut off the head of Isaac. It is the cut between God's *jouissance*, insofar as this is imagined and idealised with the sacrifice of Isaac, a flawless victim, and what may present itself as God's desire, but introducing into the *in-between*, the anxiety inherent in flaws. God's son as bearing all the flaws in the world will be sacrificed. The scandal of Isaac's sacrifice thus introduces anxiety into the gap between mythical enjoyment and desire. And anxiety can be overcome by love (transference love). The overall architectural interplay, in which all the levels play in concert, is what is at stake in the introduction of the Name-of-the-Father.

2   The real of the Name-of-the-Father

Firstly, the name and the proper name. For Bertrand Russell, the proper name is reduced to an index referring to a thing; any point on the board could be named "John", for example. Lacan objects that Russell will never interrogate the point "John" in the hope that it would begin to speak. The proper name – *referring to a person* – necessarily something that could speak, essentially raises the question of the Other. The proper name as such (starting from the locus of the Other and *jouissance*) immediately evokes the question of the Name-of-the-Father. Name is translated into Hebrew as *shem*. Touching as it does on the real, the unpronounceable, Lacan adds that he would not have uttered it had it not been for the announcement of his exclusion from the psychoanalytic community.

What is the name of God? To Moses, who was interrogating him, Yahweh answers: "You will tell them that I am what I am". This is either a tautological – "I am what I am and you can go to hell" – or an ontological answer – "I am he who is, I am the identity of Being", the beingness of all beings, the supreme Being, the *Ens Supremum*, on which all other beings in creation depend. But this interpretation is absurd, because God who speaks to Abraham, Isaac, Jacob, Moses, etc., is not the God of the philosophers, is not the supreme Being, the creator of all beings. He is encountered in the inaccessible, unpronounceable real. And he is revealed through anxiety. In contrast to the Being of all beings, who would be understood on the symbolic side, the God of Abraham, of Moses is encountered in the real, as real.

The God of the philosophers – the *Ens supremum*, the supreme Being – appears as all-powerful insofar as all other beings symbolically depend on him. *El Chaddaï*, the Almighty in the encounter with *the real,* is something completely different, and Lacan makes it clear that he would not have pronounced his name without having been excluded from the IPA. And he adds: "I will never give the *Names-of-the-Father* seminar". This is because it is a question of the real, and the real must be taken into account, somehow or other. It is from the real that the fundamental place of angels, of "messengers", is established. In a discussion with Teilhard de Chardin, Lacan firmly defended the existence of angels, precisely because of the question of the real. The angel is not a simple messenger, an intermediary between two speaking beings (between two symbolics); on the contrary, it is a question of making the real of God pass into the symbolic of man. Lacan implicitly presents himself here as the angel of the real, this being the very question of the Names-of-the-Father. It is also what happens in the S_1–S_2 signifying process. An angel passes ["un ange passe" = silence reigns].

The real is not imaginable; in the Hebrew tradition, there is no image. To get his message across, in this lesson, Lacan nevertheless invokes two similar images, the difference between them allowing us to hear the voice of the real. Two paintings by Caravaggio depict the sacrifice of Isaac. In one painting (in the United States), the ram that is going to replace Isaac is represented; not so in the other (at the Uffizi Museum in Florence). Can the real be represented or not? It cannot be a simple representation: the ram rushes to the place of sacrifice and what it represents is *God sacrificed* in place of Isaac, the big Other sacrificed. And the *jouissance* of God becomes the jouissance of the Other (not without anxiety). The phobic animal, a defence against anxiety (the ram), is not a simple metaphor for the father; it doesn't just imply the murder of the father (the father of the primal horde), which would still amount to basing the question of the father on a positive image. Rather, it implies the void in the ram's horn, the shofar, the nothing that precedes the very question of the father.

One can say that the Name-of-the-Father presupposes the emptiness that underlies and allows any question, precisely what is at stake in anxiety, always to be respected in order to sustain the gap between desire and *jouissance*. Overcoming this anxiety is the question of transference love, which respects the question of the nothing, of the void, of *minus phi*, of the voice from which speech might spring. It is the question of the Name-of-the-Father.

Notes

1 Lesson of 3 July 1963. Chapter XXIV in the Seuil edition.
2 Jeremiah 5–21 and Matthew 13–13.
3 Just as in ancient Greece, where a triad of tragedies ended with a comedy.
4 Lesson of 20 November 1963. In Jacques Lacan, *Les Noms-du-Père*, Paris, Seuil, p. 65ff.

References

Fierens Christian, *Lecture de l'Identification de Lacan. De l'utopie d'identité au moteur de l'invention*, Louvain-la-Neuve, EME, 2020.

Fierens Christian, *The Jouissance Principle. Critique of Practical Reason (Kant), Kant with Sade (Lacan)*, Louvain-la-Neuve, EME, 2020. Translated by Kieran O'Meara, London, Routlege, 2022.

Freud Sigmund, "The Interpretation of Dreams" in *The Standard Edition of the Complete Psychological Works*, Volume 4 and 5, translated and edited by James Strachey, London, Hogarth Press, 1953.

Freud Sigmund, "On the Universal Tendency to Debasement in the Sphere of Love" in *The Standard Edition of the Complete Psychological Works*, Volume 11, translated and edited by James Strachey, London, Hogarth Press, 1957.

Freud Sigmund, "On Narcissism: An Introduction" in *The Standard Edition of the Complete Psychological Works*, Volume 14, translated and edited by James Strachey, London, Hogarth Press, 1957.

Freud Sigmund, "Instincts and their vicissitudes" in *The Standard Edition of the Complete Psychological Works*, Volume 14, translated and edited by James Strachey, London, Hogarth Press, 1957.

Freud Sigmund, "The Unconscious" in *The Standard Edition of the Complete Psychological Works*, Volume 14, translated and edited by James Strachey, London, Hogarth Press, 1957.

Freud Sigmund, "The 'Uncanny'" in *The Standard Edition of the Complete Psychological Works*, Volume 17, translated and edited by James Strachey, London, Hogarth Press, 1955.

Freud, Sigmund, "The Psychogenesis of a Case of Homosexuality in a Woman" in *The Standard Edition of the Complete Psychological Works*, translated and edited by James Strachey, Volume 18, London, Hogarth Press, 1955.

Freud, Sigmund, "Beyond the Pleasure Principle" in *The Standard Edition of the Complete Psychological Works*, Volume 18, translated and edited by James Strachey, London, Hogarth Press, 1955.

Freud, Sigmund, "Group Psychology and the Analysis of the Ego" in *The Standard Edition of the Complete Psychological Works*, translated and edited by James Strachey, Volume 18, London, Hogarth Press, 1955.

Freud Sigmund, "Inhibitions, Symptoms and Anxiety" in *The Standard Edition of the Complete Psychological Works*, Volume 20, translated and edited by James Strachey, London, Hogarth Press, 1959.

Freud Sigmund, "New Introductory Lectures on Psycho-Analysis" in *The Standard Edition of the Complete Psychological Works*, Volume 22, translated and edited by James Strachey, London, Hogarth Press, 1964.

Heidegger Martin, *Being and Time*, New York, Harper Perennial Modern Thought, 2008.

Hegel Georg Wilhelm Friedrich, *The Phenomenology of Spirit*, Oxford, Oxford University Press, 1977.

Hoffmann Ernst, *The Sandman*, London, Alma Classics, 2014.

Kant Immanuel, *Critique of Practical Reason*, Cambridge, Cambridge University Press, 2015.

Kant Immanuel, *Critique of Pure Reason*, London, J.M. Dent, 1993.

Lacan Jacques, "The Function and Field of Speech and Language in Psychoanalysis" in *Écrits: The First Complete Edition in English*, translated by Bruce Fink, New York, W. W. Norton & Company, 2006.

Lacan Jacques, "The Direction of the Treatment" in *Écrits: The First Complete Edition in English,* translated by Bruce Fink, New York, W. W. Norton & Company, 2006.

Lacan Jacques, "Kant with Sade" in *Écrits: The First Complete Edition in English*, translated by Bruce Fink, New York, W. W. Norton & Company, 2006.

Lacan Jacques, "The Subversion of the Subject and the Dialectic of Desire" in *Écrits: The First Complete Edition in English*, translated by Bruce Fink, New York, W. W. Norton & Company, 2006.

Lacan Jacques, *Le séminaire livre I, Les écrits techniques de Freud*, Paris, Seuil, 1975.

Lacan Jacques, *The Ethics of Psychoanalysis 1959–1960, The Seminar of Jacques Lacan: Book VII*, London, Routlege, 1992.

Lacan Jacques, *Anxiety, The Seminar of Jacques Lacan: Book X*, Cambridge, Polity, 2014.

Lacan Jacques, *La Troisième*, Paris, Navarin, 2021.

Rancière Jacques, *Le maître ignorant*, Paris, Fayard, 1987.

Sartre Jean-Paul, *Critique of Dialectical Reason*, London, Verso, 1984.

Index

Note: *Italic* page numbers refer to figures and page numbers followed by "n" denote endnotes.

For Product Safety Concerns and Information please contact our EU
representative GPSR@taylorandfrancis.com
Taylor & Francis Verlag GmbH, Kaufingerstraße 24, 80331 München, Germany

9 781032 762760